TUNING

NEW GENERATION ENGINES

for power and economy

A. GRAHAM BELL

ISBN 0 85429 609 3

© A. Graham Bell

First Published September 1988

A FOULIS book

Published by
Haynes Publishing Group
Sparkford, Yeovil, Somerset BA22 7JJ, England

Haynes Publications Inc
861 Lawrence Drive, Newbury Park, California 91320 USA

British Library Cataloguing in Publication Data
Bell, A. Graham
    Tuning new generation engines.
    1. Cars. Petrol engines. Tuning – Amateurs'
    manuals
    I. Title
    629.2'504

    ISBN 0-85429-609-3

Library of Congress catalog card number
88-82210

Editor: **Jeff Clew**
Cover design: **Graffiti**
Layout design: **Rob Pattemore**

Printed in England by J.H. Haynes & Co. Ltd.

Contents

Preface 7
Chapter 1 Introduction 9
Chapter 2 The Cylinder Head 15
Chapter 3 Fuel and Compression Ratio 31
Chapter 4 The Camshaft 44
Chapter 5 The Valve Train 62
Chapter 6 The Exhaust 71
Chapter 7 Carburation 82
Chapter 8 Fuel Injection 108
Chapter 9 The Ignition System 127
Chapter 10 Turbocharging and Intercooling 149
Chapter 11 The Bottom End 169
Chapter 12 Lubrication 181
Chapter 13 Cooling 189
Chapter 14 Pollution Control and The Law 195
Chapter 15 Dyno Tuning 213
Chapter 16 Gearing 217
Chapter 17 Suspension and Brakes 222
Chapter 18 Economy and the Driver 231
Appendix Table of Useful Equivalents 234
Index 235

Preface

Four stroke engines have entered a new era; an era of pollution controls, unleaded and low lead fuel, and electronic engine management systems. For the engine and car enthusiast the situation may appear perplexing and confusing, in fact some engine tuners pine for the "good old days". They feel that high performance and engine tinkering is now on the way out. This couldn't be further from the truth; performance is here. New generation engines offer a greater potential for performance and economy than those of previous times.

Today's engines feature better cylinder heads with large valves, and port and combustion chamber designs far superior to those available in the past. Many feature fuel injection, along with high flow inlet and exhaust manifolds. Ignition systems able to provide precisely timed combustion for more power and efficiency. Lightweight, but stronger pistons, connecting rods and crankshafts which give greater reliability and allow higher rpm. Small turbos and sophisticated management systems have allowed high power outputs without turbo lag. The list could go on, for from whatever aspect new generation engines are examined, the irrefutable conclusion has to be that these engines provide a fine base for performance-oriented development.

In this book I have set out to show the enthusiast how electronic controls and emission controls work, and how new generation engines can be modified for performance with cam, exhaust and carburation changes, and still pass emission inspections in those lands with such requirements. The end result is a book which I believe outlines in a non-technical manner simple and inexpensive tuning modifications for road and occasional club competition engines, with the emphasis on economy and useable street power. I am sure that you will find this publication an informative and valuable tuning aid.

A. Graham Bell

Chapter 1
Introduction

New generation engines are like the engines from previous times. They still have many of the same mechanical features and respond in a similar way to cam, head, exhaust and carburation changes. Where they differ is to many enthusiasts a mysterious black hole of both misinformation and confusion. Like most engine tuners I feel comfortable and confident with mechanical things, things which I can see, touch and compare. I can see that a big bore carburettor will flow more air. Likewise I can see and know from experience that a stiffer distributor advance mechanism spring will slow down the rate of ignition advance. However, how do you compare one black box with another, by sight how do you compare one computer "chip" with another which has a different part number? The truth is you can't, which is why I, like many tuners, felt intimidated, even threatened by this new technology. When I looked around the engine bay of a new car I saw all those hoses, sensors, wires and computer modules and concluded that I could never figure out any of it. Then I started seriously reading the factory workshop manuals. After a time I began to understand a little about what the various systems are for and what they do. This re-education is still going on because manufacturers are finding new ways of dealing with the complexities of performance, emissions and economy.

Later chapters deal with the function of the various electronic and vacuum control devices. However, I would still recommend that you obtain a copy of the factory workshop manual and carefully read the sections dealing with the engine management system and emissions devices after you have read this book. Approached from the correct perspective these devices are neither mysterious nor intimidating. Even if initially you are unable to fathom how these systems function, by understanding basically what they do you will be in a better position to make sensible, workable engine modifications. For example, you may not know exactly how a carburettor works, blending fuel and air in the correct proportions under a quickly changing variety of circumstances. But by knowing what a carburettor basically does, what its function is, you are able to make a number of tuning decisions which may not

Many enthusiasts are intimidated by what they see when they lift the hood of a new generation car. A careful study of the workshop manual will show what all of those hoses, wires and sensors are for, thus aiding you to make workable tuning modifications.

be directly related to carburettor science and tuning. You can choose a cam, exhaust and head work, for instance, without full knowledge of how a carburettor works; however you must know the basics about carburettors otherwise you could quite easily wind up with mis-matched components which don't work too well together. The same principle applies when it comes to electronics and pollution controls; your modifications must be compatible with these systems so some knowledge of their function, what they do, is necessary.

Possibly the worst outlook that you can start out with is that the manufacturer didn't know what he was doing and that all pollution controls are bad news so remove them or render them inoperative. It is true that many car makers do not make performance-oriented decisions and of course this is understandable when it is considered that millions of cars spend the majority of their time moving at a crawl in bumper to bumper traffic as their owners travel to and from their place of employment. However, the fact that the engine has been built to function under these, and a wide variety of other conditions in no way indicates that the manufacturer doesn't know much about performance engineering. In fact it surprises many enthusiasts to find just how much performance potential is built into new generation engines. Engines may begin life as fairly hot performance units and then during their development be deliberately de-tuned for a number of reasons. It is reported by those within the factory that the intercooled Buick 3.8 turbo has its output limited by changing the computer "chip" because the standard rear axle isn't quite up to the task

Performance is alive and well in spite of the constraints imposed by pollution controls and unleaded fuel. To get back lost performance and meet emissions standards manufacturers have turned to twin cam multi-valve cylinder heads and fuel injection for many new generation engines.

11

of drivers regularly doing drag starts. In some lands the Datsun 300ZX turbo is governed by a speedo-tripped fuel shut-off to a top speed of 127mph in the interests of affordable insurance premiums. Others can be de-tuned in the interests of economy, and so on.

I see many cars which have had their performance and economy spoiled simply because the owners had the "all smog gear is bad" mentality. True, some pollution devices do detract from performance and economy, but some improve both performance and economy. The early fuel evaporation system (EFE) is an example. Many carburated engines use this system to rapidly heat the inlet manifold, providing quick fuel evaporation and more uniform fuel distribution when the engine is cold. The rapid heating of the induction system allows slightly leaner carburettor jetting and reduces the length of time the choke is required. Exhaust emissions go down, cold driveability and performance improves, and fuel consumption decreases. Basically a good system, but many enthusiasts disconnect it, making their cars a real pig to drive when cold.

The air injection reactor system (AIR) is both good and bad, depending on the engine. On turbo engines the AIR system contributes to performance by significantly increasing exhaust gas volume and velocity at lower engine speeds. This aids the turbo to spool up to speed more quickly, increasing boost and reducing lag and low speed sluggishness. These and other pollution control systems will be dealt with in detail in a later chapter; however, these two examples illustrate the point that we need the correct outlook before making tuning decisions.

In fact at all times we need to make logical, not emotional, tuning decisions if we are to be truly happy with the end result. Avoid over-enthusiasm and accurately access your engine. Write down what are its good and weak points. Write down what you want to achieve and then carefully think the matter through. I personally feel that too many modifications are made simply as something to brag to friends about when in truth the enthusiast is quite disappointed with the result. So many modified cars are horrible to drive because the cam or the carburettor is too big. The only way to avoid this type of problem is to think the matter through carefully. Don't make changes for the sake of change. If the valves are large enough then why waste money fitting larger ones? If the standard carburettor is large enough and gives good economy then why fit a Weber or a Holley?

Think too about how long you want the engine to last. If the standard engine is plagued with rapid cam lobe wear, then a modified cam will aggravate the situation so consider if you really want to replace the cam and rockers, say, every 15,000 miles. Perhaps you don't, so consider other ways of achieving your goal. Does the engine manufacturer fit a hotter cam in another model which would do the job, could the standard cam be advanced, would it be wise to leave the standard cam alone and get the desired result by cleaning up the head? All these options deserve to be considered. Maybe the engine is prone to fast valve guide wear. Obviously a high lift cam will exaggerate this weakness so think about the choices available to you. Roller tip rocker arms, chrome valve stems, bronze valve guides, a cam with less lift and so on.

Another consideration is the electronic engine controls. Many function interdependently so you can't disconnect or change any single part of the system; the total package has to be considered. For instance, the engine may be equipped with an electronically-controlled carburettor. Changing to a conventional carby will just foul up the electronics, so your modifications have to be planned around the retention of the standard electronic carburettor. Possibly the ignition is tied into the computer. This means that unless alternative "chips" are available, the advance curve cannot be altered. Hence camshaft options will be limited to what will work with the standard ignition advance curve. Also, the electronics probably incorporate a rev limiter, so if the engine is governed to, say, a maximum of 6000rpm, then component choices must be made with that fact in mind.

The four strokes; induction, compression, power and exhaust which take place in every cylinder each two revolutions (720°) of the crankshaft.

The same principle applies with fuel-injected engines. Most road fuel injection systems are a little fussy about cam changes. All will tolerate non-stock cams, but some systems have trouble getting the idle speed and mixture right unless a cam with a certain duration and lobe phase angle is selected. Some injection arrangements are air flow limiting; the runners may be small to give a broad torque curve or the throttle body could be on the modest side. Either situation restricts air flow so it would be useless planning a 200hp conversion if the induction system will flow enough air for only 180hp. Similarly with the injectors; if because of cost considerations the standard injectors have to be retained and they have a fuel flow potential of 150hp, then engine modifications need to be planned around that reality.

So that there is no misunderstanding of the basics of engine operation I will explain what goes on in each cylinder every two revolutions (720°) of the crankshaft. This type of engine is called a four stroke or four cycle engine because of the four distinctive cycles which occur during 720° of crankshaft rotation. These cycles are the induction stroke, the compression stroke, the power stroke and the exhaust stroke. First, as the piston goes down, the inlet valve opens fully and admits air and vaporised fuel to fill the cylinder (the induction stroke). On the compression stroke the piston rises, but compression does not commence until part way up the stroke when the inlet valve closes. As the piston approaches top dead centre (TDC), the spark plug ignites the fuel/air mixture. Compression of the burning mixture continues as the piston rises to TDC. The resulting pressure drives the piston down on the power stroke. Part way down on this stroke the exhaust valve begins to open and as the piston rises again to TDC, the burned gases are expelled out past the open exhaust valve (the exhaust stroke). Just before the piston actually reaches TDC, the inlet valve starts to lift off its seat to allow in the fuel/air mixture when the piston descends on its next induction stroke.

I have endeavoured to keep this book as non-technical as possible and eliminate information which would apply primarily to race and rally engine development. If you require more detailed information then I would suggest that you also read another of my books *Performance Tuning in Theory & Practice – Four Strokes* published by the Haynes Publishing Group. In that publication I delve far more deeply into combustion; cylinder head, exhaust and camshaft design; how Holley, Weber and SU carburettors work and how to tune them. Also included is an extensive Appendix providing data on most engines; oversize valve sizes, rebore limits and best performance cylinder head casting numbers etc.

Chapter 2 The Cylinder Head

Cylinder head design has come a long way in recent years and many new generation engines now incorporate features which a decade ago would have been found only in purpose-built race engines. Most of the advances in port and combustion chamber design have been adopted as a direct result of pollution control. Early emission engines were inefficient, low hp fuel guzzlers. To get back lost power and efficiency car makers had only a limited number of options open. Camshaft design couldn't be changed without upsetting emissions and economy. Exhaust design was already quite efficient so no easy gains could be made here. This left only cylinder heads and carburation. Some adopted fuel injection as an interim solution and most began intensive research into porting and combustion chamber design. The result today is a good number of family sedans sporting cylinder heads not too far removed from that found on the Cosworth DFV V8 Formula 1 race engine.

This is not intended to imply that the cylinder heads fitted to new generation engines cannot be improved upon. They can be, but the modifications now required are much more subtle than in the past. Today's heads usually do not require the removal of very much metal from the ports or combustion chambers in performance/economy applications. Frequently the valve size is adequate too. For a long time I have maintained that big ports and big valves are not the way to go, particularly for street engines, and that principle is still true.

A large number of amateur head modifiers and even cylinder head shops still spend a lot of time doing what I call "sparkle and glitter" head jobs. They don't really change the shape of the ports or combustion chamber, and it is probably just as well they don't, given their obviously limited knowledge. What is more usual is to grind out the first couple of inches of port close to the manifold face, because that is the part easiest to get at with a grinder, and then finish off with a high polish. The combustion chamber is next to receive a sparkle job and probably big valves as well. The end result is a head that looks pretty and has cost a lot of money, but which in truth actually reduces power and economy at most points in the rev range.

Many ordinary family sedans now feature high flow cylinder heads with large valves right from the factory. Only subtle port and valve modifications are necessary to unleash extra hp.

On a performance/economy engine we particularly need to keep gas speed up otherwise the fuel will drop out of suspension and dribble into the combustion chamber in non-combustable droplets. This wastes fuel, reduces performance, washes lubricant from the cylinder walls and ups emissions. Hence we do not need to hog out the ports; some stock ports are a little too big anyway. Big casting protrusions can be ground down but don't waste time smoothing and polishing. With few exceptions the majority of stock ports give good flow up to about 0.400in valve lift, some up to 0.450in lift. The principal impediment to high lift flow is the valve itself and the valve pocket (also called valve bowl) which is the area between the valve guide and the valve seat. Obviously then, the valve pocket is the part of the port on which to concentrate our modification efforts.

To understand better what happens when the ports are hogged out and big valves are fitted, take a look at Table 2.1 which shows the gas flow through two Chev heads. The first head with casting number "993" was originally fitted to low performance 350 cu in cars and trucks in the early 70s. By American standards it is not a bad head, but it certainly isn't close to what is coming out of Japan and Europe. Note that inlet air flow fell on its face at about 0.400in valve lift, which is about where we would expect a stock head to stop increasing in flow. The second head was a full race head with big ports and valves modified to give good power up to 8000rpm with a high lift roller cam. For the price of just one of these you could buy a full set of alloy wheels and high performance low profile tyres! The flow figures seem to indicate that the race head was far superior right through the valve lift range. (Incidently the race head kept on flowing well right up to 0.650in lift). However, for little more money than a reconditioning job the low performance emission heads were modified to produce the third set of test figures. As can be seen these mildly modified heads outflowed the full race heads right up to 0.400in valve lift and at 0.450in lift, which is about the maximum we can reliably use on the street anyway, they were not too far behind. Actually, the flow figures at maximum lift are not terribly important as the valve only dwells there for an instant; however, it spends much more time at lower lifts opening and then closing as well.

Table 2.1   Chev Cylinder Head Flow Test

Valve Lift   Cubic Feet Per Minute Air Flow

	Test 1		Test 2		Test 3	
	Inlet	**Exhaust**	**Inlet**	**Exhaust**	**Inlet**	**Exhaust**
0.100in	33	23	38	32	42	30
0.150in	49	34	57	50	63	48
0.200in	66	42	75	65	85	63
0.250in	84	55	93	74	105	70
0.300in	98	62	108	88	116	85
0.350in	110	67	120	96	124	94
0.400in	116	71	131	108	131	102
0.450in	117	74	141	115	133	105
0.500in	117	76	150	118	135	110

Test 1 – standard Chev 350 head with 1.94in inlet and 1.5in exhaust valve

Test 2 – fully modified Chev 350 race head with 2.055in inlet and 1.625in exhaust valve

Test 3 – slightly modified Chev 350 head with 1.94in inlet and 1.6in exhaust valve

Except for the valve pocket area, the ports on the emission heads were not touched. In the inlet valve pocket the first job was to cut away the lip formed by the original factory-machined 75° throat cut. This lip was not ground right down to leave a straight wall as many would think, rather it was radiused as shown to assist the air to turn into the cylinder past the valve head. The short radius on the port floor also required careful blending and smoothing. Next, the valve guide boss was slimmed down, but not shortened in the interests of long life, and the port roof at the sides of the boss radiused and smoothed. After this, the port was very gently blended into a conventional three angle valve seat.

On the exhaust side it was decided to replace the 1.5in valve with a standard Chev 1.6in exhaust valve. Some Chev heads can be only properly modified for good exhaust flow after a 1.6in valve is used, otherwise the valve throat shape ends up all wrong. Also these heads were to be fitted to a Corvette which was being stroked from 350 cu in to 383 cu in and I wanted good exhaust flow. The first job was to cut a new seat to accept a 1.6in valve. A large 60° cut was taken under a normal 45° seat to allow a generous radius to be ground on both the long and short side of the port. This again is where many would-be head modifiers go wrong. They tend to bore or grind the valve

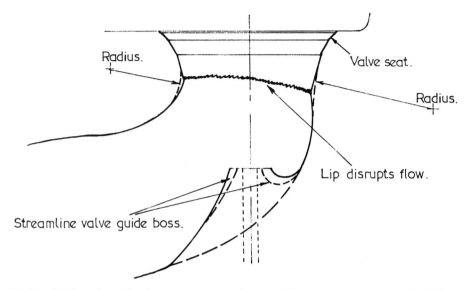

Radiusing the lip where the throat cut meets the cast inlet port promotes good air flow into the cylinder. If the port is ground right out to the edge of the valve seat flow is spoiled.

throat parallel below the 45° seat cut, which drastically reduces low and mid-lift exhaust flow. After blending the 60° throat cut into the port, the valve guide boss was then slimmed and the port roof at the sides of the boss blended and smoothed.

To further prove the point that ports do not have to be made larger to give good flow in performance/economy engines, look at the example of a VW Golf 1.6 litre head. Standard, these heads flow fairly well, but they are restricted by tiny 1.34in inlet

Table 2.2   VW Golf Cylinder Head Flow Test

Valve Lift			Cubic Feet Per Minute Air Flow			
	Test 1		Test 2		Test 3	
	Inlet	**Exhaust**	**Inlet**	**Exhaust**	**Inlet**	**Exhaust**
0.075in	21	17	22	22	24	23
0.150in	37	30	45	42	46	43
0.220in	51	38	64	53	65	57
0.290in	63	42	78	60	80	64
0.360in	65	47	86	66	86	72
0.430in	66	50	88	68	93	75
0.470in	67	51	89	70	95	78

Test 1 – standard 1.6 VW Golf head with 1.34in inlet and 1.22in exhaust valves

Test 2 – as above with 1.61in inlet and 1.34in exhaust valves

Test 3 – as above with ports modified

and 1.22in exhaust valves, and in the minds of many tuners by small ports as well. To dispel this idea just take a look at the flow figures in Table 2.2. On the inlet side flow dropped severely after 0.290in lift but in the exhaust port flow still wasn't too bad right up to 0.430in lift. In view of the small valves fitted it was decided not to waste time working on the valve pocket area or reshaping the valve underhead profile. Instead, suitably large valves would be fitted right from the start and then we would find out what sort of port modifications work.

The first step was to remove the standard valve seat inserts and fit high quality inserts (the standard inserts crack frequently), able to accept large 1.61in inlet and 1.34in exhaust valves. The standard ports were then roughly flared into the inside diameter of the inserts without any fancy work radiusing the throat or anything like that as I wanted to see just how well the standard head would work for a minimum outlay. As you can see from Test 2, the result was quite spectacular, proving that the small standard ports were well up to the task, even with a large increase in valve size. However, flow was still tapering off above 0.360in lift so some port modifications were tried to rectify this situation. The first move was to properly taper the valve pocket area right from the valve guide into the valve seat. This modification produced the figures shown in Test 3. Every modification tried after this gave better flow only at 0.470in lift which was of no value with a road cam, and as expected, some modifications reduced flow at all lifts up to 0.290in. On the exhaust side tapering the valve pocket into the wider valve throat didn't do anything one way or the other. The only modification which did any good, was to square the top of the exhaust port, where most flow occurs, over its entire length. This change produced the exhaust flow shown in Test 3. In view of the extra expense involved this work could not be justified for a road car as the larger exhaust valve by itself produced acceptable exhaust flow.

A nice straight inlet port like in the Golf and many ohc new generation engines can be quite small and give good flow while pushrod engines with more tortuous bends require a larger port to allow acceptable flow. Looking at the illustration of the Chev inlet port you note that there is less flow on one side of the valve because the tight bend in the floor of the port restricts flow around that side of the valve. In fact in some heads flow along the floor of the port, and around the short radius into the combustion chamber, can be as little as 25% of the flow along the port roof and around the opposite side of the valve. Except at low valve lift the majority of mixture flows along the roof and around the more gentle radius into the engine. Hence with this type of head a larger port is necessary than if the port is good and straight, as the straight port has little variation in flow between the port floor and port roof.

Just how large the inlet port should be depends on a number of factors such as cylinder size, engine operating rpm, port shape, valve size etc. so a definite answer is not possible. However, it is true to say that the port must be more than 0.82 times the valve diameter in the case of round ports, or more than 0.67 times the valve area in the case of rectangular or oval ports. Table 2.3 sets out inlet port sizes which I have found to work well in many applications. These are maximum recommended sizes; many engines will give fine performance with round ports up to 6% smaller in diameter and rectangular or oval ports up to 11% less in area.

Three and four valve heads usually do not require any change in inlet port diameter. If you wish to check, the port diameter should be 0.77 to 0.79 times the valve diameter.

Porsche 944 inlet port.

Chev 350 inlet port.

Comparison of these Porsche and Chev inlet ports illustrates why many new generation engines flow so well with relatively small but straight inlet ports.

Table 2.3   Inlet Port Size For Two Valve Engines

Cylinder Size (cc)	Port Diameter (in)	Port Area (sq in)
250	1.13	1.0
325	1.2	1.13
400	1.25	1.23
450	1.32	1.37
500	1.35	1.43
550	1.4	1.54
600	1.48	1.72
700	1.6	2.0

Note: with round ports the port must not be more than 0.82 times the valve diameter and with rectangular or oval ports the port area must not be more than 0.67 times the valve area

As mentioned earlier, the part on which port modifications should be concentrated is in the area directly above and below the valve seat. To help the air turn into the combustion chamber the inlet pocket must not have straight walls as this destroys flow. Rather a venturi must be formed, as illustrated. At its narrowest point it should be 0.85 to 0.88 times the valve diameter. Sometimes manufacturers just do not leave enough metal in the valve pocket to form such a venturi, which leaves just two options. Either we have to be satisfied with less flow or if there is sufficient room in the combustion chamber and the budget is large enough, we can fit larger valves to give the required neckdown in the valve pocket.

Exhaust ports basically require similar modifications to the inlets. The valve pocket area must be radiused and have a throat diameter of 0.85 to 0.86 times the valve diameter. Then the port can open out to about 0.95 times the exhaust valve diameter as it approaches the manifold face. In road applications this is not terribly important as many engines work quite well with a port diameter only 0.89 times the exhaust valve size (for rectangular ports port area is 0.81 times exhaust valve area). If the exhaust ports are too small then grind the top half of the port larger, where most flow occurs. Round and oval ports can be squared at the top while rectangular ports can be made wider in the upper half. Do not lower or widen the floor of exhaust ports as this will create turbulent flow and encourage exhaust gas backflow into the engine.

Raise and widen small exhaust ports.

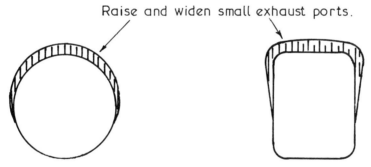

Exhaust ports which are too small should be raised and made wider in the top of the port, where most flow occurs.

A major constriction exists in the exhaust ports of emission engines with the AIR (Air Injection Reactor) system dumping directly into the exhaust port. To adequately support the air injector nozzle a substantial boss is cast in the port roof where most exhaust flow should take place. If it is possible to remove the AIR system, this should be done, then screw plugs in the holes left by the air injectors and grind the bosses away. This often will not be possible so it may be necessary to grind the injector nozzles and bosses down as far as practical, so as not to cause cracking of the port if the roof is fairly thin. If your engine does not have an air injector system but comes from a family of engines equipped with AIR, on some models the exhaust ports may have unused bosses cast in them which will have to be ground away for good exhaust flow. Turbo engines should not have the AIR system removed or rendered inoperative as it actually contributes to performance by increasing exhaust gas volume and velocity at lower rpm. This helps the turbo spool up to speed more quickly, reducing lag and low speed sluggishness.

AIR injector nozzle.

AIR injector nozzle and support boss badly impede exhaust flow because they partly block the top half of the exhaust port.

Because the inlet and exhaust valves can pose a considerable restriction on flow both in and out of the engine, they must be of adequate size and of the correct shape to reduce flow impediments to a minimum. Many tuners by habit replace the stock valves with oversize items and in some instances, as with the 1.6 litre VW Golf, this is a wise move. However, many engines already have sufficiently large valves for road applications. What is required often is a subtle change to the stock valve shape to effect a good flow gain. There are advantages in retaining standard valves too; they are usually much cheaper than oversize racing valves, they are easy to obtain, the shape and length etc. doesn't change from one batch to the next, and they are usually available in a number of oversize stem sizes which allows the stock valve guides to be reamed out rather than replaced when the time comes to recondition the head. Some people worry about the quality of material used in standard valves but as a rule this is no longer a problem. All emission engines, and in particular unleaded fuel engines, are very hard on valves, hence only good heat and erosion-resistant materials can be used in stock engines. In fact many stock engines use materials in the valve heads very similar to that in competition engines. The secret to getting long valve life in today's engines is not better valve materials but more frequent reconditioning. A little valve guide wear and a rough or carboned up valve seat will soon lead to burned valves no matter what valve metal is specified. Some engines require a head reconditioning job as frequently as every 15,000 to 20,000 miles while others will still go 45,000 to 60,000 miles between valve jobs just like in the good old days.

Standard inlet valves flow much better when a simple 30° backcut is applied. The standard 1.94in Chev valve is typical of many mass produced valves but note in Table 2.4 how much flow improves when it is backcut as illustrated. As you can see, mid-lift flow was improved by up to 12%, which is as much flow gain as could be accomplished with many hours of grinding in the ports. Another relatively simple

Inlet valve.

Undercut .015 to .0175in.

30° backcut.

45° seat .075 to .090in wide.

Square corner.

Margin width .040 to .060in.

Simple valve modifications can produce as much flow increase as a lot of work in the ports. Inlet valves should be ground with a 30° backcut to blend the seat into the underhead radius. The stem is undercut over the distance between the valve guide and the underhead radius. A square corner between the valve margin and valve face reduces inlet backflow when a performance cam is fitted.

Table 2.4   Chev Inlet Valve Flow Test

Valve Lift	Test 1	Test 2	Test 3
0.050in	18	18	18
0.100in	33	35	38
0.200in	66	74	79
0.300in	98	109	112
0.400in	116	120	121
0.500in	117	117	118

Test 1 – standard Chev 1.94in inlet valve

Test 2 – standard valve with 30° backcut

Test 3 – standard valve with 30° backcut and 0.035in stem undercut

modification is to undercut the valve stem by 0.035in. In the Chev it produced a 7% flow gain at lower lifts. Care is needed with this latter modification to avoid valve stem fatigue and eventual cracking. The undercut area must be carefully polished and blended into the valve head and also the uncut portion of the valve stem.

Table 2.5 indicates the gains to be made from simple exhaust valve modifications. A 1.5in Chev exhaust valve was chosen for this comparison because of what looks like a very poor underhead shape. A 30° backcut improved the valve shape but flow went up only 3%, which just proves that backcutting does not work on some valves. Next a good radius was applied to the valve face/margin area. This modification picked up flow by over 12% at lower lifts. A 45° cut around the valve face would have worked just as well, but this tends to weaken the valve more than a radius job. The valve stem was not undercut as the exhaust valve stem shape in engines is

Table 2.5   Chev Exhaust Valve Flow Test

Valve Lift	Test 1	Test 2	Test 3	Test 4
0.050in	14	14	15	17
0.100in	23	23	27	29
0.200in	42	43	48	53
0.300in	62	64	66	75
0.400in	71	73	74	80
0.500in	76	77	77	81

Test 1 – standard Chev 1.5in exhaust valve

Test 2 – standard valve with 30° backcut

Test 3 – standard valve with 30° backcut and radiused face

Test 4 – 1.5in competition valve with 30° backcut, radiused face and 0.035in undercut stem

Exhaust valve.

30° backcut.

45° seat .065 to .080in wide.

Radius corner .030in.

Margin .060 to .100in wide.

Standard exhaust valves can be modified as shown, with a 30° backcut and a radius to break the margin/valve face corner. If high quality one-piece austenitic stainless steel valves are fitted, the stems may be undercut to reduce their diameter by 0.035in.

very carefully established by factory testing for reliability. I know many exhaust valves have a terrible underhead stem shape which does restrict flow. However, that stem shape is required otherwise the heat of the exhaust gases combined with their long term corrosive effects would erode the underhead area, precipitating minute cracks which eventually allow the valve head and valve stem to part company. The way around this is to fit expensive high grade competition exhaust valves with nice slim stems. These are of one-piece construction, not a head welded to the stem like many stock valves, and as such require a special aluminium bronze valve guide material to avoid stem scuffing and seizure. By way of comparison, Test 4 shows just how much flow improvement is possible when a competition valve with the correct underhead profile is used. This particular valve comes from the manufacturer with a 0.035in stem undercut. All that was added was a simple 30° backcut and a face radiusing job.

Table 2.6 sets out the valve sizes which I like to see in a performance/economy engine with a two valve head. The performance difference between the minimum and preferred valve size is not very much in heads developed to give a good spread of power and economy. Theoretically, the bigger valves should flow more air at lower valve lifts and thus increase power output a little right through the range but it frequently does not work out that way. Car manufacturers have been doing a lot of cylinder head work both in-house and with the help of outside consultants for a few years now and they have fairly well worked out what size valves are most suited for road use.

In the quest for more power and reduced pollution, a number of car makers are now offering engines with three and four valve cylinder heads. The arrangement of two inlet and either one or two exhaust valves in the combustion chamber allows for an increase in valve area over that possible with a two valve head, but contrary to what many believe and write, this increased valve area is not the real reason for the superior performance of a multi-valve engine. The power increase comes about primarily because the combustion chamber is a better shape with a spark plug igniting the fuel mix right in the centre of the combustion space. This brings about a more complete and progressive burn and results in more power. Additionally, with more valves there is more valve flow area at all lifts. Remember that air does not flow through a valve but around its periphery, thus flow area is equal to valve circumference multiplied by valve lift. An engine with a 1.725in valve has a valve area of 2.34 sq in, while one with two 1.22in valves has a valve area also of 2.34 sq in. However, the single large valve has

Table 2.6   Valve Sizes For Two Valve Engines

Cylinder Size (cc)	Inlet Valve Diameter (in)		Exhaust Valve Diameter (in)	
	minimum	preferred	minimum	preferred
250	1.32	1.37	1.14	1.18
325	1.4	1.5	1.15	1.32
400	1.5	1.63	1.22	1.35
450	1.55	1.67	1.26	1.38
500	1.6	1.72	1.31	1.42
550	1.63	1.77	1.35	1.47
600	1.67	1.84	1.42	1.53
700	1.72	1.9	1.5	1.6

about 40% less flow area at all valve lifts which restricts its maximum power potential.

Obviously regardless of the number of valves or their size, the combustion chamber wall must not block flow around any of the valve circumference if their full flow potential is to be realised. Years ago most heads had a restrictive bath tub combustion chamber which allowed reasonable flow around only approximately 40% of the valve's circumference. Fortunately today very few heads have such tight combustion chamber walls masking the valves. However, all heads with in-line valves do suffer from some valve masking no matter how well designed, and all the more so if oversize valves are fitted. The way to ease the problem is to grind away the combustion chamber wall which is in close to the edge of the valve. Ideally it would be good if we

Combustion chambers with in-line valves will require some grinding to unmask the valves. A balance must be struck between high flow and good combustion. If the chamber wall is cut back as far as possible to improve flow, combustion may be slowed excessively and emissions could increase.

could have a passage between the edge of the valve and the chamber wall which is equal to the valve lift so that at 0.100in lift the wall is 0.100in from the valve, at 0.200in lift it is 0.200in from the valve and so forth. Such a chamber would probably flow reasonably well but the compression ratio would be very low and the mixture burn would be slow and inefficient. Hence a practical compromise has to be struck. The two ends of the chamber can only be ground back as far as the head gasket fire ring outline otherwise the head gasket will not seal. Around the inlet valve we want the chamber wall approximately 0.9 times the valve lift from the valve edge on the "live" or high flow side and about 0.65 times the valve lift from the edge of the valve on the "dead" short turn radius side. The chamber wall can be in much tighter around the exhaust valve; about 0.7 times the valve lift on the high flow side of the valve and approximately 0.55 times the valve lift on the short turn radius side of the valve.

More and more new generation engines are fitted with heads featuring semi-hemi or pentroof combustion chambers and inclined valves. With a few exceptions, such as the twin cam Fiat/Lancia, the combustion chamber does not shroud the valves to any extent in these designs. So unless there is an obvious deficiency, leave these combustion chambers alone and spend your time getting the valve pocket and valve seats right.

All heads need accurately ground multi-angle valve seats to give good flow, and more importantly a perfect gas-tight seal for many thousands of miles. The actual seat angle should be 45°, 0.050in wide for the inlet and 0.070in wide for the exhaust. The outside diameter of the seat is 0.015–0.020in less than the inlet valve diameter and up to 0.010in less than the exhaust valve head diameter. The top cut to blend the seat into the combustion chamber is at a 30° angle and just wide enough to blend the 45° seat into the chamber roof. The throat cut is usually made at 60° but this is best determined

The inlet valve seat is cut 0.050 to 0.060in wide for long life. The outside diameter of the seat should be about 0.020in smaller than the valve head diameter. Because we want the valve as high as possible for good flow, the 30° topcut is kept less than 0.040in wide. The 60° undercut will be about 0.100in wide, blending into the factory throat cut.

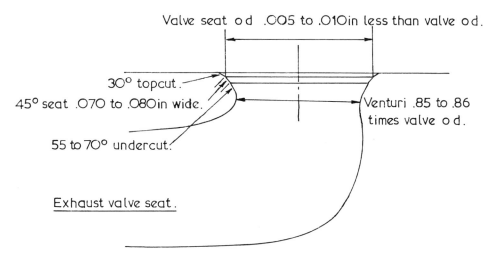

Valve seat o d .005 to .010in less than valve o d.

30° topcut.

45° seat .070 to .080in wide.

55 to 70° undercut.

Venturi .85 to .86 times valve o d.

Exhaust valve seat.

The exhaust valve seat is a little wider than the inlet to help get rid of the additional heat. The outside diameter of the 45° cut is almost the same as the valve head diameter because the valve will grow when hot. The width of the 30° topcut is not critical. In fact sinking the exhaust valves a little can help reduce mixture draw through and exhaust reversion. If a flow bench is not available, stick to a 60° undercut and radius it into the venturi.

on the flow bench as some inlets show superior flow with a fourth cut of 70–75° and exhausts can need a single cut of from 55–70°.

Some tuners like to use valve seats much narrower than I have suggested but this is not wise for road engines. Narrow seats flow better than wide seats only at very high lifts and at low and mid-lift they do not flow as well. Additionally, narrow seats pound out quickly which can lead to valve burning or lost performance. A valve gets rid of its heat primarily through the valve seat so if the seat becomes rough the valve head overheats, warps and finally burns.

The other heat flow path for the valve is via the valve guide to the engine coolant, so do ensure that the guide and stem are not worn excessively. Primarily, the valve guide is responsible for accurately guiding the valve onto the valve seat, to effect a gas seal. When the guide and valve stem wear, this allows the valve to wobble as it seats, wearing the seat to an irregular shape. Again heat transfer is reduced so the valve head warps and eventually burns. In some engines though the problem can be much more serious than a burned valve; it can lead to a major blow-up! What can happen if the valve is very hot and the engine is running at higher rpm, is for the valve head to bend a couple of degrees relative to the valve stem. Each time the valve seats it bends back a different way, eventually fatiguing the stem. The valve head drops off and proceeds to hole a piston. Usually, welded two-piece valves are blamed for this type of blow-up but it is worn valve guides and worn valve seats which are the real problem.

Valve guides can only be accurately measured for wear after all the carbon baked into them has been removed. Generally, the clearance should be 0.001–0.003in for the inlets and 0.0015–0.004in for the exhausts. Don't rely upon your sense of feel, actually measure the clearance to ensure that it is within limits. If the clearance is excessive, the guides will have to be reamed and valves with oversize stems fitted. Alternatively, new valve guides may be fitted and the old valves can have their stems "paralleled".

Just as worn valve guides allow oil into the engine, upsetting combustion and perhaps causing detonation, so too can the absence of effective valve stem seals and oil splash shields. Personally I do not like the Teflon-type seals which press over the valve guide. In race engines that never see worn valve stems or guides they work fine but for road use where the stem to guide clearance is ideal for only a few thousand miles they just do not work. If there is sufficient room I prefer to use the common "umbrella" type valve stem seal which fits firmly on the stem up under the valve spring retainer. Unfortunately, this seal will not fit inside some inner valve springs or dampers, and it may interfere with valve spring retainer to valve guide clearance with some high lift cams. The other common seal is the "O" ring type which is concealed between the valve stem, the collets and valve cap. This type is not as effective as an "umbrella" seal but will work well when used in conjunction with Teflon-type seals or under-retainer oil splash shields.

Faulty or the wrong type of valve stem seals, and the removal of oil splash shields, are probably the most common cause of excessive oil consumption, and a problem which is frequently underrated or overlooked. I have had freshly reconditioned engines brought to me which showed exhaust smoke at idle. Investigation showed that the oil splash shields had been left off. Replacing the shields stopped the smoke and cut oil consumption. Many race teams are now using umbrella seals in their production-based long distance race engines. Oil consumption has been halved in some cases. Overhead cam engines with inverted bucket type cam followers, which fit over the valve stem and valve spring, sometimes do not have valve stem seals fitted at the factory because this type of cam follower stops oil from getting onto the valve stem. However, oil vapor can be drawn down the inlet valve guide under high vacuum conditions. To prevent this, Teflon seals which press over the valve guide may be fitted on the inlets, cutting oil consumption and carbon deposits under the valve head and in the combustion chamber.

For the head to seal against the engine block it must be flat, with a stable and rigid deck and, of course, the correct type of head gasket must be used. Most alloy heads will experience sealing problems, due to a thin flexible deck, if more than 0.030–0.040in is machined off to reduce the combustion chamber volume. Some cast iron heads have such a thick deck that it is possible to mill off 0.100in if necessary, without any problems. 0.050–0.060in is a safer upper limit and this amount should suffice in most instances to restore chamber volume lost from unshrouding the valves. Chev cast iron heads made after about mid-1977 were cast thinner to reduce engine weight.

Heavy head.   Thin Chev head.

Lightweight Chev cast iron heads are very thin in the deck and should not be milled more than 0.020in to avoid gasket problems.

These should not be machined more than 0.020in to avoid gasket problems. Whereas the earlier heavy heads have a straight deck edge under the spark plugs, the light heads have a projection between the head bolt holes under each spark plug.

Very few new generation engines suffer head sealing problems in performance/ economy tune if a little care is taken to select the correct type of head gasket. Usually the manufacturer's standard head gasket will be suitable; however I would not use a copper asbestos gasket or a stainless steel gasket. Naturally if the engine has been radically overbored, against my recommendation, then the standard gasket may lap over the bore and be unsuitable. Also some car makers have changed over to alloy heads for their latest engines so do be sure to get the correct gasket set which suits an alloy head. A thin mild steel shim gasket will work well enough, if fitted the correct way up, with cast iron heads, but they will not effectively seal aluminium heads. The correct way to fit mild steel gaskets is with the channel rolled into them facing up as if to hold water. Mostly though head gaskets are a composition type with a mild steel fire ring. Some are coated around the water and oil holes with a sealer to prevent leaks. This sealer should not be removed with solvent as it does a good job of stopping water or oil seepage between the head and block. Regardless of the gasket material I always use a very thin coating of sealant; Rolls-Royce Hylomar for copper/steel/asbestos gaskets and non-hardening Permatex No. 3 for mild steel and composition gaskets. If the gaskets are factory pre-coated with a sealer I apply the sealer only around the gasket fire ring area.

When the head is fitted, the head bolts should have their threads buffed and oiled to ensure good tensioning. If the threads break into the water jacket delete the bolt thread oiling and apply a silicone sealant such as Silastic RTV. Then tighten the head bolts in the sequence recommended by the manufacturer. Note that this sequence is reversed for head removal. I always tension the head in progressive steps to prevent warpage. If the head tension was 80lbf ft I would first take all the bolts down to 30lbf ft, then 50, 70 and finally 80lbf ft. In about 15 minutes go over the bolts again. That's it for the moment if the head is alloy. With cast iron heads bring the engine to normal operating temperature and then re-tension the bolts. Final gasket set should take place after about 300 miles of driving, so then re-tension the head, either alloy or iron, again. This should not be done if the bolts break into the water jacket as leakage past the threads may result.

To avoid head warpage the manufacturer's tensioning sequence should be followed. Remember to increase the tension in about four stages. When removing the head, the tensioning sequence is reversed.

Chapter 3
Fuel and
Compression Ratio

I don't think anyone has to be told that today's fuels are not what they used to be. Not too many years ago 100–103 octane five star fuel was freely available, allowing the use of compression ratios approaching 11:1. That situation has changed dramatically in just a few years because of pollution control and steep rises in crude oil prices in the early 80s. Today, the best leaded fuel is usually no better than 97–98 octane and the lead content is down from about 3 grams per gallon to 1.5 grams per gallon in many countries. In the UK and Canada it is about half that figure and in some parts of the USA there is so little in so called "leaded fuel" that it should be illegal in my opinion to call it leaded. In countries where pollution has become an issue, new cars have to make do with unleaded fuel. Some countries have only one grade of unleaded, of about 91–92 octane, while others have a high octane unleaded of 96–97 octane as well. Even with premium unleaded being freely available in most parts of the USA, 16% of cars designed to use unleaded are being illegally refueled on leaded.

Since much confusion exists as to what octane ratings are all about it is best to have a look at the subject before we get into what options are open to us to improve the poor quality fuel situation which exists. Most people realise that we can get more power and better fuel economy with a high octane fuel because we can use a higher compression ratio, and perhaps more spark advance, without running into a detonation problem. However, many don't realise that simply changing from, say, 97 octane pump petrol to 100/130 Avgas, which has an octane rating of about 110, will not necessarily give any power increase. Actually, you could lose power if the engine was not modified, or could not be changed in any way to take advantage of the octane increase.

To understand this more easily, we have to delve back into history to see why a number system was introduced to grade fuels, and discover exactly to what the octane numbers refer. About the time of World War 1, aircraft engines would suddenly self-destruct, through detonation. An engine might run just fine on one load of fuel, but punch holes in the pistons on the next batch. The fuels seemed to be the same, weigh the same, and may perhaps have come from the very same refinery.

The fuel companies tried chemical analysis in an endeavour to achieve parity from one lot of petrol to the next but, in spite of an intensive programme, they were not able to weed out the batches which were prone to produce engine knock. Therefore special fuel research engines, with a variable compression feature, were constructed to evaluate and grade fuels. Such a standard heavy-duty, single-cylinder test engine would be warmed up to a standard test temperature, run at standard rpm and load, and then have the compression ratio increased until the fuel being tested just produced engine knock. Its anti-knock quality would then be specified as its Highest Useable Compression Ratio (HUCR).

Even with every fuel test lab supplied with the same type of test engine, and using the same standard test procedure, it was discovered that the same fuel could test out with differing HUCR numbers in different laboratories. It was next decided that some unvarying standard was needed by which to calibrate the lab test engine. Two pure substances were chosen as reference fuels. The high reference fuel chosen was 2-2-4 trimethylpentane, what we commonly call iso-octane, while the low reference fuel was normal heptane (n-heptane).

Now it was decided that a fuel under test would be run in the variable compression test engine and its HUCR determined. Then a series of runs would be made with various mixtures of iso-octane and n-heptane until a blend was found which produced knock behaviour identical to the fuel being tested. At this point the quality of the test fuel would be rated in relation to the percentage of iso-octane in the reference fuel mixture which gave identical test results. For example, a fuel which behaved the same as a mixture of 90% iso-octane/10% n-heptane would be called 90 octane fuel. Using this standard test procedure, fuel of constant quality could be refined and supplied for a variety of applications.

Since that time a number of test procedures have come into use to simulate a variety of engine operating conditions. Motor spirit is usually rated according to the Research or Motor test methods. Both measuring techniques use the same single-cylinder, variable-compression test engine, but as indicated in Table 3.1 the Motor method employs a greater engine speed and a higher inlet mixture temperature than the Research test. Hence the Motor method is a more severe test, and generally yields octane numbers 6 to 12 less than the Research test as shown in Table 3.2. This distinction is important, as it informs us that the Motor Octane Number (MON) is more relevant to today's engines, and in particular turbo engines which operate at high inlet temperatures, than is the Research Octane Number (RON).

The spread between the Motor and Research numbers is known as the fuel's sensitivity and it is very important to understand what this distinction is exactly. Because intake temperature affects different fuel compounds in various ways it is possible for a company to come up with a fuel which has a high Research number (or a high Pump Octane Number) of say, 97 but by the Motor test that same fuel would only rate as, say, 85 octane. Hence it would perform as an 85 octane fuel in a modern emissions or turbo engine with high inlet temperatures. However, on another day the same fuel company could use a different blend of fuel compounds, depending on what was available in storage or the type of crude oil being "cracked", and produce a fuel again with a Research octane of 97, but with a Motor number of 89. This is why there is this frequent complaint of "bad fuel". The Research number may legally be up

where the company says it is, but because of the sensitivity of the blending compounds

Table 3.1   Comparison of Motor and Research test procedures

	Motor Octane Test	Research Octane Test
Inlet air temperature	148.9°C	65.6°C
Engine jacket temperature	100°C	100°C
Engine rpm	900	600

Table 3.2   Octane test comparison

Research Octane Number	Motor Octane Number	Pump Octane Number
90	83	86.5
92	85	88.5
96	88	92
98	90	94
100	91.5	95.8
105	95	100
110	99	104.5

Note: the octane numbers in this table are approximate only and will vary by as much as 2 from one fuel to another

the fuel could be performing like low octane stuff because of the high inlet temperatures common in new generation engines. Years ago, when high lead levels were usual, this sensitivity problem seldom surfaced as lead tends to "cushion" fuel sensitivity. However, with today's unleaded and low-lead fuels, fuel sensitivity will continue to cause us problems in modern engines for as long as Research octane figures are used as the industry standard to rate commercially available fuels.

In America the service station pumps carry a Pump Octane Number (PON) rather than the Research Octane Number usual on pumps in other parts of the world. This rating is the average of the RON and MON:

$$\frac{RON + MON}{2}$$

but it does not completely overcome the problem of fuel sensitivity. For example, a 92 PON fuel may have an 88 Motor rating and a 96 Research rating. However, fuel with a 92 PON from the same company may test out at 86 Motor and 98 Research because of the blend of compounds used in another batch. Hence even with this system the octane could vary by 2 points (88 to 86 Motor) as the engine of today with high inlet temperatures sees it.

The Supercharge test is applied to aircraft fuels which exceed 100 octane numbers, as the other tests obviously become meaningless at anything over 100 octane. The Supercharge Octane Numbers (SON) are really performance numbers obtained by linearly extending the scale beyond 100. In this test the reference fuel is iso-octane plus lead. Two tests are involved, the F3 and F4, which explains why aircraft fuels have a dual rating such as 100/130. The first number refers to the F3 test, which simulates a supercharged engine running on a chemically-correct fuel/air mixture, as when cruising. The F4 number gives an indication of the fuel's performance rating with an enriched mixture and increased supercharge boost, as would be supplied during aircraft take-off or during combat conditions.

There are really only two types of Avgas freely available today, both rated 100/130. The old green coloured 100/130 is a high lead variety with 4.5 to 6 grams of tetra-ethyl-lead (t.e.l.) per gallon while the newer blue coloured Avgas has 2 to 2.7 grams of lead per gallon.

The anti-knock properties of hydrocarbon fuels are related to their molecular structures. The paraffins, such as normal heptane and kerosene, are long chains of carbon and hydrogen held together by weak molecular bonds which are easily broken by heat. Iso-octane is a member of the iso-paraffin family. These have a branched chain structure that form stronger bonds to resist detonation better. The cyclo-paraffins (or napthenes) also have good anti-detonation properties with their hydrogen and carbon atoms well bonded in a ring-shaped molecule. The aromatic fuels, such as toluol, have a ring-shaped structure with very strong bonds. This explains why they have such good anti-knock characteristics.

The chemical composition determines just how rapidly the fuel will burn and whether it will be resistant to detonation at high compression pressures and temperatures. The fuels with weak molecular bonds break up and burn spontaneously (ie., without being ignited by the combustion flame initiated by the firing of the spark plug) at lower temperatures and pressure than fuels with strongly bonded structures. Some fuel additives, such as the aromatics, make excellent anti-detonants because they burn slowly and don't oxidise or burn completely until combustion chamber temperature and pressure is very high. Such additives therefore inhibit, or slow down, combustion. Hence a high octane fuel will not increase power unless the engine actually needs a fuel which is chemically stable at high temperature and pressure. Obviously, if the engine does not have a compression ratio and spark advance great enough to produce high combustion pressure and temperature, then the high octane fuel will not burn completely, resulting in loss of power.

Table 3.3 shows the results of fuel tests carried out on a 4.1 litre Buick. Because the engine was being developed to run on 92 octane unleaded the compression ratio was kept down to 8.8:1. The cam was a Phase III grind with 210° inlet and exhaust duration and 0.425in lift. In each test the total ignition advance was changed to achieve the maximum hp figures indicated, at 5000rpm. In all, six different fuels were tested; two different brands of 92 unleaded "summer" blend, a 92 unleaded "winter" blend from the same company as fuel B, a 97 unleaded, a 97 leaded with 1.8 grams per gallon, and "green" Avgas.

In the first series of tests the inlet manifold was heated to check the sensitivity of the fuels and in the second series the manifold heat passage was blocked to prevent flow through it. Note that this modification may not be suitable in cooler climates as

Table 3.3   Comparison fuel test of 4.1 litre Buick

Fuel	Test 1 hp	Test 1 Advance	Test 2 hp	Test 2 Advance
92 unleaded "summer A"	212	28°	220	31°
92 unleaded "summer B"	219	30°	223	32°
92 unleaded "winter B"	208	26°	215	29°
97 unleaded "summer A"	215	30°	222	33°
97 leaded "summer A"	218	30°	221	33°
100/130 Avgas "green"	222	40°	224	44°
100/130 Avgas "green"	210	30°	213	33°

Test 1 – heat to inlet manifold

Test 2 – heat blocked off to inlet manifold

the engine could lose some economy and cold driveability. As can be seen, the high octane unleaded was very temperature sensitive, as was the low octane unleaded from the same company. Both fuels only worked really well with reduced intake charge temperature. The 100/130 Avgas, as expected, made good power but required a lot of advance. When the advance was cut back, the power dropped.

The 92 winter blend was thrown in to show what effect fuel volatility can have on performance. In summer (or at higher altitudes) we don't want the fuel vaporising too easily and causing vapour lock. However, in the winter the fuel must vaporise easily, and stay in vapour to allow easy starting and acceptable driveability while the engine is below normal operating temperature. To achieve these fuel characteristics the fuel companies change the fuel blend according to the season and the altitude. At the risk of over-simplification what they do is blend in more of the volatile "front-end" molecules (also called "light ends") which vaporise and fire more easily. This brings another problem; that of reducing the shelf life and the octane rating as these molecules are released into the atmosphere. The more light ends, the shorter the shelf life, and the quicker the fuel loses octane level, which can be as much as 2–4 octane numbers. Apparently this is a problem with some high octane unleaded as well, so if you live away from the city in a location where there is a lower turn over of fuel you may often be getting old or out of season fuel which will require the use of a lower compression ratio to compensate.

The compression ratio has always been of interest to engine tuners, even more so today with the need to achieve the best possible fuel economy and power on low octane and unleaded fuel. In the past tuners liked to see the compression ratio pushed up as high as possible because high compression has always been equated with high horsepower. I agree that the compression ratio should be as high as practicable, but often the manufacturer has already found the limit and built his engines accordingly. If this is the case then all we can do is check that production tolerances have not lowered the ratio significantly below that which the makers intended.

The actual value of compression ratio which may be used in any engine is dependent on the design and size of the combustion chamber, the cam timing and   35 overlap period, and the fuel octane rating. In the case of turbo engines we need to add the boost pressure and intake charge temperature as well. Generally speaking, small "fast burn" pentroof and semi-hemi combustion chambers and longer duration cams permit the use of a higher compression ratio than bathtub or wedge chambers and short duration cams. For example, the 1.6 litre four valve Toyota Corolla with a 81mm bore and pentroof chamber will run quite happily with standard cams on a 9.4:1 compression ratio burning only 92 octane unleaded fuel. With mild cams the compression can be upped to 10:1. Conversely, the 5 litre Holden with open wedge chambers and a 101.6mm bore will tolerate no more than a true 8.8:1 compression ratio with a mild cam on the same fuel. Increasing the fuel octane rating to 97 permits a compression ratio of 9.3:1 to be employed.

Research has indicated that increasing the compression ratio from 8.5:1 to 10.5:1 will result in a 10 to 12% fuel saving, with improved torque and acceleration as a bonus. Unfortunately, such a large jump just will not be tolerated with the fuel now available. Some tuners feel that the compression ratio can be pushed way up and then the ignition timing backed off to stop detonation. If this is done, the engine loses responsiveness and fuel efficiency. Table 3.4 indicates the result when this was tried on a 5 litre Holden. A Phase IV cam with 212° inlet and exhaust duration and 0.443in lift was used in all tests. In the first test, stock compression was used. It was supposed to be 8.5:1 according to the manufacturer, but in reality was a true 8.2:1. The engine made good power and torque on 30° total ignition advance. For Test 2 the compression ratio was increased to 10.8:1 but the engine wouldn't take full load without detonating severely so the timing was backed off until the detonating was eliminated at 19° total advance. With the distributor recurved to suit, the engine produced the figures indicated. The test was a disaster, with power down at all engine speeds. Added to this

Table 3.4   Compression ratio comparison test of 5 litre Holden

rpm	Test 1 hp	Test 1 Torque	Test 2 hp	Test 2 Torque	Test 3 hp	Test 3 Torque	Test 4 hp	Test 4 Torque
2000	109	286	102	269	117	306	112	294
2500	141	297	136	286	150	315	144	302
3000	174	304	167	292	183	320	179	313
3500	208	312	196	294	216	324	211	316
4000	237	311	219	288	248	326	241	317
4500	251	293	232	271	265	309	256	299
5000	257	270	241	253	270	284	265	278
5500	247	236	219	209	256	244	249	238

Test 1 –   8.2:1 compression ratio, 30° total advance, 97 octane fuel

Test 2 – 10.8:1 compression ratio, 19° total advance, 97 octane fuel

Test 3 – 10.8:1 compression ratio, 35° total advance, approximately 106 octane fuel

Test 4 –   9.3:1 compression ratio, 27° total advance, 97 octane fuel the engine sounded dead on the dyno and without the crispness that it had previously shown. Perhaps the "rattling" while the ignition timing was being sorted had damaged the pistons and rings which could have contributed to the poor power figures. Before stripping the engine to determine if this was a problem, a 50/50 fuel mix of 97 unleaded and Avgas 100/130 (106 Research octane approximately) was prepared to see if the engine would respond to good fuel. Test 3 shows the results with the distributor recurved and 35° total advance. The engine really responded to the change and showed just how much high compression and good fuel is worth in outright power. For Test 4 the compression was brought down to a more realistic 9.3:1. The distributor was recurved and total advance set at 27°. This increased maximum power by 8 hp at 5000rpm over that in Test 1 and would have resulted in a fuel saving of around 5 or 6% on the highway. These tests clearly show that getting the compression ratio up within the limits of available fuel will give better performance. However, going too far and then backing the timing off will not solve the problem. The result will be lost power and generally sluggish performance.

Although a fuel blend was used during the testing of this engine I do not really recommend mixing fuel for road use for a number of reasons, namely; inconvenience, no guarantee of blending agents being freely available in all localities, possible damage to catalytic converter and oxygen sensor, danger to health from compounds being mixed, danger from fire. However there is an exception: in some lands high octane leaded (97–100 Research) is now very hard to find, but many service stations carry high octane unleaded (usually 95–97 Research) and low octane leaded (91–93 Research) in their pumps. Now a one third mix of the low octane leaded stuff to two thirds 95–97 unleaded should yield a leaded fuel with an octane rating equal to or up to 1 point less than that of the unleaded. In countries where high octane leaded and unleaded are both available in the pumps, then a 50/50 blend can be used to increase the octane rating by 1–3 points over that of the base fuels. So 96 octane unleaded and 97 octane leaded would yield a 97.5–99.5 octane fuel.

If your engine is designed to operate on leaded fuel do not use straight unleaded otherwise the valves and seats will soon be damaged. Running the occasional tank of unleaded through the engine will not hurt, providing leaded is used for the next fill. Using leaded fuel in a car designed to burn unleaded will not cause engine damage, in fact it will make life easier for the valves; however the lead will wreck the catalytic converter and in time also the oxygen sensor.

For those enthusiasts who engage in a little weekend competition driving, a little more advanced fuel blending may be in order providing the engine components are up to handling more turbo boost or more spark advance to take advantage of high octane fuel. At the present time there are a large number of concentrated octane booster additives on the market which are designed to convert pump petrol, either leaded or unleaded, into racing fuel. When blended in the correct proportions boosters which work will raise the octane rating of fuel about 5 points; double strength they raise the octane by up to 8 points. Some companies claim that their boosters will produce 108–110 octane fuel, equivalent to Avgas 100/130, but I have not found this to be true. In fact a number of boosters will give only a 2 octane increase. One booster which does work is *104+*. Mixed at normal strength this booster will give a true 5 points octane increase, allowing about 2–4° increase in spark advance or around an extra 2–3lb boost. Mixed double strength *104+* has little additional effect on some fuels, but with many fuels will yield an 8 point octane boost. To take advantage of this increase another 6–8° spark advance or up to 3–5lb more boost would be required.

When using these concentrated additives, there are two points you must keep in mind. The first is that American concentrates are usually marketed in US quarts, which equal 946cc as opposed to the Imperial quart of 1136.5cc. Therefore, if you live outside the USA you will have to carefully work out the blending ratio for the liquid measure used in your country. The second point is with regard to mixing technique. Don't just pour a can of octane booster into a drum of fuel and expect it to blend properly. What is preferable is to mix the concentrate with about 2–3 gallons of petrol, give the drum a good shake, and then add this mixture to the untreated fuel.

Avgas 100/130, either "green" or "blue", is also an excellent octane booster for weekend competition, but remember if the catalytic converter is left in place this leaded fuel will wreck it. Mixed one part Avgas to three parts petrol gives a 3–6 point octane boost, depending on whether the base fuel is leaded or unleaded, eg 25% Avgas to 75% 97 octane unleaded will yield about a 103 octane fuel; with 97 octane leaded it will be closer to 100 octane. A 50/50 blend should give as much octane as is required for weekend competition, around 106 octane with 97 unleaded and about 104 with 97 leaded.

Toluol, marketed under the name Methyl Benzine by Shell, may be blended in proportions up to 1:2 (ie 33%) with leaded petrol to produce a 4–5 point octane increase. More than 33% toluol is not recommended as starting difficulties may be encountered. A 25% toluol/75% petrol mix raises the octane of leaded petrol approximately 2–3 points. A predictable or large octane increase can not be guaranteed when toluol is added to unleaded fuel as at times the base fuel may already contain a good amount of toluol, benzole or acetone. Hence a 25% toluol mix may permit a 3lb boost increase at times, but on another occasion you may punch holes in the pistons because the octane level has not risen significantly due to the blending agents used in the base fuel.

For a few years now water injection has been hailed by some as the perfect knock suppressor. I do not agree and apparently none of the car manufacturers do either. Water does not contribute to the combustion process, rather it takes heat and hence energy out of the combustion flame as it is converted to steam. This slows combustion, so unless the water is actually injected when the engine is under a heavy load, power and economy are lost. Many systems which I have seen inject too much water, not properly vaporised, and at the wrong level of engine loading. Some people use a 50/50 water/alcohol mix because the alcohol at least does contribute to the combustion process. However, this is not without its problems either; the alcohol in combination with water causes top cylinder and piston ring corrosion, shortening the life of the engine.

Because a number of new generation engines have a knock sensor which relays back to the ignition chip that ignition retard is momentarily required, some tuners indiscriminately push up the turbo boost or the compression ratio. They figure that since this system is in place they will let it prevent engine knock. This is definitely not the way to go. You may impress a few people telling them how much boost or compression that your engine is able to run, but that is about the limit to what you will gain out of the exercise. As shown earlier in Table 3.4 too much compression just reduces maximum power no matter how good the ignition retard system. Some manufacturers also deliberately run too much compression and leave it to the knock sensor to keep them out of trouble. This usually is done to improve part throttle fuel economy, which is good for advertising, but also in America the manufacturers have to meet the government corporate fuel consumption levels averaged over the total number of vehicles produced. A higher compression than desired will allow some engine models to squeeze through without upsetting the delicate equation for the other engine models. For the same reason you will find that some engine models are available in very limited numbers and then only with a certain gearbox and rear axle combination so as not to put a dent in the corporate average fuel consumption figures.

Just how much compression or boost is desirable with today's pump fuel? As I indicated earlier there are far too many factors involved to give an accurate answer, but the figures shown in Table 3.5 will give a guide to the compression ratio suitable for naturally aspirated engines with a reasonably quick burn combustion chamber, a Phase II or Phase III cam, and a squish clearance of no more than 0.045in. For a turbo engine I like to see the compression ratio up at 8:1 to give reasonable part throttle economy and acceptable off-boost performance. For the engine to live with an 8:1 compression ratio boost will have to be limited to the level indicated in Table 3.6. Note that the boost levels with an intercooler refers to an effective unit which reduces the intake charge temperature by 50–60°C. Some intercoolers are far less effective, reducing charge air temperature by only 25–30°C.

The actual compression ratio is the relationship between the total volume of the cylinder, head gasket and combustion chamber, with the piston at BDC (bottom dead

Table 3.5   Compression ratio for naturally aspirated engines

Bore diameter mm	91–92 octane	96–97 octane
76	9.3:1	9.8:1
83	9.2:1	9.7:1
90	9.0:1	9.5:1
100	8.6:1	9.0:1

Table 3.6   Turbo boost/compression ratio

Compression ratio	91–92 octane	96–97 octane
7.7:1	7 psi	9.5 psi
7.7:1 intercooled	11 psi	14 psi
8:1	6 psi	8.5 psi
8:1 intercooled	10 psi	13 psi
8.5:1	5 psi	7 psi
8.5:1 intercooled	7.5 psi	10 psi
9:1		5.5 psi
9:1 intercooled		8 psi

centre) and the volume contained in the space between the piston crown, head gasket and combustion chamber at TDC (top dead centre). This is expressed by the formula:

$$CR = \frac{CV + CCV}{CCV}$$

where CV = cylinder volume
CCV = combustion chamber volume

Naturally CV is the engine capacity in cc divided by the number of cylinders. CCV however is not so easy. This volume is made up of the combustion chamber volume, plus the volume that remains above the piston when the piston is at TDC, plus the volume caused by the thickness of the head gasket, plus the volume of the dish if dished pistons are used, or minus the amount displaced by high top pistons if these are fitted.

When we know what compression ratio we want then we can calculate what the volume CCV should be to give that ratio using the formula:

$$CCV = \frac{CV}{CR-1}$$

Assuming the engine has 500cc cylinders and we want a compression ratio of 9.2:1 then:

$$CCV = \frac{500}{9.2-1} = \frac{500}{8.2} = 61cc$$

The combustion chamber volume is measured using a burette. For road engines the volumes do not have to be carefully equalised.

To find what the actual value of CCV is in our engine we first must physically measure the volume of the combustion chamber using a burette filled with liquid paraffin (kerosene). Incidentally, the combustion chambers should have been equalised in volume so that for road engines, there is not more than a 0.1 change in compression ratio from cylinder to cylinder. This means that if the pistons are the same level below the top of the block at TDC then an engine with 300cc cylinders will have a variation of no more than 0.5cc between the largest and smallest combustion chamber. For a 500cc cylinder the spread between the largest and smallest should not exceed 0.8cc and for 700cc cylinders the spread is 1cc.

When dished or high top pistons are fitted, or if the piston crown has valve cut-outs, the volume has to be measured so as to ascertain the compression ratio.

If the engine has pistons which are either dished or high top, or have valve cut-outs, then the increase or decrease that they are causing has to be measured. For instance, if the cylinder bore is 90mm in diameter and the piston crown at the edge is 6mm from the block deck, using the formula:

$$V = \frac{\pi D^2 \times H}{4000}$$

where π = 3.1416

D = bore in mm

H = height between piston crown edge and block deck in mm.

this volume should be:

$$V = \frac{\pi \times 90^2 \times 6}{4000} = 38.2cc$$

If on measuring the volume with a burette it is found to be 27.2cc, the lump on top of the piston decreases CCV by 11cc (38.2 − 27.2 = 11).

If the piston in this example had a dished top and the volume as measured by the burette was 52.7cc then the dish volume would be 14.5cc, increasing CCV by 14.5cc (52.7 − 38.2 = 14.5).

The above formula is also used to find the volume of the head gasket by measuring the thickness of a used, and thus compressed, gasket. If the pistons are flat tops and they are below the block deck at TDC, the same formula is used to find this volume as well.

To assist in equalising compression and combustion pressures, the crown of every piston should rise to approximately the same point in each cylinder. This is called the deck height or deck clearance. I like to keep the squish clearance between 0.035 and a maximum of 0.045in to assist combustion and cylinder scavenging. Hence if the compressed thickness of the head gasket is 0.030in then the deck clearance required will be 0.005 to 0.015in. Usually, to achieve this figure the top of the block will have to be milled. Note in a road engine that it is not essential for all pistons to rise to the same height in each cylinder; a variation of 0.005in is acceptable.

Head gasket.

Squish clearance.

A tight squish clearance of 0.035 to 0.045in speeds up combustion. The squish clearance is the sum of the compressed thickness of the head gasket and the piston deck clearance.

Most people take the easy way out and simply mill the head to change the compression; however, I feel that this should only be done, if necessary, after the deck clearance has been reduced. As I said, I like to build a good deal of squish into an engine by having the piston rise to 0.035 to 0.045in from the face of the cylinder head. This causes the piston to squish the fuel/air charge from the edges of the cylinder toward the spark plug. The fast moving gases meet the spark plug and quickly carry the combustion flame to the extremity of the combustion chamber, thus reducing the risk of detonation.

With the passing of time more benefits of building squish into the engine have come to light. The mixture being purged across the combustion chamber from the squish areas homogenises the fuel/air mixture more thoroughly and also mixes any residual exhaust gas still present with the fuel charge. This serves to speed up combustion by preventing stale gas pockets from forming. Such pockets slow down, and in some instances can prevent, flame propogation.

Turbulence caused by the squish effect also serves to enhance heat transfer at the spark-initiated flame front. Without proper heat transfer, jets of flame would tend to shoot out toward the edges of the combustion chamber, prematurely heating the surrounding gases to start off the cycle leading to detonation.

If you can't get the compression ratio up where you want it from milling the block and the head then do not go and fit high top pistons. These have no place in a road engine, and I don't like using them in race engines either. A big compression lump on the piston crown masks the spark plug and retards flame travel after ignition, and then often upsets complete cylinder scavenging during the exhaust cycle. After ignition, we want the flame to travel uniformly across the piston dome and back toward the squish area. Any abrupt protrusion on the piston crown will disrupt the flame front as it moves across the piston, leaving pockets of mixture that are only partially ignited or completely unburned. A low, 2–3mm high, flat or circular dome is necessary with some semi-hemi combustion chambers to get the compression ratio up. These low domes do not cause much trouble if they do not mask the spark plug and are free of abrupt edges.

Chapter 4
The Camshaft

A cam swap is an easy and inexpensive way to transform most new generation engines. With the right cam a ten per cent power increase is usually attainable without any loss in fuel economy. Buf if the wrong choice is made, it could transform the car into a sluggish fuel guzzler which fails emissions inspections.

In spite of all that advertising would have you believe, a camshaft is a simple device designed to open and close the inlet and exhaust valves in harmony with movement of the piston within the cylinder. The inlet lobe pushes the inlet valve open just before top dead centre (TDC) on the induction stroke and keeps it open until well after bottom dead centre (BDC) to let the inertia or momentum of the high velocity fuel/air mixture literally ram in additional mixture as the piston moves upward on the compression stroke. The exhaust valve is opened by the camshaft exhaust lobe during the combustion stroke. Most of the effective expansion power of combustion is over by mid-stroke so the exhaust valve is opened well before BDC to allow the cylinder pressure to "blow down" before the piston commences up on the exhaust stroke otherwise power would be lost pushing the gas out of the cylinder. The valve is left open until a little past TDC to use exhaust gas momentum to scavenge the cylinder efficiently. The inlet valve is opening again during this period, called the overlap period, to allow the small vacuum created by the movement of exhaust gas out of the cylinder to assist in drawing fresh fuel/air mixture into the inlet tract and cylinder.

The theory sounds good but in practice it does not work out like this, except over a narrow 2000–3000rpm range. At low engine speeds the incoming fuel mixture has little velocity and correspondingly little momentum, so as the piston starts up on the compression stroke, mixture is pushed out past the open inlet valve into the inlet tract. Less mixture is available for combustion, hence a 3 litre engine can perform as though it is a 2.0 litre unit.

Swapping the standard camshaft for a performance item is one of the most cost-effective changes which can be made. However, selecting a cam that it too wild will wreck low speed driveability and fuel economy, and could cause failed emissions tests.

At lower rpm late closing inlet valves allow mixture to be pushed out of the cylinder back into the inlet tract.

A similar situation occurs with late exhaust valve closing. Because the outgoing exhaust gases have low inertia at low rpm, the downward movement of the piston, now on the inlet stroke, will actually cause burned gas to turn around and be drawn right back into the cylinder. These hot gases occupy considerable cylinder volume, volume

Closing exhaust valve.

Opening inlet valve.

Piston descending at start
of induction stroke.

At lower rpm late closing exhaust valves allow exhaust gases to be drawn back into the cylinders.

that should have been filled by combustable fuel mixture. This exhaust gas goes on causing trouble by slowing combustion of much of the fuel mix and blocking combustion of the remainder. As will be discussed later, some manufacturers use both late inlet and exhaust valve closing, by retarding the cam or wide lobe separation angles to reduce cylinder pressure and combustion flame speed. This lowers the emission of nitrogen oxides (NOx). Good for emissions but potentially destructive of performance and economy.

The other flaw in inertia gas flow theory is evident during the overlap period. At certain higher engine rpm, dependent on exhaust system and combustion chamber design, the fuel/air mix will be drawn down the inlet tract, across the combustion chamber and then out past the open exhaust valve due to the inertia created by the spent exhaust gas leaving the cylinder from the previous cycle. The larger the cam overlap period and the more efficient the exhaust system, the greater the potential for this to occur. The end result is more pollution, excessive fuel consumption and less power.

By now it should be evident that selecting the ideal performance/economy cam involves more than merely reading some persuasive advertising in a car magazine and picking a cam timing figure that seems appealing. To assist in your understanding we must go back to the basics. Then you will grasp more of what the camshaft numbers game is all about.

Inlet and exhaust valves both
open during overlap period.

Mixture flows down the
inlet tract and out
the exhaust port.

Piston near TDC at the end
of exhaust stroke.

At mid-range and higher rpm, mixture may be drawn out past the open exhaust valve due to exhaust gas inertia and a long valve overlap period.

The illustration depicts the various features of every cam lobe. The base circle should be a constant radius from the cam centre. It allows the valves to seat and dissipate heat and permits the valve train time to settle from shock after each opening/ closing cycle. The ramp (or clearance ramp) takes up slack in the valve train and commences gently lifting the valve. The flank rapidly accelerates the valve open, the nose slows valve train motion to a stop, and the following flank accelerates the valve

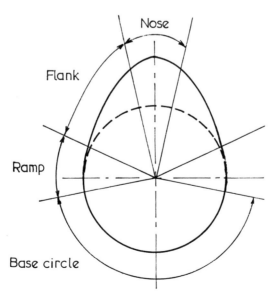

Nose

Flank

Ramp

Base circle

A performance cam has lobes with shorter ramps than stock and longer, steeper flanks to open the valves more rapidly and keep them open longer.

47

back down toward its seat where the closing ramp takes over to gently lower the valve onto the valve seat.

That is all very simple; the problem arises when you wish to purchase a cam and you want to compare one manufacturer's cam timing figures with another. In the USA nearly everyone times their cams from a 0.050in cam lift point but most car makers time their cams from when the lifter (cam follower) commences to move. In all countries no standard system is used. Some are timed at 1mm cam lift, others at 0.004in, 0.006in, 0.010in, 0.015in and 0.020in. To further confuse the situation a number of cam grinders time their product at 0.010in valve lift for hydraulic lifter cams and at "lash point" (when valve clearance is taken up) for mechanical (solid) lifter cams. It has been suggested that comparing cam timing figures is much like comparing buildings by measuring the length of their shadows without taking into account the position of the sun in the sky. To illustrate the problem with which the enthusiast is confronted when trying to make some sense of advertised timing figures we will consider the mild Chevrolet "929" cam which I classify as a Phase I cam. According to the factory, the intake valve opens 26° before TDC and closes 90° after BDC while the exhaust opens 84° before BDC and closes 46° after TDC. Durations of 296° inlet and 310° exhaust, figures which are taken at lash point, could have one thinking that this is a wild race cam. Measured at 0.006in lift the duration is approximately 254° inlet and 262° for the exhaust, figures which could still indicate a sporty cam. However, measured at 0.050in lift the true nature of the cam is revealed; 195° duration for the intake and 202° for the exhaust, a truly mild cam! Hopefully, one day everyone will adopt the same system, such as has been done by American cam manufacturers.

Table 4.1   Camshaft Duration for Performance/Economy

Duration at 0.050in cam lift

Rocker arm ratio	1:1		1.15:1		1.25:1	
Cam type	Inlet	Exhaust	Inlet	Exhaust	Inlet	Exhaust
Phase I	208–212°	210–216°	204–208°	206–212°	202–206°	204–210°
Phase II	216–220°	214–224°	212–216°	210–220°	210–214°	208–218°
Phase III	224–228°	218–226°	220–224°	214–222°	218–222°	212–220°
Phase IV	230–232°	220–228°	226–228°	216–224°	224–226°	214–222°
Phase V	236–242°	224–230°	232–238°	220–226°	230–236°	218–224°

Rocker arm ratio	1.4:1		1.5:1		1.65:1	
Cam type	Inlet	Exhaust	Inlet	Exhaust	Inlet	Exhaust
Phase I	197–201°	199–205°	194–198°	196–202°	190–194°	192–198°
Phase II	205–209°	203–213°	202–206°	200–210°	200–202°	196–206°
Phase III	213–217°	207–215°	210–214°	204–212°	206–210°	200–208°
Phase IV	219–221°	209–217°	216–218°	206–214°	212–214°	202–210°
Phase V	225–231°	213–219°	222–228°	210–216°	218–224°	206–212°

In Table 4.1 I have set out a variety of cams to suit a number of performance/ economy considerations. The numbers refer to cam duration measured at 0.050in cam lift.

What I refer to as Phase I cams are very mild, good low speed torque grinds. The exhaust duration should be no greater than 6° more than that of the inlet. Valve lift would be around 0.390in inlet and up to 0.410in exhaust. Cams of this type are fitted to pre-emissions 350 Chevs, current 350 Chev Corvettes and the Porsche 911 turbo.

Phase II cams also are mild, good low speed torque grinds, but there will be a minute loss of torque below about 1200rpm. The exhaust duration should be no greater than 4° more than the inlet. Valve lift would be up to 0.415in on all lobes. Usually these cams will give better fuel economy than the standard cam providing driving habits do not change to take full advantage of the additional power available.

Phase III cams are my preferred performance/economy compromise grind. A little torque is lost below 1500–1700rpm but there is no problem with power brakes, power steering, air conditioner operation or a standard torque converter in auto transmission vehicles. The idle is smooth but a "cammy" note may be discernible if rowdy straight-through mufflers are used on some 6 and 8 cylinder vehicles with hydraulic lifters. The exhaust duration should be 4–6° less and certainly not more than that of the inlet, otherwise economy may be lost. Valve lift would be up to 0.420in however, if roller tip rocker arms are used, or if it is an overhead cam engine which doesn't have rocker arms, such as the VW Golf, the lift could be up to 0.440in on the inlet. I do not like lifting the valves too far in road engines as valve guide wear increases rapidly. Depending on driving style there should not be any loss of fuel economy. This is the warmest cam that I would recommend for turbo engines as the low compression ratio which is necessary with turbocharging combined with a longer duration cam would seriously reduce low speed power and flexibility.

Phase IV cams are really not an economy grind in engines larger than approximately 3.5 litres and should not be used in any vehicle which is overgeared. Engines smaller than 2 litre do not show any loss in economy and engines up to 3.3 litres would normally suffer a serious loss of economy only under stop-start driving conditions. There is a loss of flexibility under 2000rpm but power accessory function is not affected. The idle will be a little "cammy" in 6 cylinder engines with hydraulic lifters. Inlet valve lift would be up to 0.460in if roller tip rocker arms are fitted. The exhaust lobe should have up to 10° less duration and up to 0.050in less lift to maintain fuel efficiency and a wide power band.

What I refer to as Phase V cams have very limited application, only in engines up to around 1.8 litres. Small aerodynamic vehicles will deliver good economy at highway speeds. Power accessory operation and idle quality will not be affected in engines with solid (mechanical) cam followers.

Some people will no doubt question using a cam with less exhaust lobe duration and lift than the inlet. True the majority of performance cams have virtually identical inlet and exhaust lobes or the exhaust lobes may have more lift and duration. However, I have found that road cars with restrictive exhaust systems gain very little performance from exhaust lobes with extended duration and higher lift. On the contrary, often low speed performance and economy is reduced because of exhaust gas "draw-back" diluting the fuel/air charge and then at higher rpm fuel consumption   49 may also increase due to fuel draw through into the exhaust during the overlap period. Cams with the inlet and exhaust lobes suggested for Phase III, IV and V may not be available off the shelf but most cam manufacturers will oblige with special grinds on request.

Table 4.2 shows the effect of cam timing on horsepower and torque. The test engine was a 229cu in (3.75 litre) Chev V6 equipped with stock 4 barrel carb and manifold, stock cast exhaust manifolds feeding into a single 2.5in exhaust, stock cylinder heads machined to raise compression to a true 8.8:1 and fitted with standard valves backcut to improve flow, and budget 1.52:1 roller tip rocker arms.

Table 4.2   Effect of Cam Timing on Horsepower and Torque

	Test 1		Test 2		Test 3		Test 4	
rpm	hp	Torque	hp	Torque	hp	Torque	hp	Torque
1750	63	189	63	190			60	180
2000	73	193	73	191	68	180	72	189
2500	93	196	96	202	88	186	95	199
3000	108	190	118	206	107	188	115	201
3500	123	185	135	203	123	184	137	206
4000	129	170	148	194	152	200	155	203
4500	134	156	153	179	173	202	165	193
4750	123	136	152	168	173	191	171	189
5000			137	144	176	185	162	170
5250					168	168	143	143

Test 1 – stock cam 0.365in inlet and 0.392in exhaust lift, 176° inlet and 194° exhaust duration

Test 2 – Chev marine cam 0.415in inlet and exhaust lift, 202° inlet and 210° exhaust duration

Test 3 – Phase IV cam 0.460in inlet and exhaust lift, 218° inlet and exhaust duration, 110° lobe centres

Test 4 – Phase III cam 0.446in inlet and 0.420in exhaust lift, 212° inlet and 206° exhaust duration, 108° lobe centres

The stock cam was very, very mild; milder in fact than most standard cams. Hence a simple cam swap unleashed more power in this example than would usually be realised. The cam used in Test 2 caused very little loss of low speed torque and in the 2500–3500rpm range where we spend most of our time driving there is a good hp and torque increase. For Test 3 another off the shelf cam was chosen to check just how well the stock carb/manifold/head combination breathed. As can be seen in the table this cam did not give good power until 4000rpm, which is way above the usual cruise speed of most 6 cylinder cars. With a better design inlet manifold, extractor-type tubular exhaust headers and twin 2¼in exhausts, this cam would have made about 195hp. A special cam with a low lift, short duration exhaust lobe was ground and fitted for Test 4. Compared with the marine cam used in Test 2, it lost a little low speed torque but had better power above 3000rpm.

The next aspect of the camshaft to be decided upon is the lobe phase angle, which can also be referred to as the lobe separation angle or just simply as the lobe

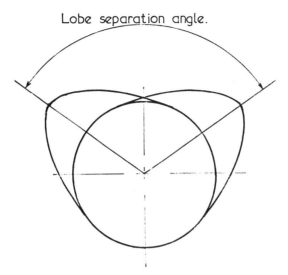

The lobe separation angle fixes the relative phasing between the inlet and exhaust lobes.

centres. This angle fixes the actual position or phasing of the lobes on the camshaft and in turn determines the opening and closing points of the inlet and exhaust valves expressed in degrees of crankshaft rotation. For example, if the lobe has been ground to push the inlet valve to its maximum lift at 110° after TDC, and to open the exhaust valve to its peak at 110° before TDC, the camshaft is said to have a lobe separation angle of 110° (110° + 110° ÷ 2 = 110°).

Predominantly performance road camshafts are ground with a lobe separation angle of from 108 to 112 degrees. In most instances a narrow angle favours mid-range power while a wider angle increases peak power at the expense of low rpm power. Just why this transpires can be better appreciated when we compare two camshafts having identical lobe contours of 270° advertised duration but lobe separation angles of 108° and 112° respectively. The cam ground in 108° centres will have timing figures of 27/63, 63/27, meaning that the inlet valve will theoretically commence lifting off its seat 27° before TDC and close back onto its seat 63° after BDC while the exhaust valve begins to open 63° before BDC and closes 27° after TDC. The 270° cam ground on 112° centres has timing figures of 23/67, 67/23.

The difference between numbers like 27/63, 63/27 and 23/67, 67/23 may not appear too significant so what makes the two cams change engine power and fuel consumption characteristics? The most obvious distinction is the valve overlap period of 54° for the cam ground on 108° lobe centres (27 + 27 = 54°) and 46° for the cam with 112° lobe centres. With mild cams the additional overlap will have little effect, except to perhaps enhance cylinder filling and power at mid-range engine rpm. Hotter cams from Phase IV and upward will have a rougher idle because of the longer overlap, and of greater concern at certain higher rpm, fuel consumption could become excessive because of mixture draw-through.

This timing diagram illustrates how changing the lobe separation angle alters the valve timing of a 270° duration camshaft.

The timing of the exhaust opening event is of little consequence and frequently can be varied by up to 8° before a change in horsepower or torque is detected. If a particular engine has an extremely inefficient exhaust it is sometimes helpful to open the exhaust earlier and increase "blow-down" time, thus reducing losses due to literally pumping exhaust gas out of the cylinder by the upward movement of the piston.

The timing of the inlet opening event is of more importance only when hotter, long duration profiles are utilised. If the inlet is opened very early, the piston's upward movement on the exhaust stroke may force exhaust gas into the inlet tract causing dilution of the fuel/air charge. This problem is compounded particularly if the entire exhaust system, including the exhaust valve and port, are very inefficient, as exhaust gas pressure could be quite high even very late in the exhaust cycle.

From a performance/economy viewpoint the intake closing event is the most important. We want to hold the intake open as long as practicable to extend the length of the induction period but we do not want the intake valve closing so late that the piston moving up on the compression stroke actually pushes a portion of our power-producing fuel mixture out of the cylinder and back into the inlet tract. This reverse flowing intake mixture (called reversion pulse or reversion flow) can cause more problems by actually blocking and then slowing intake flow into the cylinder on the next induction stroke. In extreme examples the reversion pulse reaches back to the carburettor venturis and disrupts the fuel metering signal. Reducing the lobe phase angle has the effect of closing the inlet valve earlier thus reducing low rpm reversion and increasing lower rpm horsepower and torque. Increasing the phase angle generally increases the peak torque and horsepower rpm because the induction cycle is extended by a few degrees (in this example 4°).

In road engines which are forced to run lower compression ratios when compared with race engines I tend to favour narrower lobe displacement angles to pick up mid-range power and improve fuel efficiency. However, this benefit can be offset to some extent because of the less efficient exhaust evident with road vehicles, which necessitates a somewhat wider lobe phase angle. There aren't any rules, because engines have no regard for rules, but I would suggest the following which I have found to apply in the majority of performance/economy applications. The majority of 4 cylinder engines require 108° lobe centres; some larger engines around 2 litre may work better with a cam ground to 110° lobe phasing. Pushrod type 6 and 8 cylinder engines with an rpm limit of up to 5500, 108° lobe displacement with Phase I, II and III grinds; 110° with Phase IV grinds. Overhead cam 6 cylinder engines with a 6500rpm limit, 110° with Phase I, II and III grinds and 112° lobe phase angle with Phase IV grinds.

Table 4.3 shows the typical effect of changing the lobe displacement angle. Initially, a cam with long duration was chosen as the owner wanted BMW-type performance with a simple cam change and head clean up. Also the exhaust had to be quieter than stock which required the use of a restrictive 2.25in system. Because of the long duration and tight exhaust, the first cam was ground on 115° centres. It produced

Table 4.3   Effect of Cam Lobe Centre Change on 3.3 litre Holden

rpm	Test 1		Test 2		Test 3	
	hp	Torque	hp	Torque	hp	Torque
2000	67	176	61	161	64	169
2500	87	183	79	165	84	177
3000	108	189	104	182	105	184
3250	122	197	118	191	120	194
3500	130	195	130	195	132	198
4000	144	189	148	194	149	195
4500	147	171	163	190	162	189
5000	140	147	171	180	168	176
5250			163	163	154	154

Test 1 – stock engine and exhaust

Test 2 – Phase V cam 0.430in inlet and 0.410in exhaust lift, 222° inlet and 218° exhaust duration, 115° lobe centres

Test 3 – Phase V cam as above with 112° lobe centres

good top end power but like a BMW it didn't accelerate too well below 4000rpm in the higher gears which frustrated the owner when driving in city traffic. Another cam was then ground on 112° centres. It knocked the power off above 5000rpm but restored some lost lower rpm power.

It does not always work out according to written theory. The 350 Chev in Table 4.4 was being built for maximum economy and anything over 250hp would be a

Table 4.4   Effect of Cam Lobe Centre Change on 350 Chev

| rpm | Test 1 | | Test 2 | |
	hp	Torque	hp	Torque
2000	121	319	120	315
2500	155	326	153	322
3000	204	357	201	352
3250	217	350	219	354
3500	232	348	233	350
4000	251	330	249	327
4500	258	301	259	302
5000	244	256	249	262

Test 1 – Phase II cam 0.453in inlet and 0.431in exhaust lift, 206° inlet and exhaust duration, 110° lobe centres

Test 2 – Phase II cam as above with 108° lobe centres

bonus. An off-the-shelf cam was fitted for the first test but as it was felt that a cam with 108° lobe centres may give even better mid-range power and economy, the second cam was then installed. The result was the opposite to that expected; the bottom end dropped off a little and peak power improved slightly. There was no detectable change in fuel consumption at half and full throttle testing on the dyno.

Another device which we can use to change the characteristics of a camshaft is timing variation by advancing or retarding the camshaft. A number of manufacturers supply their cams ground advanced or retarded. This can be discerned by checking the timing figures. For example, the timing may be 30/60, 66/20. The first step is to find the inlet and exhaust lobe duration. The inlet is 30° + 180° + 60° = 270°; while the exhaust open period is 66° + 180° + 20° = 266°. Next we calculate when the inlet and exhaust valves are at their maximum lift in relation with the crankshaft. Unless the cam has asymmetrical lobes (we will discuss these later) the full lift point must be mid-way between the opening and closing point. Hence in this example the inlet valve will be at peak lift 135° (270° ÷ 2 = 135°) after it begins to open and the exhaust valve will be lifted to its maximum 133° after it commences opening. For the inlet we subtract the valve opening point (30° before TDC) from the half duration figure (135°), so the valve is fully open at 105° after TDC (135° − 30° = 105°). The exhaust calculation is similar except that we subtract the exhaust closing angle (20° after TDC) from the half duration figure (133°). Hence the exhaust lobe is at its peak lift point 113° before TDC (133° − 20° = 113°). To find the lobe separation angle the full lift angles are added together and divided by 2, with the answer being 109° (105° + 113° ÷ 2 = 109°). If the cam had been ground or installed with split timing (called "straight up") maximum inlet lift would have occurred at 109° after TDC instead of 105° after TDC, and the

Advancing a cam causes the valves to open and close earlier, which improves mid range power and economy.

exhaust valve peak lift would have been at 109° before TDC and not 113° before TDC. This tells us that the cam has been ground 4° advanced ie. the inlet and exhaust valves are opening and closing 4° earlier than in the straight up position.

The timing diagram illustrates the effect of advancing a cam having identical inlet and exhaust lobes with an advertised duration of 270°. The first cam has the lobes ground on 112° centres with a timing of 23/67, 67/23. The second cam has the same lobe profile but ground with a displacement angle of 108°, which gives a timing of 27/63, 63/27. By advancing the first cam 4°, using an offset timing gear key, the timing becomes 27/63, 71/19. Closing the inlet valve 4° earlier reduces reversion and improves power and economy in the rpm range where we drive most of the time. Also, opening the exhaust valve 4° earlier may help exhaust efficiency a little.

Now by comparing the cam on 112° centres advanced 4° with the cam ground on 108° centres, you may wonder why bother going to the trouble to have a cam specially ground with the timing advanced, or why bother making an offset timing gear key to do the same thing when the inlet opening and closing events finish up the same 27/63? Why not simply install a cam with 108° lobe centres? Well, it could be that we want less overlap to improve idle quality and fuel economy in some Phase IV and wilder cams. Also, we may wish to open the exhaust valve very early (71° before BDC compared with 63° before BDC) because of an inefficient exhaust.

Again there are no rules, but there are few instances where I would run a cam straight up or retarded. Usually, I install cams with 108 to 110° lobe centres 4 or 5° advanced to keep low rpm cylinder pressure as high as possible. This is very important if the compression ratio has to be purposely low because of turbocharging or the compulsory use of unleaded or other low octane fuel. Some tuners and a number of car manufacturers install their cams retarded by anything from 2 to 8°. Usually, tuners do this because they are convinced that high compression ratios must be better, if only on paper in their advertising, and to get away with high compressions they have to ensure that some mixture is pushed back out of the cylinder past a late closing inlet valve, to avoid pinging at low rpm under load. Also, the exhaust lobes frequently have up to 14° longer duration than the inlet to ensure that exhaust gas is drawn back into the cylinder before the exhaust closes. The exhaust gas then dilutes the fuel/air mixture with non-combustible molecules, which disrupts and slows combustion and avoids detonation. Manufacturers retard their cams, usually not to run higher compression ratios, but to reduce the emission of nitrogen oxides (NOx). Fuel mixture diluted by exhaust gas burns more slowly and cooler, reducing the formation of NOx. The end result is reduced driveability at lower rpm and increased fuel consumption at cruising speeds.

Many enthusiasts inquire as to whether they should "degree-in" their performance cam or just line up the stock timing marks and hope for the best. Obviously what you decide will dictate just how much benefit you can expect from a cam swap. If you are confident that your cam supplier always takes the time to correctly and accurately set his cams in his camshaft grinder, you may decide to take the risk with Phase I and II grinds and also with milder Phase III grinds. After all, manufacturers even of exotic cars don't degree-in their cams. They are willing to accept a timing error which usually amounts to ±2°. However, if the maximum performance and economy potential of a cam is to be realised, the cam should be degreed, and the hotter Phase III, IV and V cams must be degreed in.

As you now understand something of the science of cam timing you are in a position to decide exactly how you wish to degree-in your cam. For example, the cam may be ground retarded by 2°, so do not be afraid to set the cam 5° advanced if you feel that is what the engine needs. On the other hand the cam may be ground 3° advanced and you want it advanced 5°, but after timing the cam you find that the cam is actually 4° advanced. This would not be worth correcting as few engines are affected by anything less than a 2° timing correction.

After the cam is fitted with the stock timing marks lined up, the next step is to find where the cam is in relation to the crankshaft. In other words, is it advanced or retarded, and by how many degrees? To check this you will need a degree wheel or a 360° protractor at least 8in in diameter which can be bolted to the nose of the crankshaft. Also needed is a dial gauge to measure cam lift and a good solid pointer that can be fixed under a convenient bolt and lapped over the front of the degree wheel.

Firstly, TDC must be precisely determined and for this a positive stop is required. If the cylinder head is fitted, the best positive stop is an old spark plug with the insulator removed and a piece of steel rod brazed in so as to project past the thread far enough to prevent the piston reaching TDC. An easier way to find TDC is with the head removed. Then a piece of steel can be fixed across the top of the bore to prevent the piston reaching TDC. Many pistons do not project out of the cylinder at TDC so it may be necessary to fit a light bolt in the centre of the positive stop bar.

With the stop bar fitted, rotate the crank as far as it will go, being careful not to damage the piston as contact with the stop is made. Take a note of the angle the pointer is on and turn the crank in the opposite direction until the piston again contacts the positive stop. Mid-way between the two stop angles is TDC so remove the stop and rotate the crank to TDC; the halfway point. Now very carefully loosen the degree wheel and move it around to align the zero mark with the pointer. To double-check, refit the positive stop and rotate the crankshaft in both directions as before. When the degree wheel is correctly positioned, the crank will stop at the same angle before and after TDC.

After TDC is found, the cam phasing can be determined. It is a waste of time attempting to degree in the cam according to the cam manufacturers advertised timing figures. If the cam grinder has quoted timing figures for 0.050in lift, these can be used as the cam follower will be off the clearance ramps and well onto the flank at that point. Solidly mount the dial gauge to read right off the lifter (not the rocker arm) and record the angles for 0.050in lift. If the manufacturer's figures were, say, 2/34, 42/−6, this would mean that at 0.050in lift the inlet opening would be 2° before TDC and closing would be 34° after BDC and the exhaust opening would be 42° before BDC and the exhaust closing would be 6° before TDC (−6 means before). This is a Phase IV cam with 216° duration at 0.050in, ground 4° advanced on 110° lobe centres. If the timing checked out 0/36, 40/−4, indicating that the cam was only 2° advanced, I would then fit a 3° offset timing gear key to bring the cam around to the 5° advanced position which I required.

If the cam company will only provide advertised timing figures such as 23/59, 59/23, it is best to work out the full lift angle (lobe centre) and go from there. This cam has split timing and is ground on 108° lobe centres. I would want to fit it with full inlet lift at 104° after TDC and maximum exhaust lift at 112° before TDC ie. 4° advanced. 57

If the cam phased out with peak inlet lift at 110° after TDC and full exhaust lift at 106° before TDC, the cam is retarded 2°, requiring a 6° offset key to move the phasing to 4° advanced.

Having determined that the cam has to be moved to degree it in, the next problem is just how to accomplish this. With some engines this is easy as they have vernier timing gears (eg. Jaguar and Alfa-Romeo). The majority, however use either dowels or keys to positively locate the cam or crank timing gears.

Dowelled drives will need offset dowels fitted and if more than a single central bolt fixes the timing sprocket to the cam then the bolt holes will require elongation with a round file. The amount of offset required is minute. For example, with the 4 cylinder pushrod English Fords 0.006in offset at the cam sprocket represents 1° measured at the crank. Hence if we wanted to advance the cam 4° then a 0.024in offset dowel would be required.

Cam manufacturers are usually able to supply a range of offset keys, offset bushes and offset dowels, to suit a variety of applications. Others are able to supply vernier crank sprockets for engines like the 2 litre Pinto, and for many American V8 engines there is a range of crank drive sprockets available with three keyways cut to change the cam phasing.

If there is nothing available for your particular engine you will have to make the appropriate hardware. Keep in mind that the dowel or key will not require hardening in most instances, as it usually does not transmit the driving force. The driving force is taken by friction between the sprocket and shaft (key located) or by pressure between the sprocket and cam created by the fixing bolts (dowel located). Incidentally, these fixing bolts should be locked using Loctite.

Many enthusiasts have difficulty understanding just which way to move a cam and by how much, to advance or retard it. To advance a cam in relation to the cam

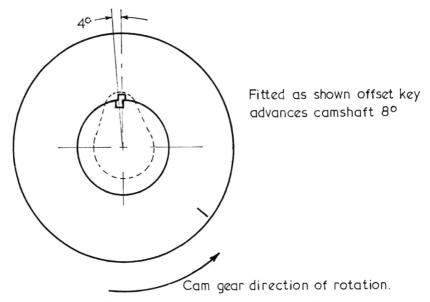

4°

Fitted as shown offset key advances camshaft 8°

Cam gear direction of rotation.

Performance cams should be "degreed in" for the best results. To advance the timing the cam is moved forward relative to the cam gear direction of rotation.

timing sprocket or gear means that we have to move the camshaft forward in the same direction of rotation as the cam timing gear. To retard the cam it is moved backward or in the opposite direction of normal rotation.

Because the cam turns at half engine speed, it only moves through half the number of degrees relative to the crankshaft. Hence if the cam timing is retarded 6° from where we want it then the cam must be advanced 6° measured at the crank, but only half that figure, 3°, at the camshaft. Therefore if the timing correction is made between the cam and cam timing gear, a 3° offset key will be needed.

To calculate just how much the key or dowel must be offset to equal 3°, we must first accurately measure the radius between the cam centre and the centre of the key or dowel. Let us assume that it is 0.594in for this example, which means that in one full rotation of 360°, the key will move around in a circle with a radius of 0.594in and a circumference of 3.732in (2 x π x 0.594 = 3.732). Therefore to move the cam within the timing gear 3° the key must be offset 0.031in (3.732 x 3 ÷ 360 = 0.031) which will advance the cam 6° measured on a degree wheel bolted to the crankshaft.

If the timing change is to be made by moving the crankshaft timing gear, the procedure is a little different. To advance the cam the crank timing sprocket is moved forward on the crank nose relative to the normal direction of crankshaft rotation. If the cam is to be retarded then the crank timing gear is moved backward or in the opposite direction to crank rotation. The amount the key has to be offset is calculated in exactly the same manner as previously, but the offset must be the full number of degrees and not half the number as when the change is being made at the camshaft. Hence if the cam timing had to be advanced 6° the key should be offset 6°.

When the valve timing is changed at the crank timing gear it is necessary to move the gear the full number of degrees and not half the number as when the change is being made at the camshaft timing gear.

A variety of cam drive systems are used by the various car makers and most will give reliable service with the milder cams which we are concentrating on in this book. Today, the most common drive arrangements employ either a timing chain or a toothed belt. Chains or belts running on steel sprockets give no problem providing the tension is adjusted correctly, but steel sprockets with nylon coated teeth, to reduce noise, should be avoided. Gear drive systems frequently give more problems as the production gears, particularly the camshaft timing gear, may be made of a silent-type material such as compressed fibre, nylon coated steel or aluminium, or compressed powdered metal. These should be replaced with either alloy or steel gears as the teeth frequently strip quite easily with just a standard cam and valve springs.

The majority of car enthusiasts look at economy purely from the viewpoint of fuel consumption. However, I take a much broader view. To my mind economy involves buying functional and not gimmicky parts at the right price and then maintaining everything properly to achieve the best service life. For example, it is false economy to fit old cam followers to run on a new cam as the old followers will soon wreck some of the lobes. It is also false economy to buy a bargain untreated cam. The lobes (not the bearing journals) should be given a treatment called by a variety of names such as Lubriting, Parkerising or Parko-Lubriting. The cam is treated after the bearing journals have been taped by being plunged into a high temperature bath of phosphoric acid. This acid etches open the pores of the freshly machined lobes so that they retain oil more effectively. Next, the cam receives a phosphate coating to aid break-in. To assist break-in lubrication even further I recommend that the lobes and followers be coated with a mixture of high pressure Hypoid 140 gear oil and moly disulphide. The first 10 to 15 minutes is the critical period for a new cam so it is essential that engine speed be maintained at 2000–2500rpm during this period to ensure adequate oil flow to the cam and lifters.

I am often asked if hydraulic lifters should be changed to a more "exotic" type and an appropriate cam fitted. Well, for many years I was no fan of hydraulic lifters and cams, but now hydraulic lifter cams give performance equal to, and in some instances better than, solid lifter cams in milder applications up to what I classify as a Phase IV grind. Solid lifter cams and roller lifter cams do have the advantage of a smoother idle with grinds hotter than Phase V and in race engines they will improve power output, but for performance/economy road engines hydraulic lifter cams work very well and there is less noise and less maintenance.

Some cam manufacturers are now producing street roller cams to suit both hydraulic roller and solid roller tappets. Again, I do not use these in economy road engines. I can get all the power that most drivers want along with good economy using simple and reliable flat tappet grinds. If, however, someone wanted his 350 Chev to make 450hp I would use a roller cam.

A little time back a few of the cam people were making a lot of noise about their special asymmetric cams which they had just developed. These are nothing new, some of the car makers have been using asymmetric grinds in their family sedans for many years, but no doubt the advertising induced a number of people to pay considerably more money in the belief that this type of profile is better or more powerful than the common symmetric profile. Actually, few cams have a true symmetric profile as many have short opening ramps and closing ramps perhaps 10° longer, but as we are really only interested in performance cams in the area past where the clearance ramps finish and commence, we normally view the lobes as being symmetric ie. the opening side of the lobe has the same profile and duration as the closing side of the lobe. Asymmetric lobes on the other hand have an opening flank a few degrees shorter than the closing flank.

60

Out of curiosity I purchased one of these super asymmetric grinds to see what the fuss was all about as previously I was convinced that whilst this type of profile basically reduced valve train noise, it didn't seem to give any extra power. What I found was interesting; yes, the cam did give a good wide power band just as the manufacturer claimed but this wasn't attributable to the asymmetric cam lobes which only varied by about 4° on the opening and closing flanks. What really helped the power band was the exhaust lobe which had around 15° less duration than the inlet.

Some of the cam advertising about high valve lift can also be misleading. As mentioned earlier, high lift increases valve guide wear, but with reground cams there is another problem. Unless a new virgin blank cam (billet cam) is used, the only way more lift can be attained is by grinding the base circle diameter smaller. This reduces the actual diameter of the camshaft, weakening the part. Thus as a cam lobe commences to push open a valve, the shaft bends a little, which changes the valve timing and also reduces the amount the valve is lifted. Therefore a cam with an advertised lift of, say, 0.430in may, in fact, lift the valve a true 0.395in if it is a solid lifter grind. Cam flex could account for 0.013in of lost lift; valve clearance 0.018in and valve train flex about 0.004in. I have seen reground cams with advertised lift figures differing by as much as 0.022in give identical valve lifts when installed, purely because the big lift cam flexed so much, due to the shaft diameter being reduced excessively.

Chapter 5
The Valve Train

The first vital link in the valve train of pushrod type engines and some overhead cam engines is the cam follower (also called tappet, lifter or bucket). It has the work of changing the rotating motion of the camshaft to up and down motion. The contact point between the lifter and cam lobe is the most heavily loaded spot in the engine. The loading can be as high as 300,000lb in², which is one reason why cam followers require more than just casual attention when a performance cam is used.

Contrary to popular opinion, lifters are not flat; they are ground with a spherical radius of 37–75in which, depending on their diameter, means that they are about 0.003in high in the centre. This spherical radius, along with a cam lobe taper angle of 3–16 minutes, and a tappet offset of approximately 0.050in from the middle of the cam lobe, causes the tappet to rotate. The rotation reduces cam and lifter wear; in fact if the lifter doesn't rotate, the lobe will be worn right down in 15 minutes. For this reason only new cam followers or re-radiused cam followers should be fitted with a new cam.

For the pushrod engine there are three basic types of lifter; the solid flat lifter, the standard hydraulic flat lifter, and the high rate bleed-down Rhoads-type hydraulic flat lifter. Some people would also include mushroom solid flat lifters, hydraulic roller lifters and solid roller lifters, but these are really only suited for use in super-performance engines.

The standard solid and hydraulic type lifters function effectively with the mild cams required in performance/economy applications. However, if you are modifying an engine which has a reputation for rapid lifter wear then it would be wise to fit lifters made of better material. These are often available from the larger cam manufacturers and component suppliers like TRW and Sealed Power.

The Rhoads hydraulic lifter was designed to allow the use of long duration hydraulic cams without losing too much low speed performance. This is accomplished by a vertical slot ground all the way down the lifter's inner piston. As

Cam follower spherical radius
37 - 75 inches.

Lobe taper 3 - 16 minutes.

To ensure long cam lobe life only new or re-radiused cam followers should be fitted when the cam is changed.

the lifter begins to rise on the cam lobe, oil is allowed to leak past the piston, thereby allowing the lifter to bleed down slightly at low rpm. Valve opening is delayed, reducing the cam duration by 10–15 degrees and reducing lift by about 0.020in at idle. The engine thus sees an improved idle and increased vacuum. As engine speed increases, there is less time to bleed off oil pressure, so by about 3000–3500rpm the cam's full potential duration and lift are restored.

From my testing I have concluded that the Rhoads lifter is a waste of time with mild, short duration cams, such as would be used for economy and performance. Used with long duration hydraulic cams of about 240–250 degrees measured at 0.050in lift they do work as claimed. I know of no good reason except perhaps less maintenance, to use such a long duration hydraulic cam. In excess of about 225 degrees duration (with 1.5:1 rockers) a mechanical cam has it all over an hydraulic. It idles more smoothly, has better low speed power and will rev about 500rpm higher. Additionally, the mechanical cam is much quieter at idle. An hydraulic with Rhoades lifters can produce a good deal of clatter at idle, particularly if the oil temperature is high or if the oil pressure is a little low.

The next link, in pushrod engines at any rate, is the pushrod. Little needs to be said about the pushrod except that it should be straight and rigid. Whenever rockers are replaced, the pushrods should also be replaced as the two wear a pattern together. For the same reason when engine rebuilding is carried out, the rockers and pushrods must be reinstalled together in the same location. In economy/performance engines there is no necessity to replace the pushrods with special chrome-moly or carbon fibre items. The standard article is more than adequate; I have seen hi-tech pushrods buckle in engines where the stock component showed no sign of failure.

Rocker arms provide the subsequent valve train link. Except for the riveted or welded pressed steel rockers found in a few engines, nearly all stock arms are suitable for use in mildly tuned engines using up to Phase V cams. The stud-type rocker arms fitted to many V8 engines and some 6 cylinder engines may require modification to avoid rocker to stud fouling when high lift cams are utilised. The clearance between either end of the rocker arm slot and the stud with the valve closed and also fully open should be measured using a wire 0.030in thick (a straightened paper clip will do).

When a high lift cam is installed it may be necessary to elongate the slot in pressed-type stud-mounted rocker arms to avoid rocker to stud fouling.

Many enthusiasts are now fitting expensive high lift roller tip rockers in their street engines. I consider this to be a waste of money which could be used in more beneficial ways to bring real performance and economy. Generally, high lift rockers are used in the belief that more valve lift guarantees more power. Yet a slightly warmer cam would have done exactly the same thing at less than one third the price. If the cam has 0.280in lift, swapping from 1.5:1 to 1.6:1, rockers will theoretically increase valve lift by 0.028in to 0.448in. The same performance increase could be had by using a cam with the same lift and about 6 degrees more duration measured at 0.050in lift. From my testing I would recommend high lift rockers in maximum performance road and race engines or in engines which have standard rockers with a ratio well below 1.4:1. For engines like the BL "A" series fitted to the Mini and Metro it is difficult to get reasonable valve lift with the standard 1.25:1 rockers. In these engines I recommend a 1.4:1 or 1.5:1 rocker and a cam duration about 10 degrees shorter than would typically be used with the standard rocker arm. To reduce valve guide wear resulting from the changed rocker geometry and increased lift, rockers with a roller tip should be used when changing from 1.25:1 to 1.5:1 rockers.

Engines fitted with high lift cams which actually lift the valves in excess of about 0.420in do have reduced valve guide wear and improved valve seat life when roller tip rocker arms are used. However, high quality extruded aluminium arms with needle roller bearings and needle roller tips are not necessary for mildly tuned engines. Competition Cams have a fine range of budget roller tip rockers available to fit popular American engines. Being only a little more expensive than the stock rocker arm they represent a good investment in maximum valve guide, and valve seat, life.

Many engines have less than ideal rocker support arrangements which can lead to reliability problems in some instances and poor valve train control in others, when modified camshafts and heavier valve springs are used. An absolute must is to have pressed-in rocker studs pinned as these have been known to pull out, even with the stock cam and valve springs. A more expensive solution which would only be justified if a cam hotter than Phase IV is installed is to fit screw-in rocker studs. The studs must be sealed to prevent seepage if the thread breaks in to the water jacket. Shaft-mounted rocker arrangements may require a number of improvements. Light alloy posts are not very rigid and should be replaced by steel posts to improve the valve train. Usually the shaft itself is up to the task, but the separation springs fitted between the rocker arms are best replaced by tubular steel sleeves. While doing this, pay attention to obtaining sleeves of the correct length to centralise each rocker over its respective valve.

The majority of new generation engines are of overhead cam design with a combination rocker arm-cam follower. Shaft-mounted units give little trouble and can be used with a new camshaft after being refaced and Parko-Lubrited, providing that play between the rocker and rocker shaft is minimal. If there is excessive play, the rockers will have to be re-bushed or replaced and new shafts will be necessary. Ball mounted rocker-cam followers such as are used in the Ford Pinto wear rapidly and must be replaced along with the ball studs when a new camshaft is fitted.

Adequate cam and follower lubrication is of major concern in either type of overhead cam engine. Hence when a new cam is fitted, and at regular intervals, thoroughly inspect all oil passages and ensure that there is a good uninterrupted flow of lubricant to each cam lobe.

Nearly all twin overhead cam engines and a few single overhead cam engines use an inverted bucket-type cam follower to transmit cam lobe motion directly to the valve. This type of follower is exceedingly durable and does not present any reliability problems, except in some super performance road applications. Unless the followers have worn flat or concave, they can be reused when new cams are installed.

One problem that is potentially damaging occurs in engines like the Fiat twin cam and VW Golf single cam which use inverted bucket tappets with a valve clearance adjusting shim inserted in the top. Because of a limited range of shims being available, it can be necessary to use "lash caps" on top of the valve stems to lift the bucket within adjusting range when reground cams with a smaller than stock base circle diameter are used. Providing a dab of grease is applied to each lash cap they will not jump out of place, creating problems during assembly; however, due to manufacturing tolerances the lash caps could be bearing against the collets rather

Machine lash caps to clear collets by 0.020in.

than the valve stem. To avoid this possibility measure the recess in each lash cap and compare the figures with the amount each valve stem projects above the collets. Any lash cap which does not clear the collets by 0.020in should be machined to increase the clearance.

Regardless of the type of valve train, very few engines present any difficulties when it comes to the design of valve spring retainers and collets (valve stem locks). If the engine has a known reliability problem in this area then steel valve spring retainers of a better material should be used; do not fit aluminium retainers. Some tuners feel that it is necessary to replace rotator-type retainers with fixed retainers, but this is usually unnecessary unless a Phase IV or V cam is being used. The rotator-type valve retainers are fitted usually to the exhaust valves of emissions engines to cause the valve to rotate. This cleans the valve and seat of carbon and evens out valve head temperatures, reducing valve erosion and burning. Rotators are not necessary on the inlets, but they do a good job of extending exhaust valve life and reduce the frequency of valve regrinds. If in your brand of engine they do not have a reputation for cracking and allowing a dropped valve, leave exhaust valve rotator-type spring retainers in place.

Not all valve rotation systems are desirable. The type mentioned above where the centre of the spring retainer clamps solidly to the valve stem usually are reliable but some manufacturers have resorted to a rotator system which creates huge problems with dropped valves. With this arrangement the collets lock solidly within

Collets must not butt together.

Grind collets to give gaps.

Collets which butt together allow the valves to float and turn. In time the collet groove wears, causing a dropped valve and probably a holed piston as well.

the spring retainer but the valve stem is a "floating" fit within the collets. This allows the valve freedom to rotate inside the collets and clean the valve seat. In time the constant friction between valve stem and collet causes considerable wear, allowing a dropped valve. If your engine has this type of valve rotation, the two collets will actually butt together when installed rather than having a gap between their ends. What must be done is grind off the faces of the collets so the two halves tightly clamp onto the valve stem and have a good gap between their ends.

In economy/performance engines the valve springs have an easier life than in race applications, hence very stiff, high rate springs, are neither desirable nor necessary. The primary requirements for a valve spring are that it must be durable and with a spring rate sufficiently high to seat the valve and keep the valve train in constant contact with the camshaft lobe up to the maximum recommended engine rpm. In road engines valve springs seldom suffer durability problems; cracking or sagging prematurely. However, it is wise to remember that they do not last forever when teamed with modern cams which feature high lift, rapid acceleration lobes. Therefore when the head is removed to freshen up the valves and seats, do measure the length of each spring uncompressed and then have the spring rate checked on a spring tester. If the compressed pressure is more than 10lb less than specified, the springs should be replaced and if any spring shows signs of sagging then all of the springs require replacement.

A number of tuners instinctively replace standard springs with high rate springs when a cam swap is made. Frequently this is unnecessary; most stock springs are adequate for Phase III cams and in some engines the stock springs require replacement only when race cams are fitted. Unless they are really essential, high rate springs actually accelerate engine wear. In addition to increased cam lobe and follower wear there is also more wear on the rockers at the pushrod cup, the pivot, and at the valve contact point. If the on-seat pressure is also high then valve and seat erosion speeds up. Engines with stud-mounted pressed metal rocker arms may experience cracking of the rockers which would necessitate the use of expensive needle roller competition rocker arms. Always consult with your cam manufacturer and ascertain just what spring rate is required with his cam. He should be able to tell you the required on-seat pressure and the full lift pressure necessary to keep the valve train in harmony at maximum engine speed. With that information it can be seen if the standard springs are up to the task.

The cam people may, for example, specify an on-seat pressure of 70lb and a full lift pressure of 180lb. On checking your workshop manual specifications you find that the car makers state that the standard springs have a pressure of 65lb at a compressed length of 1.5in and a pressure of 135lb at a compressed length of 1.25in. This may not appear to be of much value as you know from measuring them that the fitted length of the valve springs (the partially compressed length of the spring with the valve seated) is 1.47in and as the theoretical valve lift is 0.435in then the compressed spring length at full lift will be 1.055in. (Note in this example valve clearance is 0.020in so true valve lift will be 0.415in, assuming no deflection of the camshaft or rockers and assuming true to ratio rocker arms; many are not, it is not unusual to find rockers supposedly 1.5:1 with a true ratio closer to 1.45:1). We can calculate from the specifications that the stock springs have a spring rate of 280lb per in because compressing the spring from 1.5in to 1.25in increased the pressure from 65lb to 135lb. Hence 0.25in compression brings a 70lb increase in pressure, therefore the spring rate is 280lb per in (70lb ÷ 0.25 = 280lb per in). Knowing the spring rate, the on-seat pressure at 1.47in and the full lift pressure at 1.055in can be easily calculated. If at 1.5in the pressure is 65lb then at 1.47in it will be 73.4lb (65 + [280 x 0.03] = 73.4lb) and at 1.055in it will be 189.6lb (65 + [280 x 0.445] = 189.6lb) so the standard springs should have sufficient pressure. However, it would be wise to actually measure the pressure on a valve spring tester.

Having determined that the spring pressure is satisfactory does not establish that the stock springs are suitable because the valve springs may stack solid with no clearance between coils before full lift is reached. All valve springs require what is termed working clearance between coils. Depending on the spring manufacturer this 67 can vary from as little as 0.005in between coils to as much as 0.020in, the majority of springs requiring about 0.010in. Perhaps the simplest way to check the minimum length the spring can be safely compressed is to slip feeler strips of the appropriate thickness (or brass shim stock) between each coil and then fully compress the spring in a vice and measure its length. For the springs to be suitable this figure must be no more than the full lift valve spring length which we calculate by measuring the length of every spring with the valve seated and then deducting the valve lift from the smallest seated length. Let us assume that the seated lengths vary from 1.45in to 1.47in and the valve lift is 0.415in (theoretical lift 0.435in minus valve clearance of 0.020in). The minimum spring compressed length will be 1.035in (1.45 − 0.415 = 1.035), hence to be suitable our valve springs would have to be shorter than 1.035in when measured in the vice fully compressed with feeler strips between all coils, to avoid coil binding and valve train and cam lobe damage.

With modern high lift cams it is also possible for the valve train to become solid due to the bottom of the valve spring retainers hitting the tops of the valve guides at full lift. It is easiest to check for this condition with the head removed and without valve springs. Firstly set a telescopic gauge or a snap gauge at the full lift valve spring length. Then fit the valve spring retainers and collets to each valve, pulling them up tightly. Next in turn push each valve to the simulated full lift position and determine that there is at least 0.060in clearance between the valve spring retainer and valve guide. If the clearance is less, metal can be ground from the retainer up to the maximum of about 0.040in. When more metal removal is necessary it will have to be cut from the valve guides.

Simulated full lift

Minimum clearance .060in.

High lift cams may cause the valve spring retainer to contact the valve guide at full lift. Therefore before assembling the head ensure that there is at least 0.060 in clearance in the simulated full lift position.

The next thing we must take care to do correctly is adjust the valve clearance (valve lash). The cam grinder will supply a clearance figure for the inlet and exhaust valve. If he gives a "cold" clearance he means just that; the engine should not have been run in the previous five hours. The "hot" clearance is for an engine at normal operating temperature. It is important to maintain correct valve clearance to allow the valve to seat properly and transfer its heat to the valve seat. If the valves are run tight to quieten them, valve burning could result.

Setting the valve clearances accurately is not difficult; it just requires a little time
and thought. Firstly, let me point out that it will be impossible to do a good job if the

contact face of the rocker or the tip of the valve stem has a dip worn into it. The feeler blade will be too wide or too rigid to fit into the dip, hence the clearances will be wrong. When we measure the clearance the lifter should be fairly close to the centre of the base circle of the cam lobe. This is no problem with overhead cam engines as it is easy to see when the cam follower is on the base circle. There is a difficulty, however, with ohc engines using rocker-type cam followers which employ a swivel foot to contact the valve stem as the foot easily rolls over, resulting in inaccurate clearance adjustments. To overcome this situation I prefer to adjust the clearance by inserting the feeler strip between the cam lobe and rocker. When doing it this way it becomes necessary to reduce the clearance because of the effect of the rocker arm ratio. Therefore if the clearance at the valve is 0.013in and the rocker ratio is 1.45:1, then the clearance measured at the cam lobe will be only 0.009in (0.013 ÷ 1.45 = 0.009).

Pushrod-type engines require a little more thought because it is not possible to see when the lifters are on the base circle of each cam lobe. Knowing that both the inlet and exhaust valve are closed at TDC on the compression stroke simplifies matters as the lifters obviously must be on the base circle at that moment. Starting with the No. 1 piston on TDC on the compression stroke (the rotor button will point to the No. 1 plug lead) adjust the clearance. Then turn the motor over to bring each piston in turn, according to the firing order, to TDC and adjust the clearances as you go. To make this task easy mark the crank pulley with TDC marks for all the cylinders; 4 cylinder engines will have one mark 180° around from the No. 1 and No. 4 mark, 6 cylinder engines will require two new marks each 120° from the original, and 8 cylinder engines will require three new TDC marks spaced 90° apart.

Adjusting the valve train of engines with hydraulic lifters is quite different. The majority of manufacturers recommend that the adjustment be done with the engine hot and running. They suggest that each rocker be slackened off until it emits a distinctive "clacking" sound and then the adjuster should be taken down one half to one full turn. To increase the rpm at which the lifters "pump up" I suggest that the adjusters are taken down only one quarter turn. An alternative method is to slacken off each rocker with the engine stopped, then run the engine for a few seconds to completely fill the lifters with oil. Next, with the engine stopped and the lifter on the base circle, turn the pushrod within the fingers, tightening the rocker at the same time. When some resistance to turning the pushrod is felt, note the position of the adjusting spanner and tighten the rocker adjusting nut a further quarter of a turn.

Unfortunately, to reduce costs a number of car makers no longer make any provision to adjust hydraulic valve systems. Hence when the head or block deck is machined, or a cam is fitted with a smaller than standard base circle, you will have to take special steps to obtain the correct valve adjustment. The simplest, but more expensive way, is to use adjustable pushrods. These are also fiddly to adjust. An effective and less expensive method is to raise or lower the rocker arms by either shimming up the rocker pedestals or machining the pedestal base to lower them. Firstly, to determine if shimming or machining is required, turn the engine so that No. 1 piston is at TDC on the compression stroke. Next fit the two pushrods and rockers for this cylinder and tighten the pedestal studs down finger tight. If there is clearance between the two rockers and valves, fully tighten the pedestal studs and then measure and record the clearance. Repeat this procedure for all the other cylinders, measuring and noting the clearance. After this divide each clearance figure by the   69 rocker ratio and then add 0.040in to 0.050in divided by the rocker ratio to each figure. This appears complicated so consider an example. The engine has 1.5:1 rocker arms. The clearance is 0.030in on the No. 1 inlet valve and 0.021in on the No. 1 exhaust. Dividing each clearance figure by the rocker ratio gives us 0.020in and 0.014in respectively. Adding 0.040in and 0.050in divided by the rocker ratio increases each figure by 0.027 to 0.033in. Hence the inlet figure becomes 0.047 to 0.053in and the exhaust figure becomes 0.041 to 0.047in. These figures represent the amount which will be machined from the base of the pedestals to preload the lifter the required 0.040in to 0.050in.

Circlip.

.040 to .050in piston preload.

Piston.

Hydraulic lifters must be preloaded otherwise the rockers and valves will clatter. Normal piston preload is 0.040in to 0.050in.

On the other hand it is possible that when the pedestal studs are taken down finger tight there is a gap between the base of the pedestal and the cylinder head. In this case measure and record the gap for each pedestal. Next, multiply each figure by the rocker arm ratio. If the resulting figures are somewhere between 0.040in and 0.050in then the pedestals can be fully tightened down as the lifter preload will be correct. However, if the figures are less than this, the pedestals will require shimming. Consider the example of an engine with 1.5:1 rockers. The gap under No. 1 inlet pedestal is 0.015in and under the exhaust 0.018in. The gap required for correct preload is 0.040in to 0.050in divided by the rocker ratio ie. 0.027in to 0.033in. Therefore shim thickness will be 0.012in to 0.018in and 0.009in to 0.015in respectively.

Chapter 6
The Exhaust

Subtle changes to the exhaust system can unleash a lot of horsepower without any decrease in fuel economy. In fact usually the opposite is true; a free flowing exhaust ordinarily reduces fuel consumption. With race and rally engines a lot of testing is necessary to get the exhaust tuning just right. However, with road engines using mild economy cams and fitted with mufflers, exhaust tuning is far from a precise art. A lot of money can be wasted buying parts which are totally unnecessary for muffled road cars.

For example, while testing a 3.3 litre Holden it was decided that a special extractor-type header was required. The owner wanted a high power output but being limited to a Phase V cam, so as not to upset the electronic fuel injection sensors, this was proving to be a little elusive. It appeared that the next obvious place with which to gain more power was from the exhaust. The standard engine came fitted with an extractor header which did not appear to be very efficient. The extractors were a 6–3–1 type with small diameter 1.375in primary pipes approximately 12 to 17in long. The secondaries were 1.625in diameter and of a similar length leading to a 2in o/d collector. What was strange considering the firing order 1–5–3–6–2–4 was the unusual primary pipe combinations. Cylinders 1 and 4 were connected, as were 3 and 5, and 2 and 6. This did not appear to make any sense except to perhaps increase work area around the engine when installed.

The first change was to fit an off-the-shelf 6–2–1 header with "standard" straight six pipe connections; cylinder 1, 2 and 3 joined together and 4, 5, 6, together. The primaries were again small at 1.375in and the secondaries were 1.75in. This exhaust made virtually identical power as the stock header above 3500rpm, but below that it lost on the average about 1hp. Next, a special one-off header was fabricated to experiment with different pipe diameters and lengths. After several trials the best exhaust was found to be a 6–3–1 system with 1.5in primaries 16in long, and 1.75in secondaries 20in long, leading to a 2.5in outlet. The primaries were connected conventionally; cylinders 1 and 6, 2 and 5, 3 and 4. The end result was an exhaust costing a lot of money which gave a mere 2 to 4 hp more than the stock pipes that had appeared to be so inefficient!

This is just one example of how money can be wasted, but invariably I find that with small cams and mufflers even very odd, inefficient-looking tubular headers work just as well as nice looking headers with big diameter equal length pipes. Cast iron manifolds sometimes are not all that bad either. Some of the Japanese and European car makers cast their exhaust manifolds very well; almost as well as tubular headers. Often it will be found that these cast manifolds virtually duplicate tubular headers. The correct cylinders are joined together and the cast "branches" are frequently up around 10 to 12in long to reduce exhaust contamination from one cylinder to another cylinder.

This Mustang V8 header doesn't look very efficient; the pipes are small in diameter and they are nowhere near equal length. However, with a mild performance/economy cam fitted the engine makes about the same power as with big diameter equal length tube headers.

Really this, along with less exhaust restriction, is the reason why tubular headers are fitted. The basic idea is to connect the primary pipes so that the exhaust gas from one cylinder will not pressurise another cylinder. Taking a typical four cylinder engine with a 1-3-4-2 firing order, it can be seen that at the end of its exhaust stroke No. 1 cylinder will tend to draw in exhaust gas being expelled under high pressure from the No. 3 cylinder when a standard cast iron manifold which connects all four exhaust ports is used. Naturally No. 3 in turn will draw in exhaust gas from No. 4, No. 4 will draw in gas from No. 2 and so on. To overcome this problem a tubular header or a cast iron manifold with branches up around 10 to 12in long is necessary on 4 and 8 cylinder engines when cams hotter than Phase III are utilised.

The exact design of the header is not really so important with economy cams. The primary tubes may be connected 4 into 1 or 4 into 2 into 1 (also called tri-y) and the tubes should be at least 12in long to be really effective. When cams up around 240° duration at 0.050in lift are used, 4–1 headers usually show more top end power and 4–2–1 headers give better mid-range power. Table 6.1 indicates the pipe size which should be aimed for when selecting a header. Actually in performance economy applications I consider ease of maintenance with the various header types fitted to be more important than the pipe sizes. For this reason I tend to favour 4–2–1 or short tube (ie. 12–16in) 4–1 headers to gain maximum working space around the engine. I regularly waste a lot of time working on customer's cars which have been equipped with ill-designed headers. The most common problem on V8 engines is not being able to get all of the spark plugs out without first unbolting the headers! Other common problems on all engines are not being able to adjust the steering box, or remove the oil filter and starter motor with headers fitted. Some header manufacturers do not seem to care very much about maintaining a safe working clearance between header pipes and such things as steering arms, firewall, starter motor, alternator, air conditioner compressor etc. It is annoying belting pipes with a hammer to gain clearance and it is expensive replacing electrical components over-heated by the close proximity of header tubes.

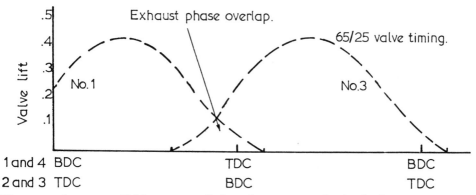

When an exhaust manifold connects all the exhaust ports of a 4 cylinder engine together, the gases exiting one cylinder can contaminate another cylinder, diluting the fuel/air mixture.

4 into 1 tubular header.

4 into 1 tubular headers cut out exhaust gas contamination between cylinders on 4 cylinder and V8 engines. However, long branch headers like these seriously limit working space around many engines.

4 into 2 into 1 tubular header.

This 4 into 2 into 1 header is for 4 cylinder engines. It allows more working space around the engine than a 4 into 1 system and mid-range power is usually superior as well.

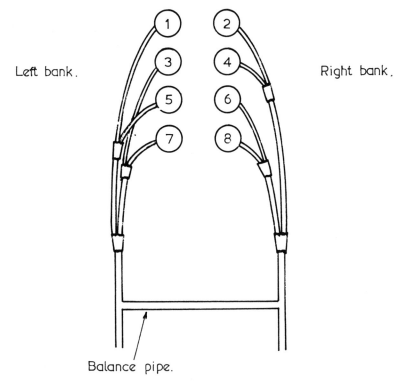

Left bank.

Right bank.

Balance pipe.

The pipe connections are quite different for 4 into 2 into 1 headers for V8 engines than those for 4 cylinder units. Note that the connections for the left and right cylinder banks are also different. A balance pipe should be fitted between the exhaust pipes of all 6 and 8 cylinder engines with twin exhaust systems.

Table 6.1 Header pipe sizes for 4 and 8 cylinder engines

Cylinder Size (cc)	4 into 2 into 1 header Primary pipe size (in)	Secondary pipe size (in)	4 into 1 header Primary pipe size (in)
250	1.25 dia x 12 to 18 long	1.5 dia x 15 to 24 long	1.25 dia x 15 to 30 long
325	1.25 to 1.375 dia	1.5 to 1.625 dia	1.25 to 1.375 dia
400	1.375 to 1.5 dia	1.625 to 1.75 dia	1.375 to 1.5 dia
500	1.375 to 1.5 dia	1.625 to 1.75 dia	1.5 dia
600	1.5 to 1.625 dia	1.75 to 1.875 dia	1.625 to 1.75 dia
700	1.625 dia	1.875 to 2.0 dia	1.625 to 1.75 dia

Note: all pipe lengths are as shown for 250cc cylinder size
all pipe diameters are outside diameters

Table 6.2 Exhaust comparison testing of 305 Chev

rpm	Test 1 hp	Torque	Test 2 hp	Torque	Test 3 hp	Torque
2000	107	282	110	290	112	295
2500	137	287	139	293	141	296
3000	169	295	175	306	178	312
3500	201	302	208	312	212	318
4000	228	300	237	311	238	313
4500	241	281	248	289	254	296
5000	252	265	259	272	264	277

Test 1 – Chev cast iron "rear discharge" manifold

Test 2 – Chev cast iron "rams horns" manifold

Test 3 – 4 into 2 into 1 headers

Table 6.2 shows what sort of power increase can be expected with various exhaust manifold types. The test engine was a 305cu in Chev V8 with emissions gear. The carb was a standard 4 barrel Quadrajet on a stock inlet manifold with a 1in spacer and the centre divider cut down. Early model 307 heads milled to increase the compression ratio to 9:1 were given a valve set and throat job. Backcut 1.84in inlet and 1.5in exhaust valves were fitted. The cam was a Phase III grind with 108° lobe centres, 212° inlet and exhaust duration and 0.412in lift. In all tests a twin 2.25in exhaust and mufflers were attached. A 2in balance pipe (cross-over pipe) interconnected both engine pipes.

In the first test Chevrolet's most poorly designed (from a performance view-point) cast iron manifolds were used. These connect each of the four exhaust ports together and discharge into the exhaust pipe at the rear of the engine. For the second test "ram horns" Chev cast manifolds were used which dump their gases into the exhaust pipe in line with the centre cylinders. Because of improved flow and reduced cylinder contamination with exhaust gas, power increased considerably right through

75

Some stock cast iron exhaust manifolds work better than others. The centre dump Chevrolet "rams horns" manifolds are much more efficient than the rear dump design.

the power range. For the final tests several tubular headers were tested with similar results. Headers with 4 into 1 primaries 1.625 dia x 28in long lost power below 2500rpm while those with 1.5 dia x 28 long primaries gave more power below 3000rpm without giving away anything at 5000rpm. The power figures shown for Test 3 were produced when 4–2–1 headers were fitted. These had 1.5 dia x 15in long primaries and 1.875in dia x 20in long secondaries. This system gave marginally superior power right through the power range than either 4–1 system. As can be seen, when a mild cam is installed and mufflers are fitted, tubular headers do not necessarily unleash a whole lot more power if the cast iron manifolds are of the centre outlet "ram horns" type.

Even small capacity engines do not show a dramatic power increase with headers. The standard cast iron manifold fitted to the Ford crossflow engine is certainly less efficient than the stock manifolds fitted to many new generation engines; however, as you can see in Table 6.3, it did not reduce the power output of this engine by a large degree. The engine was rebored to 1.7 litres, and was fitted with a 32 DFM Weber mounted on a GT inlet manifold. The head was reworked and fitted with 1.625in inlet and 1.375in exhaust valves. A Phase V cam with 224° inlet and 217° exhaust duration and 0.420in theoretical valve lift was used.

Table 6.3   Exhaust comparison testing of 1.7 Ford x/flow

	Test 1		Test 2	
rpm	hp	Torque	hp	Torque
2000	38	99	34	89
2500	48	101	46	96
3000	60	105	59	103
3500	71	106	67	101
4000	79	104	80	105
4500	90	105	87	102
5000	98	103	95	100
5500	104	99	103	98
6000	107	94	102	89

Test 1 – Tubular 4 into 2 into 1 headers, 1.5 in x 15in long primaries, 1.625in x 20in long secondaries

Test 2 – Ford cast iron manifold

No doubt you have seen advertisements claiming huge power increases when headers are fitted and there was probably a nice graph showing the relative power outputs to prove the point. I won't say that such claims are untrue but usually these power comparisons are made with a standard manifold and standard small bore exhaust to prove how inefficient the manifold is, and then for the second test headers and a large bore system, or perhaps no exhaust system at all if the company is totally unscrupulous, are used to prove how headers benefit power output. This is not to say that headers are of no value as they will show some power improvement. However, this improvement should be weighed carefully against their cost and the inconvenience which headers can cause. I would not consider their use on 4 and 8 cylinder engines with small Phase I or II cams as headers really only begin to show their worth with Phase IV cams and warmer.

Six cylinder exhaust manifolds fall into two categories; very good or plain horrible. Fortunately, very few straight sixes use a cast iron manifold which connects all exhaust ports together and dumps through a single outlet. This type of manifold creates a lot of exhaust back pressure and because of overlapping exhaust open periods each cylinder will draw in high pressure exhaust gas from two other cylinders during its exhaust cycle. Even Phase I cams are out if this type of manifold is retained.

Nearly all new generation straight sixes utilise a "split" type cast manifold which joins cylinders 1–2–3 to one outlet and joins cylinders 4–5–6 to a second outlet. The split manifold works very well even with wild road cams as there is very little overlap of exhaust cycles. Tubular headers will give marginally more economy because exhaust gas flow is a fraction better, but they will not give an increase of more than a couple of horsepower when performance/economy cams are fitted.

"Split" type cast manifolds allow good exhaust flow on 6 cylinder engines. This 2.6 litre Mercedes produces 162hp with full emissions gear and CAT converter; enough to push the 190E to 130mph.

Table 6.4   Exhaust comparison testing of 229 Chev

rpm	Test 1 hp	Test 1 Torque	Test 2 hp	Test 2 Torque	Test 3 hp	Test 3 Torque	Test 4 hp	Test 4 Torque
2000	68	180	71	186	69	182	70	184
2500	88	186	90	190	89	187	91	191
3000	107	188	113	198	107	188	111	195
3500	123	184	129	193	125	187	129	194
4000	152	200	162	213	154	202	162	212
4500	173	202	183	214	176	205	185	216
4750	173	191	187	207	177	196	191	211
5000	176	185	188	198	179	188	190	200
5250	168	168	184	184	173	173	187	187

Test 1 – Chev cast iron manifolds, single 2.5in exhaust and muffler

Test 2 – Chev cast iron manifolds, dual 2.25in exhaust and mufflers and 2.0in balance pipe

Test 3 – Tubular 3 into 1 headers with 1.625in dia. x 28in long primaries, single 2.5in exhaust and muffler

Test 4 – Tubular 3 into 1 headers as above, dual 2.25in exhaust and mufflers and 2.0in balance pipe

Table 6.4 shows the effect of exhaust manifold and exhaust system changes on a 229cu in V6 Chev. The engine was outfitted with stock 4 barrel carb and manifold, stock cylinder heads milled to raise compression to a true 8.8:1 with a valve seat and throat job, stock backcut inlet and exhaust valves, Phase IV cam with 218° inlet and exhaust duration at 0.050in lift and 0.460in inlet and exhaust lift, and 1.52:1 budget roller tip rocker arms.

It can be seen that headers raised the power level only a little over what was produced with stock cast iron manifolds. However, swapping to a free flow dual exhaust gave very good results. At cruise speed the engine developed about 5hp more and in the upper power range power was up by 10 to 16hp. This is a big power increase for a small amount of work and a minimal outlay of money.

Nearly all large engines over about 3.3 litres will show a 10 to 20hp increase just from fitting a good dual exhaust system. However, to avoid a loss of mid-range torque a balance pipe must be fitted to interconnect the two exhaust pipes. The best location, power wise, for the balance pipe is close to the front of the gearbox. Preferably it should be as short as possible and of the same diameter as the exhaust. If there are clearance problems use a pipe size which can be comfortably accommodated in the available space.

Because of limited space or the need to retain just one catalytic converter, it may be necessary to use a single large diameter exhaust. This can pose a problem in V6 and V8 engines as many "Y" pipes are very restrictive at the place where the two engine pipes connect. What we want is a nice smooth, free-flow "Y" connection.

By now it should be obvious that in performance/economy applications the actual exhaust system rather than just the exhaust manifold should attract our attention in the quest for more power. Naturally the system must have gentle bends and a good size bore to reduce flow restriction. Table 6.5 sets out the pipe sizes which should be aimed for. Unfortunately it is difficult to find sufficient space under many modern cars to fit such large exhausts and still maintain good ground clearance. If this is a problem remember that it is quite acceptable to "flatten" the exhaust by up to 0.25in over a 6in length, to fit it closer to crossmembers etc. Also, because exhaust gases cool and contract as they pass along the system, the pipe diameter can be reduced for the last half of the system's length. This won't have much effect on power

Free flow joint.   Stock factory joint.

When it is necessary to retain a single large diameter exhaust system in V6 and V8 applications every effort should be made to make the "Y" connection between the two engine pipes as free flowing as possible.

Table 6.5   Exhaust pipe sizes for good flow

Engine sizes (litres)	Preferred size	Minimum size
1.0	1.75in	1.625in
1.3	1.875in	1.75in
1.6	2.0in	1.875in
2.0	2.25in	2.0in
2.4	2.25in	2.125in
2.8	2.5in	2.25in
3.2	1 x 2.5in 2 x 2.0in	2.25in
3.5	2 x 2.25in	1 x 2.5in 2 x 2.0in
4.2	2 x 2.25in	2 x 2.0in
5.0	2 x 2.5in	2 x 2.25in

Note: all pipe diameters are outside diameters

output and it may help reduce noise, allowing the use of a less restrictive muffler.

The type and number of mufflers fitted will depend on how quiet you want your car. Personally, I prefer a quiet mellow tone which doesn't give me a headache when I drive and which doesn't attract the attention of the law. If fitted as far to the rear of the car as possible, well-designed mufflers will not reduce power by more than about 3–5%. Fitted closer to the engine, where the exhaust gases are very hot, they cause more flow restriction and power loss.

There are many muffler designs but the types most suited for performance applications are of either straight-through or reverse flow (also called "S" flow) design. Most people think of straight-through mufflers as only suitable for loud boy racer-types, but many high quality quiet mufflers are of this design. I prefer this type although two mufflers are usually necessary to stop exhaust "popping" on the overrun. The quietest designs often have an open resonating chamber in the middle to further reduce popping. Many high performance mufflers are now of the reverse flow design. These generally do not contain any sound absorbing material so they are a little lighter than straight-through types. Reverse flow mufflers can be very quiet but many are noisy, and the noisy ones frequently do not make any more power. Usually, reverse flow mufflers are not prone to popping on the overrun so often only one muffler, or a muffler and a small resonator, will be all that is required to produce an acceptable exhaust tone.

Turbo cars also frequently have inefficient exhaust systems. It would appear that a number of car makers do not have much confidence in their customers as they purposely "plug-up" the exhaust to keep the boost pressure and power down. One manufacturer, for example, equips their 2 litre turbo with a 2in exhaust, yet just before the final muffler a restrictor plate with a 1in hole is fitted! This prevents the turbo from spinning up to full boost and cuts power dramatically. Removing the restrictor results in another 1.5 psi boost. I have not been able to determine why this was done. Could it have been to meet emission standards? Or was there a reliability problem at higher boost on unleaded fuel? I do not know, and the manufacturers are not telling.

The very first modification required on nearly all turbo cars is a free flow exhaust. If the exhaust is not free flowing then all other engine modifications will be a complete waste as the back pressure will prevent the engine making good boost and turbo lag could become quite a problem. Table 6.6 shows the exhaust system size required. This table refers to pipe sizes on the downstream side of the turbo as normally in performance/economy applications an increase in pipe size between the manifold and turbo will reduce performance or increase turbo lag. In some

Table 6.6   Turbo exhaust size

Engine size (litres)	Preferred size	Minimum size
1.3	2.0in	1.875in
1.6	2.125in	2.0in
2.0	2.25in	2.125in
2.3	2.5in or 2 x 2.125in	2.25in
3.0–4.0	2.75in or 2 x 2.25in	2.5in

Note: all pipe diameters are outside diameters

applications the turbo outlet may be of a larger diameter than the preferred exhaust diameter. In this situation the first 20 to 24in of the exhaust should be larger than indicated and then tapered down over a length of about 6 to 8in to the size required. Cars with 2.3 to 3 litre engines may not have sufficient underbody clearance to accommodate such large diameter exhausts. If this is a problem, the exhaust should be of the size specified for the first 30 to 35in and then it may be tapered down over a length of approximately 6in to a size which can be conveniently fitted. Alternatively, the exhaust may be split into a twin system of the size indicated, not less than 15in from the turbo.

Chapter 7
Carburation

The basic requirement for any carburettor is that it meters the fuel and air in such proportions as to be easily combustible, enabling the engine to produce good power over a wide rpm range with good economy. For best power the mixture we need is around 1:12 or 1:13, ie., one pound of petrol (gasoline) to every twelve or thirteen pounds of air. Such a blend is just right for full throttle operation, but for other conditions such as ordinary light load running we want an "economy blend" of around 1:14.5 to 1:16. Table 7.1 indicates the fuel air requirements for a number of operating conditions. Obviously the carburettor has to "sense" the engine's operating conditions accurately and adjust the fuel-air mix to suit. If the carburettor is not able to do this, flat spots and engine surging will result, spoiling performance and economy. For this reason we have to be very selective as to the type and size of carburettor that we choose; a carburettor which provides good performance may not give the desired economy and vice versa.

Clearly to understand more fully what we should be looking for in a carburettor, we have to go back to the basics and get to know a little about how a carburettor works. All carburettors employ a fuel inlet system, an idle system and a main running system. Many in addition also have an acceleration pump system and a power system.

The inlet system consists of the fuel bowl, the float, and the needle and seat. The fuel, before passing to the metering systems, is stored in the fuel bowl, and it is maintained at the correct level by the float and the needle valve (needle and seat). If the fuel is not at the correct level in the fuel bowl, the carburettor metering systems will not mix the fuel and air in the required proportions. A high fuel level will increase fuel consumption and may cause erratic running. In extreme cases fuel spillover through the carburettor discharge nozzle and/or vent during cornering or braking could give rise to the engine faltering or stopping. Such a condition may be the result of an incorrectly adjusted float, or a needle and seat which is not seating properly and shutting off the fuel inlet when the float reaches the correct level. This is usually due to

Table 7.1   Fuel/air Requirements

Running condition	Mixing ratio by weight Fuel : air
Starting	1 : 3 – 4
Idling	1 : 6 – 10
Low speed running	1 : 10 – 13
Light load economy running	1 : 14.5 – 16
Heavy load performance running	1 : 12 – 14

excessive wear of the needle and/or seat, but may also be due to dirt if the fuel system does not incorporate an inline fuel filter. A low fuel level on the other hand causes flat spots because of lean-out in corners and when accelerating. Very serious is the possibility of melted pistons due to reduced fuel flow capacity. Such a condition may

Electric automatic chokes are adjusted by turning the thermostat assembly to a leaner (L) or richer (R) position. A choke which does not open fully or which is slow to open increases fuel consumption.

be due to a float set too low, low fuel pressure, a restrictive or partially blocked fuel filter, or a needle and seat too small to flow sufficient fuel to keep the fuel bowl full.

The cold starting system provides mixture enrichment to allow starting when either the engine or the air temperature is cold. Most carburettors employ a choke plate which restricts air flow into the engine, thus providing a rich fuel/air mixture. As

Vent tube.

Idle air bleed.

Fuel.

Throttle plate.

Idle jet.

Mixture screw.

Emulsified fuel/air mixture.

The idle system provides fuel at idle and low speeds. In the majority of carburettors turning the mixture screw in leans the mixture and turning it out richens the mixture.

nearly all new generation engines employ carburettors with an automatic choke, it is necessary to regularly check that the choke is opening fully, and in the prescribed time; usually about 3 minutes. A choke which is slow to open or which is not fully opening severely increases fuel consumption.

The carburettor idle system provides a relatively rich mixture at idle and low speeds, when not enough air is being drawn through the venturi to cause the main system to operate. When the throttle plate (butterfly) is nearly closed, the restriction to air flow causes a high vacuum on the engine side of the throttle plate. It is this high vacuum which causes the idle system to operate. The outside air pressure of 14.7 psi acts on the fuel in the float bowl, forcing it through the idle jet, and past the idle mixture screw into the air stream. To emulsify the fuel before it reaches the mixture screw, an air bleed is included in the system. Increasing the size of the air bleed leans the idle mixture, if the size of idle jet remains constant.

The progression or transfer holes are a part of the idle system and allow a smooth transition from the idle fuel circuit to the main fuel system without "flat spots", provided the carburettor size has been correctly matched to the engine displacement. As the throttle is opened a little wider past idle, the progression holes are uncovered by the throttle plate, and begin to flow fuel metered and emulsified by the idle jet. At this time fuel flow past the mixture screw decreases and gradually tapers off as the next progression hole is uncovered by the throttle plate.

When the throttle is opened further, the pressure differential between the idle-progression holes and the air pressure acting on the fuel in the fuel bowl decreases,

84

Main system flow commences.

Emulsified mixture flows from progression and idle holes.

Progression/idle flow tapers off.

The progression system is an extension of the idle system. It flows fuel when the throttle is opened a little past idle.

causing fuel flow in the idle system to decrease. Finally, the pressure is too low to push the fuel up the full height of the idle jet and the idle system ceases to supply fuel. Fuel flow through the main metering system though will have commenced before flow in the idle circuit is reduced, providing a carburettor of the right size is fitted.

The main system meters fuel for cruising and high speed. As the throttle is opened and engine speed increases, air flow through the venturi rises, bringing the main system into operation. The heart of the carburettor is the main venturi, as it causes the pressure differential necessary to push the fuel from the fuel well, through the main jet, and up to the discharge hole in the auxiliary venturi (boost venturi).

In the internal combustion engine, a partial vacuum is created in the cylinders by the downward stroke of the pistons. Because atmospheric pressure is higher than the pressure in the cylinders, air rushes in through the carburettor to equalise the pressure difference. On its way through the carburettor the air passes through the venturi, which initially necks down the inrushing air and then allows it to widen out to the throttle bore. To get through the venturi, the air must speed up, thus reducing the pressure inside the venturi to below atmospheric. This pressure differential, commonly referred to as the "signal" of the main metering system, causes the system to discharge fuel. No fuel issues from the discharge nozzle until air flow through the venturi produces a pressure drop or signal of sufficient strength for the atmospheric pressure, acting on fuel in the fuel bowl, to push fuel through the main jet and up to the discharge nozzle. Pressure drop or vacuum within the venturi varies with engine

The main system is activated by the air speed through the main venturi creating a vacuum of sufficient intensity to draw fuel up from the fuel bowl. It functions at cruise and higher speeds. The power valve is a diaphragm-type valve controlled by manifold vacuum, adding fuel to the main system at above normal cruising loads. This type of power system is found in Holley carburettors and fixed venturi downdraught Webers such as the 32DFM and 32/36 DGAV.

speed and throttle opening. Wide open throttle and peak rpm give the highest air flow, and consequently the highest pressure difference between the fuel bowl and discharge nozzle. This in turn gives the highest fuel flow into the engine.

To compensate for various engine displacements and engine operational speeds, a range of carburettors with a variety of venturi diameters are available to create the necessary pressure drop to bring the main fuel circuit into operation at the proper time. A small venturi will provide a higher pressure difference at any give rpm and throttle opening than a large diameter venturi. This is a very important aspect of carburation, which partly explains why the biggest is seldom the best. If the signal being applied by the venturi is too weak, due to the venturi being overly large, this could delay fuel discharge in the main system, causing a flat spot. To cover over this flat spot the idle will have to be richened up, which could spoil low speed running due to an overly rich mixture, or the acceleration-pump jet size could be increased. Increased fuel consumption will be evident as a result of either solution.

The auxiliary venturi functions as a signal amplifier for the main venturi, allowing for more precise and quicker fuel flow responses. This is important in new generation engines as it allows the use of a slightly larger, less restrictive main venturi than would normally be possible, without sacrificing throttle response. The tail of the auxiliary or boost venturi discharges at the point of lowest pressure in the main venturi. Thus the air flow is accelerated through the boost venturi, and because of this, the air and fuel emerging are travelling faster than the surrounding air passing through the main venturi. This has the effect of assisting fuel atomisation, and subsequently improves the quality of combustion.

The actual fuel metering in the main system is controlled by the main jet, the air bleed jet, and the emulsion tube. Some carburettors also feature a metering rod to control fuel flow through the main jet as part of the power system.

The main jet controls fuel flow from the fuel well. An increase in diameter richens the mixture, but more is involved as the shape of the jet entry and exit, as well as the bore finish, also affect fuel flow. Carburettor manufacturers measure the flow of every jet to ensure precise fuel flow and low exhaust emissions, and number the jet to its flow characteristics, not acording to its nominal bore diameter. For this reason jets should not be drilled to change their size. The only exception would be if alternative jets are either unobtainable or difficult to obtain, and then only if the engine has a single carburettor with a single main jet.

The air bleed reduces the signal from the discharge nozzle, so that there is a less effective pressure difference to cause fuel flow through the main jet. This fine tunes the main metering system, preventing the mixture from becoming too rich at higher rpm. A larger air bleed leans the mixture, particularly at wide open throttle and high rpm. Additionally, the air bleed introduces air into the emulsion tube, to emulsify the fuel passing up to the discharge nozzle. This produces a lighter, frothy mixture of fuel and air which improves atomisation when the fuel is released from the discharge nozzle. It also serves to lower the viscosity of the fuel, making it lighter and able to respond more rapidly to changing signals from the auxiliary venturi. Thus the main system can keep more in step with the fuel requirements of the engine.

The emulsion tube has the task of emulsifying previously metered air issuing from the air bleed jet with the fuel coming from the main jet. Its influence is more marked at less than full throttle and during acceleration. The diameter of the emulsion tube and the size and location of holes to emulsify the fuel all affect and influence its operation. Usually, a change of emulsion tube will necessitate a main jet and an air bleed change.

Many carburettors also have a power system for mixture enrichment at heavy load operation. This system supplies additional fuel to complement the main metering system at above normal cruising loads. The added fuel supplied by the power system is controlled by manifold vacuum. As the load on the engine increases, the throttle must be opened wider to maintain a given speed. This lessens the restriction to air entering the engine, which in turn reduces manifold vacuum. In carburettors such as the Carter, Quadrajet and Varajet, at high vacuum the power piston is drawn down against the pressure of the power piston spring but when the vacuum level drops, as engine load increases, the spring pushes the power piston upward which in turn raises the metering rod out of the main jet. This increases fuel flow in the main system, effectively richening the mixture.

In Holley carburettors, and downdraught Webers with fixed venturis (eg. 32DFM, 32/36DGAV, 38 DGAS), the power system is controlled by manifold vacuum operating on a diaphragm type valve. At high vacuum the diaphragm is drawn down against the pressure of the power valve spring, thus holding the valve closed. When the vacuum falls (usually to around 6–10in Hg), the spring overcomes manifold vacuum and the valve opens. Fuel flows from the float chamber, through the open valve into

In carburettors such as the Carter, Quadrajet and Varajet the main fuel system metering is controlled by a main jet and metering rod. As engine load increases, the power spring pushes the metering rod upward out of the main jet, allowing more fuel to flow through the jet and enrich the mixture.

the main fuel channel, and adds to fuel flow from the main jet. The fuel level immediately rises in the emulsion tube well, enriching the mixture.

Another type of power system, called the pull over enrichment system, is used in addition to the power systems previously described in a number of carbs. This system becomes active when the engine is operating at high engine speeds. Only when the pressure differential reaches sufficient strength at high air flow can fuel be pushed from the fuel well up the immersion tube, to be discharged out of the pull over enrichment nozzle. An air bleed in the carburettor air horn introduces air into the system to emulsify the fuel and also bleeds off vacuum as the air flow decreases, to prevent the system from siphoning fuel out of the float chamber.

The accelerator pump system complements all of the other systems and fills in for them, so as to eliminate flat spots. It does this by injecting raw fuel into the air stream for sufficient time to allow the other systems to catch up to the fuel demands of the engine. If the throttle is opened quickly, the manifold vacuum instantly drops to a pressure not much above atmospheric, allowing the fuel to drop out of vapour and wet the manifold and port walls. (A high manifold vacuum helps to keep the fuel in vapour; remember an increase in altitude, which results in a lower atmospheric pressure, lowers the boiling point of water; likewise with petrol, lower the atmospheric pressure or increase the vacuum and it vaporises more readily). To make up for the lean condition caused by the fuel clinging to the manifold and port walls, and to avoid

The pull over type power system adds fuel to the air stream at higher speeds when air speed through the carburettor is sufficiently high to pull fuel up through the immersion tube. It supplements fuel flow through the main system to maintain the required fuel/air mixture strength.

a flat spot, it is necessary instantly to inject more fuel into the air stream.

Having discussed the various carburettor systems it should be obvious that some carburettors are more suited to performance/economy applications than others. Some are just too restrictive due to their small size; others do not have metering systems with changeable jets; and others while being good performance carburettors just do not give the economy or the low speed driveability required. However, do not assume that unless your standard carburettor, which has been fitted by the car's makers, is a Weber or a Holley, it isn't any good. Many standard carburettors work fine and additionally you will not have any problems with "visual" emission inspections if the standard carburettor or a carburettor from a factory high performance version of the same engine is in place. I find that a lot of enthusiasts make decisions either based on hearsay which is totally unfounded or based on what they see on race engines. Consequently some carburettors gain a bad reputation without justification and conversely some carburettors have status which is undeserved in road applications. For example, most V8 enthusiasts wouldn't consider anything but a Holley. Now from a performance viewpoint a Holley is quite good, but when you begin to consider economy and low speed driveability, other carburettors make a lot more sense. A Carter 625cfm or a Quadrajet will give at least 2 mpg better economy for the loss of about 10 and 15hp respectively on a 300hp engine.

At the other end of the scale we can consider the Metro which comes from the British Leyland factory with a single 1¾in SU carburettor. In modified form many tuners wouldn't consider anything less than a pair of 1½in SUs or a 40 or 45 DCOE sidedraught Weber. This is totally incorrect reasoning for a road car; twin SUs or a 89

Table 7.2   Carburettor comparison test on BL Metro

| rpm | Test 1 | | Test 2 | | Test 3 | |
	hp	Torque	hp	Torque	hp	Torque
2000	27	72	23	61	23	60
2500	37	77	34	72	33	69
3000	47	82	41	71	42	74
3500	59	88	56	84	57	85
4000	69	90	68	89	69	91
4500	79	92	76	89	82	96
5000	87	91	83	87	89	94
5500	92	88	89	85	94	90
6000	98	86	99	87	101	88
6500	100	81	99	80	102	82
7000	103	77	95	71	104	78

Test 1 – single SU on prototype manifold

Test 2 – Single 45 DCOE Weber with 34mm venturis on swan-neck manifold

Test 3 – as above but with long runner race manifold

Weber just increase the insurance cost with little or no power increase when a mild road cam is used. Table 7.2 shows the result of dyno testing done on a Metro bored to 1328cc and fitted with a modified head, a Phase IV cam and 1.5:1 rockers. As can be seen from Test 1 this little engine was quite a performer even with the "handicap" of a single SU. Fitting a 45 DCOE Weber on a typical swan-neck manifold just destroyed the performance right through the range. This wasn't the fault of the carburettor though, the manifold was the problem. The only reason for the existence of the swan-neck type manifold, as far as I can figure it, is to make fitting a sidedraught Weber within the confines of the engine bay as straightforward as possible. For Test 3 a long runner, free flow race manifold was fitted. This allowed the Weber to perform up to expectations, but as can be seen it lost out to the standard carb up to 4000rpm. Clearly there is more involved in increasing power than simply fitting a high performance carburettor. A point to note is that on a race engine the Weber would have been unquestionably superior to the SU.

The choice is yours when it comes to selecting a carburettor, but do remember that the carburettor meters fuel according to the signal being received in the fuel well. A carburettor too large for the engine produces a weak signal, consequently the metering system cannot function correctly. There are, however, other good reasons to use a carburettor with venturis of the right size. A high air velocity through the venturi lowers the air pressure, creating a partial vacuum, which makes the fuel more volatile and easily atomised. You probably already know that water will change from liquid to gas (steam) at a lower temperature on the top of a mountain than at sea level, because the air pressure is lower. Likewise with petrol, vaporisation improves with a decrease in air pressure. Additionally, the high air speed itself assists in breaking up the fuel and vaporising it. Properly atomised fuel blends more evenly with air, so fuel distribution from cylinder to cylinder improves. The power goes up because the quality of combustion is enhanced, due to the fact that liquid fuel or fuel in droplets will not burn at the correct rate to produce power. Also, with improved fuel distribution from cylinder to cylinder it is often possible to change the jetting to lean the mixture, thus benefiting fuel economy.

Before concluding that it is the carburettor which is impeding power output, it is worthwhile investigating other areas of the induction system, as the carburettor may not be at fault at all. As you know, the four stroke engine is really only a specialised air pump; the more air that can be introduced into the cylinders, the higher the power output. Already in this book several chapters have been devoted to improving the air pumping efficiency of the engine, and naturally, the induction system has an influence as it is at the starting point of air flow through the engine. However, beside actually modifying the engine so that it will pump a large volume of air, we also have to concern ourselves with improving the quality or density of air inducted. Obviously a litre of cool air will contain more molecules of power-producing oxygen than a litre of hot air. To introduce as much oxygen into the engine as possible, it is necessary to keep the inlet charge cool. This is not without problems though; in cold climates low speed performance and economy might suffer.

There are several areas in the induction system where the inlet charge is being heated. Many inlet manifolds are heated by the engine's exhaust gases or by hot engine coolant. This is done to assist fuel vaporisation when the engine is cold or operating at low rpm. Water heating isn't such a problem and is usually best left connected as it makes a significant contribution to economy. Exhaust heat is another matter as it puts considerably more heat into the inlet charge. Some systems constantly heat the inlet manifold; this is not good for performance and increases the chances for high speed detonation. On V6 and V8 engines the constant flow of hot exhaust gases throught the inlet manifold's heat passage can be stopped by using a special inlet manifold gasket which blocks the heat passage. Such a gasket should be used only between one cylinder head and the inlet manifold so that hot gas can still heat the manifold a little, otherwise economy will drop off and cold driveability may be poor. Fortunately, many carburated new generation engines use an early fuel evaporation (EFE) system of manifold heating which gives quick manifold heating when the engine is cold, but then diverts exhaust gases away from the inlet manifold when the engine is up to temperature. This system should be left in place on inline engines as it benefits cold driveability without having an adverse effect on intake charge temperature when the engine is up to operating temperature. Do check to ensure that the EFE system is functioning correctly. The thermo-vacuum switch can fail and the linkages operating the various butterfly valves do occasionally seize; the most common problem I find is that of tuners connecting the vacuum hoses to the incorrect ports on the thermo-vacuum switch which results in the inlet charge being continuously heated.

If the inlet and exhaust manifold are bolted together as a unit, heat transfer can be reduced by inserting an asbestos insulator at the joint. Additionally, because the inlet manifold will be heated by radiation from the exhaust manifold, fit an unpainted aluminium heat shield between the two. If the inlet manifold is aluminium, leave it unpainted, so that it reflects heat rather than absorbing it. Cast iron manifolds are best painted white or silver for the same reason.

Another source of induction heat in V6 and V8 engines is hot oil from the valley area splashing against the manifold. The modification required is to fit a shield to keep the oil, and heat being radiated from the valley, away from the underside of the manifold.

Many cars draw in air that has been heated after passing through the radiator. This also reduces air density and performance in hot climates where the ambient temperature is usually over 25°C. The most advantageous system involves sealing the carburettor air inlet and air filter in a cold box so that hot air from around the engine cannot be drawn in. The cold box is then supplied with cool air from the front of the car by a 3in heater duct tube. The front end of the tube will require some type of deflector to prevent water and insects damaging or blocking the air filter.

An air filter also reduces the air density, particularly if it is clogged full of dust, by restricting air flow into the carburettor. Obviously the filter could be done away with, but as long engine life and effective air filtration are very closely related, this is not an acceptable option. Contrary to popular opinion, a clean air filter of good design and of sufficient size, does not reduce power output by very much at all. However, the filtration system on many cars does have a devastating effect on performance due to the use of a tiny air filter and a restrictive air box, designed to cut down induction roar and thus reduce noise inside the car.

If induction noise isn't a consideration or a remote filter mounted at the front of the car is fitted, I would recommend the use of K & N cotton gauze type filters. These filters will flow more air than any paper element or foam filter that I know of, even with a good coating of dust. As a rule K & N filters seldom reduce flow by more than about 2–3%, and in some instances they actually increase flow by nearly that amount.

When emission inspections are a consideration, the standard filter body will have to be retained. As you can see from Table 7.3, this results in the air flow being badly impeded. Just note the large jump in air flow when the standard filter body was cut down, leaving the filter element open to draw air from around its entire circumference. Obviously such a modification will not pass unnoticed by alert inspectors so a more subtle approach may be necessary. A modification which isn't

Table 7.3   Air filter air flow comparison
Weber 32/36 DGAV with 26/27mm venturis tested at 1.5in Hg

Test conditions	cfm air flow
Carburettor without air filter	232
Carburettor with K & N sports air filter	229
As above with foam filter	217
Standard totally enclosed paper element with single snorkel air intake	181
As above with filter body cut down flush with base	212
Standard filter body and paper elment with filter base cut away	209
As above with K & N element	223

easily detected is to cut away part of the air filter base. This increases flow and performance considerably, particularly if a K & N element is fitted. One disadvantage of this is that cold air induction is not possible unless a cold air box is fabricated around the air filter and carb.

Cutting away part of the air filter base reduces air flow restriction into the engine and ups power.

Just how much effect a low restriction air filter has on performance can be gauged from Table 7.4. The engine, a 2 litre Ford ohc, had a head clean-up and a Phase IV cam, but apart from these modifications it was basically standard, even down to the cast iron exhaust manifold. Below 4000rpm the standard filter body and element didn't cut hp very much, but at 6000rpm they were knocking off 10hp or about as much as would be lost by refitting the standard camshaft.

Many enthusiasts, and tuners too for that matter, are fooled into thinking that they have gained many horsepower by fitting twin 40 or 45 DCOE Webers to fairly mildly tuned engines, like the one described above. Often, the improvement in power is more the result of the removal of the standard air filter than from the larger carburettors. An engine with a mild cam could gain a similar hp increase retaining the standard carburettor and manifold, with a simple air filter body modification and replacement of the element with a free flow element such as a K & N. Usually, the carburettor will require slightly richer jetting.

The other part of the induction system which can also impede air flow is the inlet manifold. Years ago many factory manifolds were of very poor design, but now there is frequently little to be gained by replacing the standard manifold. With a   93

Table 7.4   Air filter comparison test of Ford 2 litre ohc

rpm	Test 1 hp	Test 1 Torque	Test 2 hp	Test 2 Torque	Test 3 hp	Test 3 Torque
2000	45	119	45	119	45	118
2500	59	124	60	125	59	124
3000	77	134	75	131	76	133
3500	85	127	81	122	85	128
4000	97	128	95	125	99	130
4500	103	120	98	114	103	120
5000	110	116	106	111	109	114
5500	115	110	109	104	111	106
6000	113	99	103	90	111	97
6500	101	82	88	71	98	79

Test 1 – engine fitted with Weber 32/36 DGAV carburettor and K & N sports air filter

Test 2 – as above but with standard Ford filter body and paper element

Test 3 – as above but with standard filter base cut away and K & N element fitted

few modifications the factory manifold will perform as well as high performance replacement manifolds when a mild performance/economy cam is used. Additionally, they often display superior fuel distribution characteristics in the lower and mid rpm ranges, allowing slightly leaner carburettor jetting and better economy. Changing to a different manifold could bring you problems if you have little knowledge of what to look for. Some manifolds do not work as well as the standard manifold, and many only qualify as high performance manifolds when combined with wild cams and large carburettors. Basically I've found that race manifolds, and manifolds designed to connect two or three Weber or SU sidedraught carburettors to four and six cylinder inline engines, work very well. On the other hand street manifolds for V6 and V8 engines, and manifolds manufactured to connect a single Weber, either sidedraught or downdraught, to inline engines may not work as well as the stock manifold or a modified stock manifold.

There are more manifolds available for the small block V8 Chev than any other engine; at the moment at least two dozen. However, of that number there are only two which I would consider using on a performance/economy engine, apart from the stock manifold. The 350 Chev which produced the results shown in Table 7.5 was a typical strong street motor, developed with good mid-range power and cruise economy in mind. It was bored and stroked to 383cu in, had a Phase III cam, head clean-up, cast iron exhaust manifolds and a Carter 625cfm carburettor. As can be seen, only the Edelbrock Performer and Weiand 2P–180 were superior to the standard manifold with this particular engine tune. Remember that the five manifolds tested were carefully selected from all of the inlet manifolds available as the items most likely to be superior to the standard manifold, but only two actually worked better.

Table 7.5   Manifold comparison test of 383cu in Chev

rpm	Test 1 hp	Torque	Test 2 hp	Torque	Test 3 hp	Torque
2000	135	355	133	349	134	352
2500	178	373	175	368	176	370
3000	221	387	214	375	216	379
3500	257	386	255	382	253	380
4000	269	353	268	352	263	345
4500	291	340	294	343	296	345
5000	277	291	273	287	278	292

rpm	Test 4 hp	Torque	Test 5 hp	Torque	Test 6 hp	Torque
2000	136	358	133	350	137	361
2500	180	379	174	366	180	378
3000	225	394	214	375	225	394
3500	263	395	257	386	261	392
4000	278	365	272	357	281	369
4500	301	351	298	348	300	350
5000	283	297	281	295	282	296

Test 1 – Stock 350 Chev inlet manifold

Test 2 – Holley "Z" manifold

Test 3 – Offenhauser Dual Port manifold

Test 4 – Edelbrock Performer manifold

Test 5 – Edelbrock Torker manifold

Test 6 – Weiand 2P–180 manifold

The obvious conclusion is that the enthusiast lacking knowledge of the subject could quite easily choose a new manifold which is inferior to the one the manufacturer fitted at the factory.

Like nearly every V8 ever manufactured, the 350 Chev is fitted with a two-plane manifold. In this type of manifold the inlet passages are arranged in an upper and lower plane, with each plane connected to half of the carburettor, if a single two or four barrel carb is used. This separates the induction pulses by 180° and allows reasonably equal cylinder filling if the manifold is a good design. Also, because the total manifold runner volume is effectively halved, there is less air mass to activate with each inlet pulse, so throttle response is usually quicker and mid-range power may be improved, as compared with a single plane manifold. The division of the manifold into two planes is, however, a mixed blessing as it causes a flow restriction at higher rpm because only one half of the carburettor flow capacity is available on any induction stroke. Additionally, there may be fuel distribution problems in the upper plane at higher rpm or at small throttle openings. What happens in some manifolds at high rpm, due to the carburettor being too close to the floor of the manifold, is that the fuel/ air mixture continues straight on after leaving the carburettor, then the air turns   95 abruptly into the port runners, throwing the fuel out of suspension onto the floor of the manifold. Fuel is wasted, combustion quality and power go down as a result. At small throttle openings another problem can arise due to the directional effect imparted to the fuel/air mixture by the angle of the throttle plate. What can happen is for the mixture to flow down the partly open throttle plate and then be directed by the angle of the throttle to one end of the manifold. This restricts flow to the other end cylinders so they don't give full power. Also, there is another problem related to this which occurs when the air flow is high, but the throttle is partially open, as when cruising. Again in this situation the fuel can be thrown out of suspension, leaning the mixture entering the opposite end cylinders. To prevent detonation, less advance or richer jetting is required, reducing both power output and economy.

There are two options available to overcome these difficulties, which by the way are not unique to two-plane V8 manifolds; some inline engines also have the carburettor mounted far too close to the manifold floor. The first and easiest option, if hood clearance is not a problem, is to raise the carburettor 1–1½in using an aluminium spacer. The spacer may be either divided or open. A divided spacer will retain the 180° pulsing of the two-plane manifold, which may assist both throttle response and cruise economy. An open spacer will definitely give more power from 3500rpm, but throttle response may suffer in engines less than 5 litres unless a Carter or Quadrajet carburettor is used. The second option, which may also be utilised in conjunction with an open spacer, if desired, is to reduce the height of the manifold divider, either over a part or over its entire length, using a mill. I prefer not to cut the divider down flush with the manifold floor, but rather to leave about ¼in in place so as to prevent wet fuel spill-over from the upper plane into the lower plane. Table 7.6 illustrates the effectiveness of these simple modifications, purely from the viewpoint of power increase, when applied to a 5 litre Holden V8.

Table 7.6   Two-plane manifold spacer/divider comparison test of 5 litre Holden

rpm	Test 1		Test 2		Test 3	
	hp	Torque	hp	Torque	hp	Torque
2000	113	297	112	294	112	295
2500	147	308	144	302	143	300
3000	180	315	179	313	181	316
3500	211	317	211	316	210	315
4000	237	311	241	317	241	316
4500	250	292	256	299	255	298
5000	257	270	265	278	260	273
5500	239	228	249	238	246	235

Test 1 – standard manifold and Quadrajet carburettor

Test 2 – as above with 1½in open spacer

Test 3 – standard manifold with divider milled down ¼in from floor

A number of stock intake manifolds with exhaust gas recirculation (EGR) experience the same problems as those which can occur in the upper plane of V8 manifolds. When EGR was first introduced in the early '70s, car makers didn't make much of an effort to homogenise exhaust gas, flowing via the EGR system into the inlet manifold, with the fuel/air mixture. The result was that some cylinders got a lot more exhaust gas than others, combustion was poor in those cylinders, emission levels and economy suffered. As emisssion laws tightened up, and the need to improve economy and driveability grew, manufacturers realised that they had to introduce less exhaust gas, but better homogenised and more evenly distributed, to the cylinders. To achieve this goal, in some engines the design of the inlet manifold was changed; but unfortunately these design changes reduced air flow and power output. Basically two designs were used; both keep the inlet mixture flowing at high speed as it exits the carburettor and then force the mixture, still flowing at high speed, down to the floor of the manifold, before causing it to make an abrupt turn into the port runners.

In the first design the manifold's carburettor mounting pad is cast quite thick, anywhere from ½ to 1¼in, with holes milled to match the carburettor throttle bores. These holes, which in reality become an extension of the carburettor, keep the air/fuel mixture velocity high so that as the inlet charge flows over the exhaust gas discharge hole the two become a more homogenous blend. Additionally, these venturi-like holes, along with the high mixture velocity, force the inlet charge to flow to the heated floor of the inlet manifold, aiding fuel vaporisation and allowing learner jetting.

Remove manifold venturis.

EGR ports and passage.

Manifold venturis aid EGR distribution but reduce high speed air flow. Therefore if the EGR system is not working, the manifold entry should be opened up to increase performance.

The second design is a development on that just decribed, and is more usual on inline six cylinder engines. Again deep venturi-like openings are used below the carb mount to ensure high fuel/air mixture speed, and to drive the inlet mixture to the floor of the manifold to be heated. However, because two inlet ports of inline sixes are right at the side of the carburettor a further modification was introduced to ensure that the inlet charge entering cylinders 3 and 4 could not short-circuit the exhaust gas homogenising, and the heating/vaporising processes. As illustrated, an inner wall was cast into the manifold, forcing the mixture flowing to cylinders 3 and 4 to flow toward the end cylinders before abruptly turning through a full 180° and then a 90° bend to enter the inlet port.

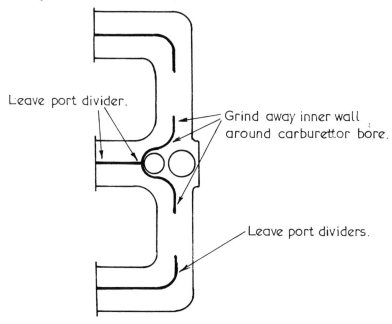

The inner manifold wall around the primary carburettor bore severely reduces air flow into all cylinders. This wall has to be ground out, but leave the port divider walls in place.

Neither design is good for performance, so if the EGR system is not working, the venturis should be milled out of the manifold to leave a single large opening for the mixture to flow through, thus allowing it to diverge after leaving the carburettor throttle bores and turn gently into the manifold port runners. Also in the case of the second design, the inner wall should be ground out to drastically improve flow in the manifold. Not only will flow increase to the centre cylinders, but because the wall effectively halves the entire manifold runner flow area close to the carburettor, flow to the end cylinders goes up as well. Note that about ⅛ to ¼in height of wall should remain in front of number 3 and number 4 cylinder port runners to prevent the flow of wet fuel into them.

Some people spend a lot of time carefully matching the manifold to the inlet port, but personally I feel that this is a waste of time in performance/economy engines. If the manifold port overlaps the inlet port by a ¹⁄₁₆in this won't cause any problems. However, the inlet port must never be smaller than the manifold runner port, allowing a reverse mis-match to occur, as this does affect flow. Another waste of time is to grind and polish inside the manifold. Grinding out the "dingle berries" will have a little effect on a race engine, but it isn't necessary for the street. Polishing the manifold ports to a mirror finish just reduces vaporisation and reduces power. I've seen carburated race engines lose 3–4% hp from this modification.

Only after you free-up the air flow path through the air filter and inlet manifold should alternative carburettors or carburettor jetting be considered. In Table 7.7 I have set out what I consider to be suitable size carburettors for performance/economy engines. Many engines come from the factory with carburettors very similar in size to what I have indicated, but the carburettor may not be branded with the same name as

Table 7.7 Recommended carburettor sizes for performance/economy
SU carburettor

Displacement (cc)

Four cylinder engine

850–1000	1½in x 1
1300–1500	1¾in x 1 or 1½in x 2
1800–2000	1¾in x 2

Six cylinder engine

2500–3000	1¾in x 2 or 2in x 2
3500–4000	2in x 2 or 1¾in x 3

Eight cylinder engine

3500–4400	2in x 2

Weber carburettor

Displacement (cc)

Four cylinder engine

850–1000	[1]28/30 or 32/32mm throttle bores, 21/24mm venturis
1300–1500	[1]32/32 or 32/36mm throttle bores, 23/24 or 23/25mm venturis
1600–1800	[1]32/32 or 32/36mm throttle bores, 23/25 or 26/27mm venturis
1900–2100	[1]32/32 or 32/36mm throttle bores, 25/27 or 26/27mm venturis

Six cylinder engine

2500–3000 open manifold	[1]32/36mm throttle bores, 26/27mm venturis or [2]38–40mm throttle bores, 27–28mm venturis
divided manifold	[2]40–42mm throttle bores, 32–35mm venturis
3500–4000 open manifold	[1]32/36mm throttle bores, 26/27mm venturis or [2]38–40mm throttle bores, 28–30mm venturis
divided manifold	[2]40–42mm throttle bores, 34–36mm venturis

[1] indicates dual barrel carb with progressive opening secondary barrel
   eg. 32/36 DGAV

[2] indicates dual barrel carb with simultaneous opening of both barrels
   eg. 38 DGAS

Carter carburettor

Displacement (cc)
Four cylinder engine

2200–2500 divided manifold   400cfm four barrel

Six cylinder engine

2500–3000 divided manifold   400cfm four barrel
3500–4000 divided manifold   400 or 500cfm four barrel
4100–4300 open manifold   400cfm four barrel
            divided manifold   500 or 625cfm four barrel

Eight cylinder engine

3600–4300 open manifold   400cfm four barrel
            divided manifold   500cfm four barrel
5000 plus   625cfm four barrel

Holley carburettor

Displacement (cc)
Four cylinder engine

1500–2100   [1]280cfm model 5200 two barrel

Six cylinder engine

2000–4000 open manifold   [1]280cfm model 5200 two barrel
3500–4100 divided manifold   450cfm model 4360 four barrel
4300 plus open manifold   450cfm model 4360 four barrel

Eight cylinder engine

3600–4300 divided manifold   450cfm model 4360 four barrel
5000 plus open manifold   450cfm model 4360 four barrel
            divided manifold   [2]585cfm model 4180 four barrel

[1] similar carb to Weber with 32/36 throttle bores, 26/27 venturis

[2] similar carb to model 4160, built for Ford Mustang 5 litre to give better
   economy than 4160.

Rochester Quadrajet carburettor

Displacement (cc)
Six cylinder engine

2500–3600   use carburettor only with divided manifold
3800–4300   carburettor may be used with either divided or open manifold

Eight cylinder engine

3500–4100   use carburettor only with divided manifold
4300 plus   carburettor may be used with either divided or open manifold

GM Strasbourg Varajet carburettor

Displacement (cc)
Four cylinder engine

1500–2300   use carburettor only with open manifold

Six cylinder engine

2000–4100   use carburettor only with open manifold

any which I have listed. Do not let this put you off using the stock carburettor. If it is of a suitable size and a good range of jets are available, then it will probably work quite well. The point is that big carburettors are just not necessary for performance/economy engines. Getting the air filter flow and manifold sorted out, and then arriving at the correct jetting is the prime consideration. I can get 200hp fairly easily from a 4.1 litre engine with a mild Phase II cam and a little head work, breathing through a comparatively tiny carburettor like the 32/36 Weber or Holley 5200. The carb has 32 and 36mm primary and secondary throttle bores and little 26 and 27mm venturis. Now many people would claim that a four barrel carb, or at least a big two barrel, is required on an engine of this size, but this just is not true. The cam is the limiting factor; a bigger carburettor would only add a few hp and in this instance fuel economy and low speed driveability would take a dive, particularly if a big two barrel were fitted.

I do not like, nor do I recommend, two barrel carburettors with simultaneous opening of both throttle plates on performance/economy engines. In general such carburettors do not offer good cruise economy or acceptable low speed driveability. I would much prefer to use a small two barrel with progressive opening of the secondary barrel (with this type of carb an open manifold design is required). A four barrel carburettor is also far superior providing that it has small primary throttle bores and small venturis. The small primary throttle bores and venturis ensure a high air speed through the carburettor at low speed and when cruising. Hence the fuel metering will be more accurate, which produces good economy and good low speed driveability, free of flat spots or surging.

When it comes to carburettor tuning, there is no substitute for years of experience. To make the situation even more difficult, tuning and jetting for the street is considerably harder overall than for race applications. A race carb basically has to meter the fuel accurately over only a narrow rpm range, and usually only in full throttle, high air flow conditions. A street carb, on the other hand, has to deliver satisfactory economy and deliver good performance over a broad rpm range and over a broad air flow range. Additionally, it must work satisfactorily when the air and engine is cold, and also when the weather is hot and the fuel is literally boiling in the float bowl, with the car stuck in stop-start bumper to bumper traffic. Hence do not expect to get the jetting and other adjustments right on the first attempt. Only with patience and a methodical approach can an acceptable level of carburettor tune be attained. I've been working with engines and carburettors for well over 20 years, but it can still take me a lot of time, and many attempts to get the tune to exactly what I require. In the case of my personal cars I prefer initially to get the carburettor basically right, and then over a period of weeks or even months do further fine tuning. The majority of tuners are happy enough if they can get the engine to idle fairly smoothly and accelerate without any sign of flat spots. However, this isn't good enough for a street engine, which is why it becomes necessary to extend the carb tuning session over an extended period of time. It will take time, for example, to ascertain accurately what the fuel economy is like. Also it takes time to determine just how the carburettor is performing under a multitude of differing driving conditions.

Before even attempting to tune the carburettor there are a number of basic checks to be made. Naturally the ignition system must be functioning correctly and the timing adjusted. Ensure that the fuel filter fitted in the fuel line is not clogged full of rubbish. Also check the filter located in the carburettor fuel inlet. The mixture ratio will be affected if there are any air leaks. Therefore check all vacuum hoses over their entire length for cracks. Examine all carburettor ports, solenoid ports and thermo-vacuum switch ports to ensure that all unused ports are capped or plugged. Previously, the carburettor should have been correctly sealed to the manifold, which in turn should have been correctly sealed to the head using the correct gaskets and the right type of gasket cement. Silicone rubber jointing materials such as *Silastic* should not be used. They are an excellent oil joint sealant, but as they are not petrol resistant they should not be used anywhere in the induction tract.

Even when the manifold and carburettor have been correctly installed, this does not guarantee that you do not have an air leak, or that a leak will not start at a later date. Some carbs have a tendency to loosen the screws that attach the body to the base, so tighten these. At the same time tighten the manifold retaining bolts, as some engines loosen these fairly rapidly. After this I test for air leaks around the carburettor throttle spindle, around the carb base, and along the face of the manifold. I've found that the most successful method to check for leaks is to squirt a little petrol out of an oil can in these areas, with the engine running. If there is a leak the engine idle speed will change, or it may run so rich that it will stop. If you use this method of leak detection do take care and have a fire extinguisher on hand. Usually there are no problems but a backfire or a cigarette smoker arriving on the scene could start a dangerous fire with all of that fuel running around. When a leak is found this will have to be rectified by replacing the offending gaskets, or if it is around the throttle spindle the carburettor will require reconditioning or replacement.

With these checks made we can direct our attention more toward the carburettor. After stopping the engine, get someone to push the accelerator pedal down as far as it will go and hold it to the floor. There should have been a good strong shot of fuel from the accelerator pump jet, if there wasn't then it is probably blocked. The primary reason to get someone to floor the pedal is so that you can check that you are indeed getting full throttle. If that is okay next investigate to see that the float level is correct and that the needle valve isn't blocked or weeping.

With these checks and adjustments made we can set about fine tuning the carburettor. Remember that nearly all driveability problems come down to the fact that at some point in its various metering systems the carburettor is either too lean or too rich. Flooding, loading up, bogging down, or black exhaust smoke are all indications of richness, while backfiring, pinging, surging, and hesitation are signs of a lean condition.

After bringing the engine up to normal operating temperature we first set the idle mixture. As discussed earlier, this system is primarily responsbile for the quality of the engine idle and also part throttle cruise and transition. The preliminary idle adjustment is to bottom the mixture screws lightly and then back them out an equal number of turns. Do not be heavy handed when seating the mixture screws as the taper on the screw and the seat could be wrecked. Additionally, a number of so called "tamper proof" carburettors now use a threaded nylon insert which is easily stripped if the screw is forced onto the seat. If the engine had previously been running reasonably well, count how many turns it takes to seat the mixture screw/s, and use this as a guide when backing the screws out. If the carb has two mixture screws they should be backed out the same amount; usually about 1 turn for Webers, 1½ turns for Holley four barrel, 2½–3 turns for Carters and Quadrajets. Now start the engine and turn the idle speed screw against the throttle linkage to provide a fast idle of 800–1000rpm. Next adjust the idle mixture screws to get the best idle, or if a vacuum gauge is being used adjust the mixture to obtain the highest vacuum reading. Remember that if the carb has two mixture screws both screws should be set very close to the same position. Finally, adjust the idle speed screw to give the desired idle speed.

Once the idle mixture has been adjusted, the overall driveability can be checked, and tuning adjustments made to rectify problems along the way. Remember to change only one thing at a time and do carry out the corrective action detailed for each step before moving on to the next step. If the sequence of steps is broken or changed it becomes much more difficult to isolate the cause of the problem.

Immediate off-idle hesitation and stumble is traceable to the accelerator pump. It may not be so noticeable when moving from a standstill so I carry out this check by negotiating a fairly tight, slow, U-turn. If there is a stumble as you get back on the throttle you can be sure that the accelerator pump is the problem. Usually it will be a lean condition, but do not automatically assume this as a rich pump shot will also cause a hesitation. The problem could be improperly adjusted pump linkages delaying the pump action or not giving the correct pump stroke, so check this aspect first and when you are satisfied that the linkages are correctly adjusted, repeat the U-turn test. Have an observer following behind to check for smoke; a puff of black smoke indicates a pump shot too big or of too long duration, grey or brown smoke usually means all is okay, and a complete lack of smoke probably indicates that a richer pump shot is required. When this has been determined, the pump jets, pump bleeds or pump cam can be changed to rectify the problem.

Next we want to check the primary main jets and the power system. These systems have their greatest influence at cruise and when lightly accelerating. If the car feels lazy, or in extreme cases misfires, when squeezing the throttle to maintain speed over a gentle rise, then either system is probably at fault. To determine this connect a vacuum gauge and gently accelerate from 1800 to 2500rpm in top gear. If the problem occurs between about 6 to 12 in Hg it is most probably the main jets, or also the metering rods and power piston spring in the case of Carter, Quadrajet and Varajet carbs. If it occurs under 5–6 in Hg it indicates that, in Holleys, a different power valve is required, and in other carburettors that the main jets or metering rods are the problem. This particular aspect of carburettor tuning is possibly the most important for a performance/economy engine, but also requires the most testing to get just right. Often it will be found that the jetting which is best for economy is not entirely satisfactory for gentle acceleration, leaving the car feeling a touch lazy or dead. Conversely, jetting to accomplish that spirited feel could lead to unacceptable fuel consumption.

With that sorted out we can then tackle the secondary jetting. I prefer to do this on the dyno in conjunction with spark plug readings. The alternative is to jet for speed, again along with spark plug readings. The jetting is richened until hp or speed drops, and then leaned back one or more steps, depending on how big the power or speed jump was with each step. Obviously if a two or three step decrease is only reducing the hp by 2% then in the interests of economy the jetting will be leaned off by that amount, unless this could give rise to detonation.

Plug reading at the very best gives only a guide to mixture strength. If the heat range for the plugs is wrong, or the engine is in less than top condition with worn rings and/or worn valve guides, reading the plugs will be a waste of time. If the mixture is excessively rich or way too lean, or if the engine's detonating, the plugs will indicate this. However, there is no way that the plugs will indicate, with pinpoint accuracy, when the jetting is correct; a couple of jet sizes either way perhaps, but that is about as close as you will get from taking plug readings.

The most accurate way to get a plug reading is to use new plugs and drive them for at least 600, and preferably 1000 miles. Then when you are checking the carb jetting take the car for a good hard run of 5 or 6 miles to burn off idling and low speed deposits. If you can't get home without sitting in traffic pull the plugs while you are out along the road, so as not to distort the reading. The plugs should have insulators all about the same colour; just off white to very light tan for unleaded fuel and the same colour range, plus as dark as rust brown for leaded. The earth electrode should be straw coloured and if there are any deposits they should have a dry, fluffy appearance. Black sooty insulators and sooty plug shells indicate an extremely rich mixture. If the mixture is too lean, the insulator may be chalky white or have a satin sheen, or even be burned a blueish colour. The centre and side electrodes will possibly have a molten appearance. If there are tiny pepper specks on the insulator, or little grey balls on the end of the spark plug shell, the engine is detonating.

Only after all of the other carburettor systems have been adjusted should the secondary opening rate be altered. If you are not able to feel when the secondary barrels open, the opening rate is correct. The car bogging down when accelerating indicates that they are opening too quickly or too early. On the other hand if you can sense the car gasping for air, or feel it hesitate during acceleration, and then suddenly take off, the secondaries are opening too late.

Now that we have taken a look at carburettor tuning procedures in general, we will consider some specific problems which may arise. (If detailed tuning information is required for Weber, SU and Holley carburettors I would suggest that you refer to another of my tuning books, *Performance Tuning in Theory & Practice – Four Strokes*, available from the Haynes Publishing Group). The most obvious problem for tuners residing in a number of lands with emission regulations is tamper-proof carburettors. These usually have seals and/or caps installed to discourage adjustment of the idle mixture screw and also the idle speed screw. Some carb makers have taken this a step further by changing the basic carburettor design and concealing some adjustments. If this latter course has been taken, the carburettor section of the workshop manual must be carefully read to discover just how to get to these hidden adjustments, and see what, if any, special tools may be required to carry out the adjustment. Where plastic or soft metal plugs or caps are used these are quite easily dislodged. Replacement plugs and caps can usually be obtained from carburettor specialists or from your local, friendly spare parts man. In some lands with emission laws, carburettors are never checked to see if they have been tampered with. However in a few places the carburettor will be given a "visual", in which case the caps and plugs must be in place.

Instead of soft plugs, hardened steel plugs are now being used in some carbs to hinder access to the idle mixture screws. Where these are used the throttle body can be quite easily broken away using a punch or chisel, allowing the plugs to be removed. On the Quadrajet, for example, the factory has even put two locator points on the manifold side of the throttle body to indicate the location and depth of the plug. By driving a punch into the body in between the locator points it is a simple matter to crack the body and remove the plug. When the carburettor is refitted to the manifold, the modification is not easily noticed, and if necessary it is a simple matter to epoxy a new plug in place once the adjustment has been completed.

When Holley redesigned their model 4160 carb for the 5 litre Mustang, calling it the 4180, they moved the mixture screws from the float bowl down to the throttle body, and hid them behind steel plugs. These plugs can be removed with a chisel as on the Quadrajet, or a part of the body can be sawed away to allow their dislodgement.

Throttle body gasket.

Idle passage restrictor.

Progression hole.

Some emissions carburettors limit idle fuel flow with a restrictor in the idle passage. If it is not possible to adjust the idle mixture successfully with the restrictor in place, it can be drilled out.

In some types of emission carbs even with access gained to the mixture screws this may not mean that you will be able to adjust the idle mixture successfully. As illustrated, an idle passage restrictor may be built into the throttle body to limit fuel flow down to the mixture screw, so if you find that many turns of the mixture screw is having no effect, this could be blocking your progress. Remove the throttle body from the carburettor and if idle circuit restrictors are evident, drill them out.

Carburettors with metering rods; Carters, Quadrajets and Varajets, appear to give many tuners problems. Personally I like this type of carburettor for the road because it meters fuel more accurately over a broader range than the majority of carbs. Consequently it is good for economy and gives the engine a good crisp feel without bogs or hesitation; providing the adjustments are right. As discussed toward the beginning of the chapter, this type of carburettor has a combined main metering/ power system, consisting of a main jet, a stepped or tapered metering rod and a power piston which is acted upon by a spring and manifold vacuum. When the engine is under a light load, vacuum in the manifold is relatively high, about 13–18 in Hg. This vacuum draws the power piston down, resisting the upward force of the power spring.

Carburettors such as Carters, Quadrajets and Varajets use metering rods which are raised or lowered in the main jet by manifold vacuum to control cruise and full power mixture requirements.

Thus the metering rod is shifted down in the main jet. With a thicker section of the rod within the jet, fuel flow is reduced. At increased engine load and wide throttle openings, manifold vacuum drops, allowing the power spring to push the power piston upward. In this position a thinner section of rod is within the main jet, allowing greater fuel flow.

Clearly the size of the main jet, the diameter of the various steps of the metering rod, and the strength of the power piston spring, all have an effect on fuel flow. However, it would appear that a number of tuners do not understand this fact because many think only of changing the main jet size, usually with unsatisfactory consequences. Obviously changing the main jet will increase or reduce fuel flow equally at all levels of engine load and speed. This probably is not what is required, particularly if idle and cruise vacuum is now lower than standard due to a cam change. With less vacuum at all engine loads the metering rod will be further out of the main jet, increasing fuel flow. If we then increase the jet size the mixture will be too rich at a number of points. The engine may then bog or hesitate, and fuel consumption will most certainly increase.

I prefer to do this type of carburettor tuning on the dyno so that I can control the engine load and then check the mixture strength at various points. First off I like to get the power spring sorted. A soft spring delays the point at which enrichment commences to a lower vacuum level, and leans the mixture from that point right through the range. Conversely, a stiffer spring begins enrichment at higher vacuum and richens fuel flow right to the limit of the metering rod lift point. (Changing from a stock camshaft lowers manifold vacuum and will tend to cause the standard power spring to function as if it were stiffer). After this, various metering rods are chosen to give the desired mixture strength at certain vacuum levels. For example, if we want to richen it up at 12in Hg vacuum, a rod a little smaller in diameter in the upper step would be chosen. If the mixture was weak under load, a rod with a smaller diameter lower section would be tested. Finally, if changing the power spring and the metering rods failed to give the required results, the main jet sizes would be fiddled, and the process repeated all over again.

Chapter 8
Fuel Injection

In a carburettor-type fuel system, the intake manifold design and carburettor size must strike a happy medium between low and high speed air flow requirements. At lower rpm air flow is very low, and in order to keep the fuel mixed with the air it is necessary to have small restrictive passages to keep the air velocity high. Conversely, when power is required, a large carburettor and larger intake passages are desirable. To accommodate these conflicting requirements a compromise must be reached which usually is optimum neither for high speed or low speed performance, but rather more suits highway cruising.

With electronic fuel injection (EFI), the elimination of the carburettor enables the induction system to be optimised more toward high speed air flow because the injector nozzles are spraying finely atomised fuel into the air stream, usually very close to the inlet valves. Hence the fuel stays in vapour as it enters the cylinders, even at low rpm when the air velocity is reduced. Because of this attribute the manifold runners can be quite long, to take advantage of pressure pulses generated by the opening and closing of the inlet valve, without fear of fuel dropping out of suspension and entering the cylinders as non-combustable raw or wet fuel. This pulse tuning of the manifold also aids performance, with the majority of manufacturers electing to use its benefits to pump up mid-range torque rather than all out power at high rpm.

I divide EFI systems into two basic camps; throttle body injection (TBI) and tuned port injection (TPI). Throttle body injection is the least desirable for a number of reasons. It is little better than a carburettor from the viewpoint of economy and frequently inferior to a carburettor as respects air flow ability. With the complications of electronics thrown in, it is not what is wanted for performance. In the TBI system a single injector, or at times two injectors, are located in the throttle body and spray atomised fuel into the air stream as air passes the throttle plate. To keep the fuel atomised, the intake manifold must be compromised with short, restrictive runners.

Otherwise at lower rpm, or when the engine is cold, the fuel would drop out of suspension on the journey from the throttle body all the way to the cylinders.

Tuned port injection is more performance and economy oriented, usually with large diameter, tuned length manifold runners. With an injector nozzle spraying atomised fuel directly at the underhead of each inlet valve there is no problem with the fuel going out of suspension and there is no chance of unequal cylinder to cylinder

These long manifold runners are made possible by using an injection system with one injector for each cylinder. The long runners take advantage of pressure pulses generated in the inlet tracts to increase mid-range power and torque.

distribution. This allows the air/fuel mix to be leaned right off under certain conditions to as little as 16:1, and cruise mix of 15:1, without fear of misfire or detonation. Today, most TPI systems have the injectors all spraying simultaneously once each crankshaft revolution. Hence each injector sprays twice each induction stroke. Sequentially timed systems, with the injectors timed to synchronise their spray period with the opening of the intake valves, are still being used on some of the latest engines but are now less common. With these systems it is usual for the injectors to be timed to commence spraying at 75° before TDC. One very sophisticated unit is programmed to stop spraying just before the inlet valve closes. The commencement of injection is determined by throttle position and engine speed. The result is improved combustion, power and throttle response at lower engine speeds over that possible with simultaneous injection. Sometimes fuel economy is also a little better.

Start of injection period.

Inlet valve open period.

▲ Ignition point.

Most injection systems spray all of the injectors simultaneously once each crankshaft revolution. The start of the injection period is triggered by the ignition pulse being received by the ECM and the injectors continue spraying for the period determined by the ECM to provide the required air/fuel mixture.

Earlier injection systems were mechanical but most fuel injection systems are now fully electronic. Mechanical injection is a simpler system. It uses an air measuring device which functions much like the piston in an SU carburettor. As illustrated, in this system air is drawn past a flap situated in an almost conical passage. The flap is connected to an arm that moves a control piston inside a metering valve. The fuel delivery rate rises as increasing air flow forces the flap to move away from the cone's small end. If the cone diverged truly conically, the mixture ratio would stay constant at all air flow rates. This is not what is wanted so the cone is shaped to cause the flap, and hence the control piston, to move to a rich biased position at idle and then leaner at mid-flow, and finally richer at maximum flow. A high pressure fuel pump delivers a continuous flow of fuel to the metering valve and a mechanical distributor allocates fuel to the injectors, which are activated to operate by the pressure of the fuel. In the purely electronic system the injector nozzles contain an electro-magnet which opens and closes the nozzle for a specific time according to the signal which it is receiving from the computer. At idle, for example, each nozzle may be held open for 2 milliseconds, while at higher engine loads this may be increased to 8 milliseconds. This is referred to as a pulse width.

Like myself initially, the majority of tuners approach electronics, and as a consequence EFI, with trepidation. To help ease you out of this frame of mind we will have a look at just how the various parts of a typical electronic tuned port injection

Air inlet

Fuel return.

Fuel inlet.

This is a basic mechanical injection system. The components illustrated are 1. injectors; 2. inlet manifold plenum chamber; 3. auxiliary air valve; 4. idle speed screw; 5. throttle plate; 6. air flow sensor flap; 7. fuel distributor; 8. fuel metering plunger; 9. pressure regulator valves; 10. fuel system pressure regulator. The high pressure fuel pump, fuel filter, fuel accumulator and fuel system control pressure regulator which also form part of the system are not shown.

Spring.

Solenoid winding.

Solenoid armature.

Pintle valve.

In the electronic injection system each fuel injector is controlled by electric pulses from the ECM. When the solenoid winding is energised, the solenoid armature and the pintle valve connected to it rises, allowing pressurised fuel to spray into the inlet tract. A spring holds the pintle valve closed as long as the solenoid is not energised, thus preventing fuel flow.

This is a basic electronic tuned port injection system with simultaneous injector operation. The components illustrated are 1. injectors; 2. inlet manifold runners; 3. throttle plate; 4. idle speed screw; 5. auxiliary air valve; 6. air flow meter; 7. air temperature sensor; 8. fuel pressure regulator; 9. manifold vacuum/boost sensor hose; 10. fuel rail; 11. fuel dampers; 12. fuel filter; 13. fuel pump; 14. fuel tank; 15. excess fuel return line; 16. electronic control module; 17. coolant temperature sensor; 18. throttle position switch; 19. exhaust oxygen sensor.

system work together to supply fuel to the engine. The basic systems can be broken down into the following: the air flow system, the fuel system and the electrical system. In turn the air flow system can be subdivided into these components; the throttle body and auxiliary air valve. The fuel system comprises; the fuel pump, fuel dampers, fuel filter, injectors and pressure regulator. The electrical system is made up of; the electronic control unit, air flow meter, throttle position switch, coolant temperature sensor, air temperature sensor, exhaust oxygen sensor, manifold pressure sensor, barometric pressure sensor, engine speed sensor.

The throttle body is located on the inlet manifold and it contains a large diameter throttle plate which is connected to the accelerator pedal; just like a carburettor. It also houses the idle speed adjuster screw. This screw allows a variance in the amount of air flowing in the passage bypassing the throttle plate, to establish a suitable engine idle speed.

The auxiliary air valve is a part of the cold start system and serves to increase the idle speed when the engine is cold. Rather than use a fast idle cam, like on a carburettor, to hold the throttle plate open and let more air into the engine, the auxiliary air valve opens and allows in more air to increase idle speed. This valve contains a slotted disc and a bimetal strip surrounded by a heater coil. When the bimetal strip is cold it is flat and the slotted disc opens the port, allowing additional air into the engine. Current flow to the heater coil commences when the ignition is switched on and continues whenever the engine is running. After a few minutes the bimetal strip warms up and bends, turning the slotted disc into a position where it closes off the port.

Fuel is supplied to the injectors by a roller-type high pressure electric fuel pump situated close to the fuel tank. In stock tune the pump delivers more fuel than the maximum requirement of the engine so that pressure in the fuel system is maintained under all engine load/rpm conditions. On leaving the pump the fuel passes into the first of two fuel dampers; the other one is located just prior to the injectors. The purpose of these dampers, as the name suggests, is to suppress fuel flow pulsations caused by the operation of the fuel pump and the injectors. Next, the fuel passes through a high flow fuel filter containing a paper element. The filter traps rubbish which may be present in the fuel, so avoiding blocked injectors. Note that to avoid high speed fuel starvation the filter must be replaced every 25,000 miles and be sure to fit it with the flow direction arrow pointing the correct way. After leaving the filter the fuel passes through the second fuel damper, and in the case of the more common simultaneous type injection system it then flows into the fuel rail and to the individual injector nozzles to be delivered, according to engine requirements, into each inlet tract as a fine mist.

To ensure precise flow through the injectors it is necessary to maintain a constant fuel pressure in the system, otherwise at higher pressures the injectors would flow more fuel than at lower pressures, even though the injector open period, the pulse width, remained the same. Hence a fuel pressure regulator is required. However, it must do more than just maintain the fuel pressure to, say, a constant 44 psi, otherwise there would still be flow differences caused by manifold vacuum variations. For example, at cruise the vacuum level in the inlet manifold may be around 15in of mercury (Hg), or stated another way, 7.4 psi below atmospheric pressure. Obviously in this situation, without compensation, the effective fuel pressure would increase from 113

44 psi to 51.4 psi (44 + 7.4) because the high manifold vacuum will actually draw fuel through the injectors during the open cycle. This would give rise to a rich mixture at a time when a lean mixture was required. On the other hand, at full throttle the manifold vacuum side will drop to zero, so the effective fuel pressure would remain at 44 psi. To overcome this undesirable situation of varying fuel pressures, a diaphragm-operated pressure regulator is used which maintains fuel pressure at 44 psi above the depression in the inlet manifold. On one side the diaphragm senses fuel pressure, while the other side is connected to the inlet manifold to react to the prevailing vacuum level, or in the case of turbo engines to the boost level. A spring is fitted in the engine vacuum side of the regulator to establish a nominal pre-load of pressure, in this example 44 psi.

With the fuel pump flowing a constant supply of fuel to the system, a situation of too much fuel at the regulator develops. When pressure greater than 44psi above the inlet vacuum builds up, the diaphragm moves, opening a valve which allows excess fuel through to flow back to the vehicle's fuel tank. Thus an accurately pressure-regulated supply of fuel is always available to the injectors to ensure precise metering. In practice, the regulator valve is always open to some extent, unless the fuel pump is too small or the filter is blocked or too small to supply the engine's fuel requirements. This gives a continuous flow of fuel through the system, ensuring that the fuel flowing to the injectors is cool and vapour free, which in turn improves metering accuracy. Plainly there are less energy producing molecules in 1cc of hot petrol than the same volume of cold fuel. Some very sophisticated systems in fact have a fuel temperature sensor to achieve even finer accuracy.

The central brain of the fuel injection system is the electronic control module (ECM), which is commonly referred to as the "black box". Its function is to receive information on the quantity of air drawn into the engine, the position of the throttle plate, air and coolant temperature, engine speed etc. and then process this information and transmit an electric signal to the injectors, which determines when they switch on and for what duration. In many of today's cars, the ECM also processes information and transmits signals to the ignition system, the torque converter, the turbo wastegate and also some pollution devices. This information will be covered in following chapters; for the moment we want to concentrate on how it controls the fuel system.

Basically, the ECM is an information processor; that sounds less frightening than calling it a computer doesn't it? It usually functions on analog signals, but also processes some digital signals. Analog simply means an infinitely varying measurement between two points. For example, a gauge with a sweep hand such as a speedo or a tachometer gives an analog reading. To receive a signal, the ECM must first send out a constant voltage electric current to a sensor, usually of 5 volts. The sensor in turn is designed to increase or decrease electrical resistance in proportion to whatever it is measuring. Hence if the ECM sends out a constant 5 volt signal to the coolant temperature sensor which is calibrated to sense from $0°C$ to $80°C$, and a 2.5 volt signal returns, it knows that the engine is still warming up as the coolant temperature is only $40°C$. With this information it would continue to send a wide pulse to the injectors, to keep the mixture rich.

At the same time it may be receiving a digital signal, an on/off signal, from the throttle position switch, indicating that the throttle has been opened past a $40°$ open angle. This would indicate that the engine is under heavy load, accelerating or climbing a steep hill, and so the pulse width would be further increased to provide the needed fuel.

Just how the control module figures out how much to increase or decrease the injector pulse width is beyond the scope of this book; however, a basic explanation is in order. During development of the engine on the dyno it is run under every possible combination of engine operating conditions to produce what is termed an engine fuel map. This process can take engineers up to 12 months, but at the end of these tests they

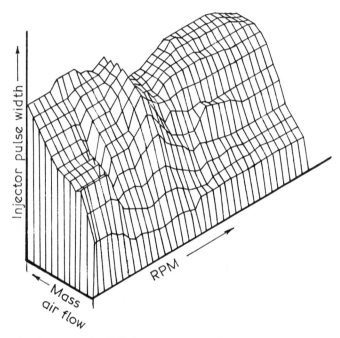

During engine development the ECM is programmed to provide precise fuel delivery for hundreds of engine operating conditions. This fuel map illustrates how the injector pulse width varies for changing engine rpm and mass air flow conditions.

know the engine's fuel requirements to meet performance, economy, driveability and emission requirements. From this store of data a computer programme is generated which implants in the ECM's memory just what time the injector pulse width should be for literally hundreds of engine operating conditions. For example, during the mapping tests it may have been found that at 5250rpm, with the engine at normal operating temperature, and a throttle open angle of 40°, the engine produced best power with an injector pulse width of 9.3 milliseconds. Along with anywhere from 300 to 800 other map reference points this information would be placed in memory. Later, when the engine was operating at 5250rpm with everything at normal temperature and a 40° throttle open angle, it would "look up" its information store and find what the pulse width should be for those criteria. It would then send a 9.3 millisecond pulse 115 to the injectors in response to that input which it had received just a few milliseconds earlier.

Under normal conditions the major portion of the control module's input comes from the air flow sensor. There are a number of designs around, but they all measure the amount of air flowing into the engine.

The most common air flow meter, designed by Bosch a number of years ago, has been dubbed by Ford a vane air flow meter (VAF). As illustrated, this simple unit passes all of the air flowing into the engine through a passage with a spring-loaded

The vane air flow meter is a relatively simple device which measures inlet air flow into the engine. The flow meter also contains the idle mixture screw. Turning the screw in reduces bypass air flow, causing the ECM to enrich the mixture.

door, or vane. As the air flows through the passage, it exerts a force on the flap, and depending on the air flow and the opposing force of the spring, it is held open to a certain angular position. Connected to the door pivot is a potentiometer, or variable resistor, which changes the control module's input voltage according to how wide the door has been blown open. An air temperature sensor is also located in the air flow meter, and from this signal, along with the air flow signal, the ECM can calculate mass air flow. Remember that air density changes with the ambient temperature, and other factors, so air flow input alone is not sufficient for accurate fuel metering. So that the flow sensor door is not disturbed by induction pulses, a compensation door is connected which works within a damping chamber. This type of air flow meter also houses an idle mixture adjusting screw and bypass passage. By varying the amount of air which is permitted to bypass the sensor flap the air flow meter signal can be changed to alter the air/fuel ratio at idle.

The other common Bosch air flow meter is a hot wire type, dubbed by General

Motors a mass air flow sensor (MAF). Basically it is a tube, often with gratings to keep air flow laminar, through which flows the air entering the engine. Stretched across this tube is a very fine platinum wire which is heated by an electric current to maintain a constant temperature above ambient. A temperature sensor in the air flow meter signals the ambient temperature to the computer module so that it sends out the correct amount of power to keep the wire at the required temperature. However, air flowing into the engine flows over the wire and cools it in direct proportion to mass air flow. Consequently the ECM must increase power flow through the wire to keep the temperature constant, and then reads this signal as mass air flow. Other manufacturers use a similar air flow meter, but instead of a heated wire, they have chosen to use a heated nickel film.

A third type of air flow meter which is gaining popularity is the vortex flow sensor. This sensor uses an ultrasonic sender and receiver to measure the rate at which vortices pass through a control passage. The signal from the sensor is measured by the control unit, corrected for barometric pressure and inlet air temperature, and used to determine the injector pulse width.

Other input signals which are received by the control module, and used to calculate the injector pulse width, vary from one injector system to another. All systems include a coolant temperature sensor (CTS) to allow for increased fuel delivery when the engine is cold. All have an engine speed input, usually taken from the ignition system, to achieve the correct pulse width and to synchronise pulses. In addition, some systems will include a manifold absolute pressure sensor (MAP), a barometric pressure sensor (BARO), a camshaft position sensor for sequentially timed injection and a VAC sensor which reads the difference between manifold vacuum and atmospheric pressure.

All types of electronic injection have a throttle position sensor (TPS). The Bosch TPS contains just two sets of electric contacts. One set monitors when the throttle is closed and the other when the throttle plate is opened wider than 40°. Both sets of contacts are attached to the throttle body and are operated by the movement of the throttle shaft. Under most conditions both sets of points are open. The closed throttle points close when the throttle is closed; as when idling or decelerating. If the engine is idling and the control module receives a signal from these points, the pulse width is changed to enrich the mixture. On the other hand if the speed sensor indicates that the engine is running at 3000rpm and the points are closed, the ECM concludes that the vehicle is coasting so it shuts off fuel to the injectors to reduce fuel consumption and lower emissions. If the engine speed continues to fall below 1800rpm the injectors are reactivated to stop the engine cutting out. Alternatively, if the throttle is opened to accelerate before the engine drops to 1800rpm, the closed throttle points would immediately open and the regular injector pulse resume. The high engine load points close when the throttle plate angle exceeds 40°. The electric signal received by the control module causes it to send a wider pulse to the injectors which increases fuel flow by about 8% to provide the fuel/air mix required for maximum power.

A less common type of TPS has a potentiometer connected to the throttle shaft which changes the control module's input voltage according to the position of the throttle plate. The ECM uses this signal, along with the inputs from other sensors, to calculate the engine's fuel requirements.

Another type of sensor, technically known as the exhaust oxygen sensor or

"Lambda Probe", but more usually called the O_2 sensor (O_2 or EGO), is common in injection systems for emissions applications. This sensor is fitted in the exhaust system, close to the engine. It is a metal-coated ceramic probe which works like a puny battery, producing about 100 millivolts when oxygen content in the exhaust is high, as when the mixture is lean. When the oxygen content falls, indicating a rich mixture, its voltage increases. If the O_2 sensor signals a rich mixture to the ECM, the pulse width is reduced under cruise conditions.

Hopefully, you now understand how electronic fuel injection works, and what all the various parts do, but before we get into reworking the system to increase power or make it function with a modified engine, there are a few terms frequently used which deserve some explanation so as to avoid confusion and misunderstanding.

The first is the "PROM chip". PROM stands for programmable read only memory, and refers to a replaceable memory chip which is used in General Motor's computers. What GM have done is build a standard ECM which is fitted in all their vehicles regardless of engine specification, transmission, or emission requirements. To tailor the ECM to specific applications a plug-in PROM chip is used. It contains detailed information, programmed in memory, to calibrate the control module to a particular car specification or emission standard. Hence it is possible for an enthusiast in the United States to obtain a Canada specification chip, for example, to perk up the performance of his Californian specification Corvette. As time passes, more companies will become involved in marketing PROM chips, just as cams with a variety of profiles are available to suit a range of applications.

The other terms which have lead to confusion are "closed-loop" and "open-loop" computer modes. In the closed-loop mode the ECM locks into a 14.7:1 air/fuel ratio programme because modern three-way catalytic converters increase hydro-carbon (HC) and carbon monoxide (CO) emissions if the mixture is any richer, and nitrogen oxides (NOx) go up if the mixture goes any leaner. The closed-loop mode operates when the vehicle is in a steady state cruise and the O_2 sensor has warmed up to 315°C. In this mode if the O_2 sensor reads that the mixture is either above or below the stoichiometric air/fuel mixture of 14.7:1, the control module immediately reacts to correct the condition. In the open-loop mode the ECM ignores signals from the O_2 sensor and calculates fuel requirements according to the input from the other sensors. For example, if the throttle is floored, the control module immediately goes open-loop to supply a richer than 14.7:1 mixture. During warm up or when decelerating, the ECM is also in the open-loop mode.

GM have for a number of years used closed-loop/open-loop control modules on carburated vehicles, as well as those with fuel injection. They call this system computer command control (CCC), using a 4 barrel Rochester Quadrajet "feedback" carburettor. This carb contains a solenoid which pulses the primary side metering rods up and down 10 times a second within the primary main jets. The ECM receives input signals similar to an injection system and then sends out pulses which control the metering rods. During each pulse cycle the ECM varies the time the rods are held down, according to the O_2 signal, or in open-loop according to other signals that it is processing. Holding the metering rods down longer leans the mixture, while holding them up richens it. The secondary barrels of this type of carb operate mechanically just like an ordinary Quadrajet.

The majority of electronic fuel injection systems are capable of handling the fuel and air required for about a 15% power increase without modification. Non-emissions systems may tolerate up to a 25% power rise. If you do not wish to become involved in modifying any part of the EFI system this must be kept in mind when you are planning your modifications. Stock fuel injection cannot handle big cams, so unless the manufacturer has fitted a fairly sporty cam, about what I would rate a Phase II grind, you are going to be limited to about a Phase III profile if the system incorporates an O_2 sensor, or a Phase IV grind if it doesn't have this sensor. Engines which come from the factory with a Phase II cam may be able to go a step further than I have suggested.

There can be a number of reasons for the fuel injection system not being able to cope with our modifications. Some systems are fuel limiting, meaning that some or a number of components in the fuel supply system are not capable of flowing the required amount of fuel at the correct pressure to enable more hp to be produced. The fuel pump or injectors could be at their flow limit, or perhaps the fuel filter or fuel lines are too restrictive. With any of these problems the engine will run fine, except at peak rpm under load. At that time the engine may just feel dead, or if there is serious starvation there will be misfiring and surging.

To check if in fact it is a fuel problem, and to isolate what part of the system is deficient, a series of tests are required, preferably on a chassis dyno. Connect a vacuum gauge to the inlet manifold and a fuel pressure gauge to the fuel rail. At zero vacuum the fuel pressure should be that specified by the manufacturer, usually 44 psi (303kPa) for Bosch injection. If the pressure is stable at all rpm levels it is probable that the injectors are limiting fuel flow. Note that if the vacuum gauge is reading above zero this figure divided by 2, when added to the fuel pressure reading, must equal the pressure specified for zero vacuum. For example, with a Bosch system designed to work at 44 psi above manifold pressure, if the vacuum gauge reads 4in of Hg the fuel pressure should at the same time be 42 psi ($44 - \frac{4}{2} = 42$). Conversely, if the engine is turbocharged the fuel pressure reading minus the manifold boost pressure gauge reading must equal 44 psi. For example, if the boost gauge reads 7 psi the fuel gauge should read 51 psi ($44 + 7 = 51$).

If the pressure isn't up to specification there must be a flow restriction or an internal pressure leak. To check for an internal leak let the engine idle and note the pressure reading. In a Bosch system if the idle vacuum is 16in of Hg then the fuel pressure should be 36 psi ($44 - \frac{16}{2} = 36$). Switch off the engine and note the gauge. If the fuel pressure falls, you have an internal leak. Leaks in fuel lines or at connections should be obvious, so we start by testing the fuel pump. Start the engine to bring the system up to pressure, switch off and clamp the pump outlet hose. If the pressure ceases falling the pump is the problem, and should be replaced. However, if the pressure continues to drop the leak must be elsewhere, so loosen the pump outlet clamp and start the engine. Switch off and quickly apply a clamp to the pressure regulator to fuel tank return line and retension the pump outlet clamp. If the pressure stops falling, the regulator must be leaking, but if the pressure continues to drop some of the injectors must be leaking, so remove the fuel rail and injectors and repeat the previous test, observing which injectors are at fault. Permissable leakage is one drop per minute.

Check for flow restrictions by connecting a hose into the fuel system at the fuel rail, and have it flow into a container. Then compare the flow attained with what is   119 specified in your workshop manual. For example, most Bosch pumps are rated at 130 litres per hour, so in 1 minute of pumping the container should collect a minimum of 2 litres of fuel. If it is less than this there is a blockage in the system. To determine if the filter is the problem, next connect the drain hose and container on the pump outlet. If the flow rate is unchanged, disconnect the pump inlet hose and connect a length of hose which is immersed in a container with at least 3 litres of fuel. Activate the pump for 1 minute and measure how much petrol it discharges. If it is less than specified, the pump requires replacement; however, if the flow rate is correct, the fuel tank pick-up is either blocked or damaged.

In some applications the fuel system may flow the amount of fuel specified by the manufacturer, but this may be less than what is required by the engine. To determine quickly the approximate amount of fuel flow needed by a road engine I use this formula: hp x 6 = cc of fuel per minute. For example, a 175hp engine requires about 1050cc, 1.05 litres, of petrol per minute. If the pump, filter and fuel lines flow less than this, the engine is probably going to experience fuel starvation at high loads and near peak hp rpm.

In the majority of cases if there is a high speed/high load fuel deficiency, it is probably due to the injectors being too small. However, before you assume this to be the case it is wise to carry out the checks which I have just outlined. Injectors are expensive, and larger than stock injectors can cause problems as will be discussed later, so first make sure that the rest of the fuel system is healthy. Injectors look pretty much the same, although the colour of the plastic varies, so the only way to determine their flow rating is to consult the workshop manual or the injector manufacturers. Knowing the flow rate of the injectors and the maximum pulse width it is a fairly simple matter to determine if they will flow the amount of fuel required for our desired power output and engine speed. For example, if we have a 6 cylinder engine producing 175hp at 6000rpm its total fuel flow rate will be 1050cc per minute, using the above rule of thumb. Dividing this figure by the number of injectors, 6, we find how much the continuous flow, or static flow, of each must be; in this example 175cc per minute. In this instance if the standard injectors were rated at 185cc/min, they would be suitable providing the maximum pulse width was 10 milliseconds.

A problem arises, however, when our power peak occurs at less than 6000rpm, because the manufacturer's flow rating no longer applies. You see, with a 10 millisecond pulse width at 6000rpm and higher the injectors are open continuously, so the flow rating has significance. Below 6000rpm with a 10 millisecond pulse width injector flow will be momentarily interrupted, reducing the flow rate below that stated by the manufacturer. Hence the injectors must be derated to 0.75 times their stated flow at 4500rpm, 0.84 at 5000rpm, and 0.92 at 5500rpm, to estimate realistically what power potential they have.

This is not intended to imply that it is preferable to have our engine producing maximum power at 6000rpm and higher so as to have the injectors flowing continuously. What can happen if the ECM has been programmed to give a maximum 10 millisecond pulse width at high engine load is for the engine to be excessively rich at 6000rpm, and then be lean by the time it reaches 6800rpm, because injector flow will not increase beyond what it was at 6000rpm. This type of problem won't occur if the stock engine produced maximum power at engine rpm above 6000, as the ECM would then have been programmed to give a narrower pulse in high load/

maximum rpm conditions, and larger injectors would have been fitted to compensate for the reduced maximum pulse width. For example, if the stock engine produces maximum power at 6300rpm you can be fairly certain that the maximum pulse width is 9 milliseconds. This means that the computer will exercise proper control over the injectors up to the engine speed where they are continuously open; 6667rpm. With a maximum 8 milliseconds pulse width continuous flow takes place at 7500rpm. It is quite easy to calculate at what rpm constant flow occurs; just divide 60,000 by the maximum pulse width stated by the manufacturer. Normally I aim to keep my maximum hp rpm at least 200 to 300rpm below the continuous flow point to avoid excessive richness then, and also keep away from a peak rpm lean out which could occur at engine speeds over the continuous flow point.

If our hypothetical 6 cylinder, 175hp engine with 185cc/min injectors produced maximum power at 5300rpm, and the maximum pulse was 10 milliseconds, the injectors would be too small, probably limiting power to about 165hp. This naturally should be verified on the dyno with the aid of an exhaust gas analyser and if found to be the case we could try larger injectors; 200cc/min injectors would do the trick, but they are not going to allow us to go much higher than our targeted power figure. Hence considering the expense it may be wise to test 214cc/min units first as these should allow up to 190hp at 5300rpm. However, this may cause us problems as the mixture will be about 15% richer at all points, as compared with the standard injectors; so fuel

A flow meter bypass tricks the ECM into leaning the mixture when larger injectors or higher fuel pressure is utilised. A motorcycle carby connected to close as the throttle is opened wider reduces the amount of air bypassing the flow meter at higher speeds thus ensuring the correct air/fuel mixture.

consumption may be excessive at cruise and the idle may be far too rich. Remember larger injectors flow almost the same percentage extra fuel at all pulse widths. Therefore if they flow 15% more with a 10 millisecond pulse, at a 5 millisecond pulse they will be flowing about 12% more than the standard injectors.

Assuming that it is decided to fit larger injectors in spite of the alternatives, which in this instance may be more suitable, there are a number of courses that could get the fuel curve back on track. Firstly, the computer could be completely re-programmed; this is expensive. The other course is to fabricate a bypass around the air flow meter. The tiny idle bypass may help to settle the idle mixture down to a tolerable level, but it won't get back cruise economy. As illustrated, what is required is a good size air flow meter bypass which tricks the computer into "thinking" that air flow into the engine is lower than it actually is, so that in turn it reduces the injector pulse width, leaning the mixture. To avoid a high load/high rpm lean out it is necessary to reduce the amount of air bypassing the flow meter at wider throttle openings. I have found that a simple way to do this is to use a small, about 18 to 22mm, motorcycle carby in the bypass. The carb throttle slide is connected to the injector throttle in such a way that as the injector throttle plate opens past 45° the carb slide commences to close. Using a motorcycle carb in the bypass avoids all of the hassles of trying different diameter hoses to get the amount of air bleed correct. At idle it is a simple matter of raising or lowering the carby slide to obtain the idle speed and mixture required. Then with a cable connecting the slide and the injector throttle plate it is possible to regulate when and by how much the slide closes to give the desired mixture strength at wider throttle plate angles.

A less expensive alternative, which again utilises a flow meter bypass to get the idle and cruise mixture right, is to increase the fuel pressure. Where adjustable pressure regulators are available these make the task much easier as you can quickly see with the aid of a dyno and an exhaust gas analyser what effect various increased fuel pressures are having. If you can't obtain an adjustable pressure regulator, the standard unit can be modified by fitting a stronger spring, or by packing up the stock spring.

Fiddling with the fuel pressure is a quick check to determine if the standard injectors are too small. It is a simple matter of disconnecting the manifold vacuum hose from the regulator, and then fitting a length of hose with a tyre valve in the end. Using a tyre pump to pressurise the regulator, first test at 5 psi, then 8 psi, and so on up to 15 psi. Assuming a standard pressure of 44 psi, pressurising the vacuum side of the regulator to 5 psi raises the pressure to 49 psi, which will increase fuel flow at all points by around 10%. If at 15 psi power is not improving, you can be reasonably sure that fitting larger injectors or fitting more injectors isn't going to help. The problem must be in the computer programme or with air flow restrictions. However, if outright power does go up at increased fuel pressure levels, it may be feasable to raise fuel flow into the engine.

In performance/economy applications I prefer not to go to the expense of fitting larger injectors or have the hassles associated with fuel pressure increases above 3 to 5 psi. If the computer can be easily tricked to increase fuel supply to the level required, I would take that course. Naturally if the injectors are just too small, no amount of computer work will get the top end rich enough. The next step then would be to raise
the fuel pressure by 3 or 4 psi. That shouldn't upset the idle or cruise economy, and

may just give the flow increase needed at higher engine loads. My next preference is to fit an additional injector nozzle up close to the throttle body. Usually a solid aluminium block will have to be machined to mount the injector on the manifold plenum. In 6 and 8 cylinder applications an injector the same as those already fitted should give the flow increase needed. For 4 cylinder engines the injector should normally be smaller. It is quite easy to determine the size required. If the flow rate desired is calculated to be 780cc per minute and the four standard injectors are rated 165cc/min, the extra injector should be around a 120cc/min unit (780 − [165 x 4] = 120). Note that to save money it is acceptable to use discarded injectors which may be a bit "dribbly" for our extra nozzle. These can frequently be obtained from vehicle repairers and injection specialists for a nominal amount, or even free! You may find when doing the internal leak test described earlier that one of the nozzles already fitted to your engine is leaky; it could be used as the auxiliary nozzle if its not leaking more than 4 drops per minute.

Unless the engine is lean right through the range it is not a good idea to connect electrically the extra injector directly to the pulse leads of the other nozzles. The most simple arrangement is to connect a wire into another pulse lead, and then run it, via a dash mounted isolator on/off switch, to the auxiliary injector. The injector is then manually turned on to receive the computer pulse signals when additional fuel is required. An alternative is to connect the injector's pulse lead through an adjustable vacuum or pressure switch into the electrical system. In this way the extra injector will receive the ECM pulse signal when the manifold vacuum falls below a preset level, usually 6 to 10in Hg; or in the case of turbo engines, when the boost increases past a certain pressure. Another arrangement which works on Bosch systems with a 40° throttle plate sensor switch is to wire a relay in line with this switch to allow the ECM pulse through to the auxiliary injector at throttle openings wider than 40°.

Rather than being fuel limiting some fuel injection systems are air flow limiting. This usually isn't a problem in performance/economy tune, but it is good to realise that this problem may be holding your engine back for making the sort of power which you desire. The manifold runners may be too small in diameter, as is the case with the 305 Camaro and the 350 Corvette. The 350, for instance, is air flow limited to about 285–290hp. Fabricating runners 3mm larger in diameter allows the engine to make another 15–25hp, with the correct cam. After that, the air flow sensor strangles the engine. With some engines the throttle body limits air flow; this usually isn't too difficult to rectify as larger units can often be found on higher hp engines, so if the linkages are similar and the same type throttle position switch is used, they can be swapped.

Fitting a high flow air flow meter, however, is much more difficult as it will send inaccurate flow signals to the ECM, resulting in excessively lean mixtures. To overcome the problem, the constant-force spring settings have to be adjusted in Bosch vane-type meters so that the larger unit has the same flap deflection for the same air flow as the standard meter. In this way the ECM can correctly adjust the mixture strength. Increasing the fuel pressure, fitting larger injectors or a full-time auxiliary injector (ie. wired to pulse with the other injectors) will also get the mixture back to an acceptable level, but the metering will not be as accurate.

Earlier we examined how the ECM was programmed to relate to information implanted in its memory as a result of engine mapping dyno tests. Clearly when the engine is modified, the ECM may no longer respond exactly as we would desire to the engine's fuel needs. For example, we may want a 12.5:1 air/fuel ratio for best power, but perhaps the computer has been programmed to give a maximum air/fuel ratio of 13.5:1 for economy reasons. Similarly, in one particular engine speed range we may be getting exhaust gas reversion due to late closing exhaust valves. If this didn't occur with the standard cam, the ECM will not have been programmed to increase the pulse width at the engine rpm where this is taking place with our modified cam. Hence the engine may be down on power at these speeds, not because the air/fuel mix is technically wrong, but because the backflowing exhaust gas has diluted the inlet charge and stifled complete combustion. Enriching the mixture from its cruise ratio of say 14.3:1 to 13.5:1 may get enough additional fuel molecules dispersed throughout the air/exhaust mix to get combustion completed in the time available, with the result that the engine makes more power.

But how do you make a computer send a longer pulse to the injectors? Well, in a maximum effort engine you would have a new ECM built with a different set of instructions locked into memory. On some General Motors models you could fit a different PROM chip. For example, a 305 Camaro will be richened up at various points with a 350 Corvette chip installed. The other way in which we can do it is to send false or misleading information to the computer.

An easy modification for Bosch injection with a throttle position switch that closes when the throttle plate has been opened wider than 40° is to place another switch into this circuit which, when closed, makes the computer think that a rich mixture is required for full power. The switch is wired in as illustrated, and may be manually operated if dash mounted, or it can be vacuum operated to close at a certain vacuum level. With the switch closed the ECM richens the mixture by 8%.

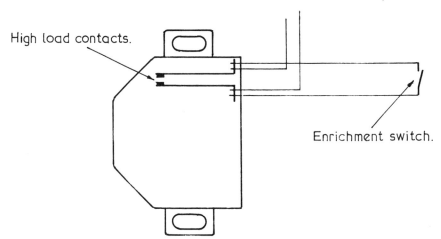

An enrichment switch wired in parallel with the throttle position switch high load contacts will, when closed, trick the ECM into enriching the mixture by about 8%.

Emissions systems utilising an O_2 sensor can be fooled to change the air/fuel ratio from 14.7:1 to a fuel mix which gives better driveability and perhaps better economy in the closed-loop cruise mode. A number of engines, because of combustion chamber design and programmed electronic spark control, just do not function efficiently at 14.7:1. Frequently richening the mix to something around 14:1 to 14.3:1 will transform cruise economy and driveability. To achieve this ratio we have to trick the O_2 sensor to send a false signal, indicating a mixture leaner than 14.7:1 to the ECM. This lean signal is induced by adding air into the exhaust just upstream of

An air metering orifice in the exhaust 3in upstream of the O_2 sensor will fool the ECM into enriching the mixture for surge-free cruising.

the O_2 sensor. As shown in the illustration, air is drawn in through a calibrated orifice due to vacuum created by the exhaust pulses. To allow experimentation it is a good idea to be able to quickly change the orifice diameter, so it is wise to weld a boss, which has been drilled and tapped for a ⅜ UNF thread, to the exhaust about 3in upstream from the O_2 probe. With that size of thread it is possible to use Carter AFB carb jets to meter air into the exhaust. Start testing with a 0.101 jet, and remember when the jet size required is established, clean deposits out of the orifice regularly.

There are a number of other modifications which can be carried out to alter the quantity of fuel metered, but these can only be undertaken by injection or electronics specialists. For example, with Bosch K Jetronic-type air flow meters the air passage profile can be machined to increase power and responsiveness. With the GM control module it is possible to remove the PROM chip and plug in a micro-computer which allows new instructions to be keyed into the ECM. In systems where an additional injector has been fitted, an auxiliary ECM can be added to control fuel flow from this injector. Then when the standard system is not supplying the required mixture, the extra injector provides what is needed. The fuel delivery map used by this auxiliary ECM will be stored digitally in a ROM (read only memory) chip. With the car on a chassis dyno and an exhaust gas analyser connected, the fuel delivery curve is set by means of an external computer which is capable of changing the delivery rate with the engine operating. To this basic curve variations are added to compensate for inlet air temperature changes. Once the fuel map is finalised, the chip is "burnt in" so that it becomes a permanent memory in the auxiliary ECM. Naturally enough modifications such as this are quite expensive. Mostly though if we haven't gone too wild with our engine tuning the stock fuel injection system will have enough built-in "latitude" to supply the additional fuel required.

In emissions engines most problems are directly related to cam changes. With increased valve overlap it is possible for mixture draw-through to be experienced at some point in the rev range. This fuel may then be ignited in the hot exhaust causing the O_2 probe to send a false signal to the ECM. For example, if this afterburn in the exhaust has consumed all of the oxygen, the probe will sense this as being due to a rich mixture. The ECM then responds by reducing the pulse width, perhaps causing excessive leanness. As a result at cruise the engine may feel unresponsive and go through a period of mild surging. To avoid this, stick to the cam designs which I have suggested, or fit the exhaust air bleed described above.

There are only two manual adjustments on electronic injection systems; for idle speed and idle mixture. The idle speed screw allows a variance in the amount of air flowing in the passage bypassing the throttle plate. Turning the screw out increases air flow, upping idle speed. If the bypass passage is too small to give the desired idle speed, drill a 2mm hole in the throttle plate, and increase the hole size in 0.25mm increments to get the idle rpm required. Before drilling the throttle plate check that the throttle body bypass passage is not partially blocked by carbon, as this will restrict the amount of idle adjustment available.

The adjustment screw on the throttle body sets the engine idle speed. Turning the screw out allows more air flow into the engine which increases the idle rpm.

The idle mixture screw, located on the air flow meter, also varies the amount of air flow in the bypass passage. Turning the screw out increases flow in this passage and reduces air flow past the air flow door. As the computer now receives a signal that a reduced mass of air is flowing past the flap, it decreases the pulse width. However, as the actual amount of air flowing into the engine hasn't altered, the throttle body bypass controls this, and the fuel/air mixture is made leaner. Alternatively, turning the mixture screw in reduces bypass flow and increases air flow past the flow meter door. The ECM senses this as increased air flow and sends a longer pulse to the injectors to enrich the mixture. Note that to discourage tampering, the mixture screw is usually out of sight, covered by a plastic cap.

Chapter 9
The Ignition System

The ignition system has the complex duty of producing high voltage surges of up to 40,000 volts, to fire the spark plugs, initiating combustion of the fuel/air charge which has been inducted into the cylinders. It must do this in the correct firing order, and at the instant necessary to properly ignite the compressed mixture. Additionally, in new generation engines the spark must be of sufficient intensity and of sufficient duration to completely fire very lean, and hence less combustable mixtures, to lower emissions and improve fuel efficiency.

Few new generation engines use a points-type distributor to time and distribute the spark. However, we will first consider the operation of this type of ignition system as this will enhance our understanding of the workings of the various electronic and computer-controlled systems.

The points-type system relies on a 12 volt battery to supply the initial electrical energy, a set of points to time the spark, and a coil to intensify the voltage of the electrical energy supplied by the battery so that it is capable of jumping the spark plug gap and igniting the fuel mixture.

As illustrated, the switching of the primary, or low voltage circuit, is accomplished by the contact breaker points which are opened and closed by the distributor cam. When the points are closed, electric current flows through the coil's low voltage primary winding, and then through the points to earth. This current flow through the low tension winding produces a magnetic field which surrounds the coil's secondary or high voltage winding. When movement of the distributor cam causes the points to open, the primary circuit is broken. Current flow through the coil primary winding stops, and the magnetic field collapses, causing a high voltage electric current to be inducted in the secondary winding. The high voltage current then flows from the coil to the centre of the distributor cap, and through the carbon brush to the rotor button. The turning rotor in turn directs the current back to the distributor cap and out to the individual spark plugs where it jumps the gap to start off the combustion process.

The points-type ignition system relies on a set of points to make and break the low voltage electrical circuit to produce a high voltage ignition spark at each spark plug.

Today's engines do not have ignition points to produce and time the ignition spark. The most basic new generation distributor uses a toothed pulse generator rotor and electronic circuitry to control current flow through a high energy ignition coil.

There are two basic problems with the conventional points-type distributor which has led to the almost universal adoption of electronic ignition. In time the points wear and pit, which changes the ignition timing, upsetting performance and emissions. Pitting reduces the conductivity of the points, lessening current flow in the coil primary winding. This in turn leads to a feeble secondary voltage which may be too weak to fire the plugs. Again performance and emissions suffer.

The other problem arises at higher engine speeds. With an increase in engine speed the time that the points are closed between each opening period is decreased. This means the coil has less time to build up a full magnetic field between firings, reducing the voltage available to fire the plugs. Today's engines, with lean mixtures and wide plug gaps, require a higher voltage to get combustion started than engines in the past, so a conventional points ignition may cause misfiring at higher engine rpm.

To overcome these deficiencies the more common electronic ignition systems use magnetic pulses and electronic circuitry to open and close the low voltage circuit, rather than mechanical contact points. A number of different designs are in use, but the basic mode of operation is similar. The distributor shaft turns a pulse generator rotor inside a stationary permanent magnet. Functioning like a mini alternator this induces a signal in the pick-up coil located within the distributor. This electric signal causes the electronic circuit to switch "on" and "off". When the circuit is switched on, current flows through the primary windings of the ignition coil, and when it is then switched off, the magnetic field collapses, inducing a high voltage in the coil secondary winding. As in the points-type system the high voltage current then flows to the centre of the distributor cap, through the carbon brush and rotor button out to the individual spark plugs. Because the system does not contain tungsten contact points which pit and burn, a substantially higher primary circuit current can be utilised to ensure that the coil is fully saturated, even in the short time available at higher rpm. Thus a high intensity spark is provided at all engine speeds likely to be encountered in road use. This had led to some manufacturers calling this system high energy ignition (HEI).

Fully computerised ignition, called by some manufacturers electronic spark timing (EST), functions in a similar way to the HEI system in that it provides a high intensity spark at higher rpm. However, the major difference with this type of ignition system is that the ignition advance is adjusted electronically by the ECM for various engine speeds and engine load conditions. The ECM receives signals from a variety of sensors and then according to its programmed memory selects the appropriate ignition advance angle to meet performance and emission requirements. The distributor may include the pulse generator to send the firing reference signal to the ECM, but at times the distributor will contain only a rotor button to direct the high voltage secondary current to the spark plugs. When this is the case, the pulse trigger may be located at the rear of the engine with "firing" pins embedded in the circumference of the flywheel. As each pin passes by the magnetic pick-up a pulse is relayed to the electronic control module (ECM) which calculates the appropriate advance angle and then switches the ignition coil primary circuit on and off. With this latter system moving the distributor body will not alter the initial ignition timing. This is determined by the location of the magnetic pick-up and the position of the firing pins.

129

With any type of road ignition system some arrangement is employed to alter the ignition timing to suit various engine operating conditions. For example, at idle the ignition may be timed to fire the plugs at anything from 5° to 18° before the piston reaches top dead centre (TDC) on the compression stroke. However, at high rpm and wide open throttle the advance required for best performance may be around 25° to 35° BTDC, while at cruise an additional 10° to 15° advance will be necessary to give best economy.

This extra advance is required to allow the fuel mixture the correct amount of time to burn properly. Clearly at 3000rpm the combustion flame has to have progressed the same amount as it would have at 700rpm, so that maximum energy is available to force the piston down as it passes TDC. The only way that this time deficit can be made up is to start the combustion flame burning earlier by firing the spark plugs several degrees advanced on the firing angle at idle.

Apart from this time factor there are a number of other reasons why the ignition firing angle must be varied for different engine operating modes, and why the advance angle changes from one engine to another. The fuel/air ratio influences the flame speed. Very lean and rich mixtures both burn slowly and require more spark advance. A mixture close to full power lean burns the fastest and requires less advance. At cruise, for example, the mixture is usually adjusted to be a touch lean in the interests of economy, hence more advance is needed. However, there is another reason why the spark lead must be increased in this operating mode; that is mixture density. With the throttle just cracked open the cylinders do not become crammed full of air and fuel, so even when compressed the oxygen and fuel molecules are slightly separated, which in turn slows the speed of flame travel through the combustion chamber. From this you will understand an increase in the compression ratio has the reverse effect, that of increasing mixture density, thus necessitating less advance. A cam change also influences mixture density. If the lobe duration is made longer, mixture density will be reduced at lower engine speeds, while in the mid-range and at maximum rpm it will be greater. To accommodate this circumstance more advance will be needed at lower rpm and reduced advance will be called for higher in the rev range. Changes to the exhaust system or in the exhaust gas recirculation (EGR) valve operation affect mixture density in yet another way. By lessening the amount of exhaust gas left unscavenged in the cylinder and by stopping EGR operation there is more room to pack fuel mixture into, hence mixture density increases. Additionally, because there are fewer inert exhaust gas molecules to separate oxygen and fuel molecules, flame travel through the combustion space is faster.

Engine design also figures in the amount of ignition advance needed for efficient combustion. The size of the combustion space and the position of the spark plug obviously affects the degree of advance wanted. The further the flame has to travel, as in a large combustion chamber, the longer it will take to burn the mixture completely. Conversely, the closer the spark plug to the centre of the chamber, as in a 4 valve pent-roof chamber, the quicker the combustion time. Some cylinder heads have been created with inlet ports and combustion chambers which induce a high degree of swirl to the inlet charge. This homogenises the mixture more thoroughly and speeds up flame propogation. Increasing the amount of squish has a similar effect. The stroke of the crankshaft, and the ratio of the connecting rod length to the length of the stroke, influence the degree of advance needed because these two factors affect the time it

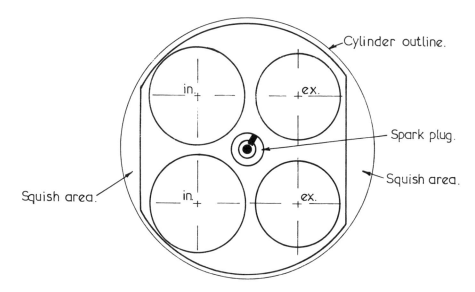

In a pent-roof 4 valve combustion chamber the spark plug is located in the centre of the combustion space so less spark advance is required.

takes the piston to move to, and just past, TDC.

Obviously in a modified engine a number of the above factors will have been changed from what they were in the standard engine. Hence the amount of advance needed under various engine operating conditions could now be different to achieve the best power and economy. Full electronic ignitions adjust the advance according to criteria programmed into the ECM as a result of ignition mapping tests carried out by the factory during engine development, and in essence cannot be modified. The ECM can be reprogrammed, but this is beyond the resources of most enthusiasts. GM systems with a **PROM** chip can have a different chip installed. As will be considered later, there are a few steps which can be taken to change the initial advance angle. Many ignitions though still use an advance mechanism within the distributor which is controlled by mechanical means. Both electronic breakerless and points distributors of this design can be modified to alter the rate of advance and the amount of advance.

With non-computerised ignition there are three types of ignition timing; initial or static advance, centrifugal or mechanical advance, and vacuum advance. The initial advance is the amount of spark advance which is provided when the engine is started up to about 450 to 1000rpm. It is measured in degrees of crankshaft rotation before TDC and is determined by the position of the distributor in the engine. Rotating the distributor body in the direction of rotation of the rotor button decreases the amount of initial advance, while turning it in the opposite direction to rotor rotation increases the advance.

Centrifugal advance adds ignition advance to the initial timing at an rpm pre-set in the distributor, usually about 800 to 1000rpm, but sometimes as low as 450rpm. The amount and rate of centrifugal advance is controlled, relative to engine speed, by

131

revolving bob weights and springs, and some type of stop. Increasing the weight of the bob weights or reducing the spring tension allows the distributor to add ignition advance more quickly. The amount of centrifugal advance which the distributor can add is limited by a stop peg that permits the distributor cam, or the pulse generator rotor in the case of electronic systems, to move a fixed amount. Reducing the amount of travel cuts down the maximum amount of centrifugal advance.

Vacuum advance adds to the combined initial advance and centrifugal advance angle, to increase the amount of advance under cruise conditions. The system consists of a vacuum canister which is connected by a vacuum hose, and perhaps a number of ported valves, to the inlet manifold and/or the carburettor. The canister in turn

Mechanical ignition systems use a vacuum canister to increase ignition advance at cruise. A range of canisters are available to change the rate and amount of advance. Selecting the correct vacuum canister is important to ensure maximum cruise power and economy.

responds to engine vacuum, moving the distributor's pole piece assembly or points plate relative to the vacuum level. With an increase in vacuum there is a corresponding increase in advance. A variety of canisters are available with differing advance rates and maximum amounts of advance.

If, for example, an engine is adjusted with the initial timing at 10° BTDC and the maximum centrifugal advance is 20° at 3000rpm measured at the crankshaft (10° at 1500rpm measured at the distributor), that means at speeds above 3000rpm with zero vacuum the total advance will be 30° (10° + 20° = 30°). However, if the vacuum canister added a maximum of 15° at vacuum levels above 12in of Hg, and the vacuum was 14in Hg, the cruise advance at 3000rpm would be 45° (10° + 20° + 15° = 45°).

Most modified performance/economy engines will require less total advance than standard, due to improved fuel/air density at higher engine speeds. However, the amount of initial advance will probably have to be increased if a warm cam is fitted. If the compression ratio has been raised, this will tend to offset the increase necessary. Naturally if the initial advance is increased, and less total advance is necessary, the amount of centrifugal advance has to be reduced. Also the rate of centrifugal advance may have to be changed; some engines may need to reach full centrifugal advance more slowly, others more quickly.

Mechanical advance-type distributors use a system of revolving bob weights and springs to regulate the rate of centrifugal advance and some type of stop arrangement to limit the amount of centrifugal advance.

All distributors limit the amount of centrifugal advance by using a slotted plate or lever that comes up against a stop peg to prevent the distributor cam moving forward any further, relative to the direction of rotor rotation. To investigate how the advance mechanism works in your distributor you will probably have to remove the points plate, or the pick-up coil assembly in electronic distributors. Now that you can peer into the internals of the distributor, hold the drive gear to prevent the shaft turning and turn the rotor button forward. In most instances the rotor and the outer shaft will rotate a few degrees until the stop peg limits further movement.

If there is no movement possible, the outer shaft must be seized onto the drive shaft due to a lack of lubrication. In this case the outer shaft will have to be dismantled from the drive shaft. To do this remove the rotor button and the oiling wad, and then remove the screw or circlip concealed underneath. Next, disconnect any springs and pull the outer shaft off the distributor drive shaft. Remove the accumulation of rust from both shafts and reassemble them, using engine oil to lubricate the two shafts. With the advance mechanism freed-up you will now be able to see what means are used to limit the amount of centrifugal advance, and work out how to reduce the degrees of advance built into the distributor.

Let's say that our standard engine had 6° initial advance, and according to the workshop manual, 23° to 27° centrifugal advance measured at the crankshaft at 4000rpm. The quoted 23° to 27° degrees is due to production tolerances. It means the factory designed the distributor to give 12.5° centrifugal advance, but some limit it to   133

11.5°, while others allow up to 13.5°. Hence if the timing is set at 6° before TDC, the total advance at 4000rpm should be somewhere between 29° and 33°. When the engine is modified it may be found from testing that the performance is best with 11° initial advance and 28° total advance at 3000rpm. Obviously the distributor will have to be modified to limit centrifugal advance to 17°, measured at the crankshaft (28° − 11° = 17°); 8.5° at the distributor. Additionally, the governor springs may have to be changed to springs with a different tension to allow full advance to be reached at 3000rpm, and to give the required rate of advance at lower engine speeds.

Reducing the amount of centrifugal advance is quite easy; for some distributors it is just a matter of placing a nylon or metal bush of the appropriate diameter over the stop peg to reduce the amount the advance mechanism can advance. Other distributors will require the limiting slot, or the nose of the advance limiting lever, to be welded to restrict the amount of travel. Calculating the distance to what we want to restrict the centrifugal advance, 8.5° in this example, is quite basic. Do remember that at the distributor the advance angle is half that at the crankshaft. The formula is:

$$D = \frac{2\pi r \times CA}{360}$$

where D = distance to which advance is limited.

$$\pi = 3.1416$$

r = radius from distributor shaft centre
to stop peg centre.

CA = centrifugal advance angle at distributor.

If in our example the distance r equals 0.75in, advance movement in the distributor must be limited to 0.111in to give 8.5° centrifugal advance.

$$D = \frac{2\pi r \times CA}{360}$$

$$= \frac{2 \times 3.1416 \times 0.75 \times 8.5}{360}$$

$$= 0.111in$$

Because advance movement may be limited by either of two stop pegs it is necessary to identify one peg, with a dab of paint, as the peg from which all measurements are referenced. This is because the pegs are often not exactly 180° apart, or exactly the same radius from the centre of the distributor shaft. When the distributor is reassembled, the advance limiting mechanism must always be aligned with the painted peg. If it is referenced to the other peg, the centrifugal advance could be a couple of degrees from what we want.

To ensure accurate timing the distributor must be in good condition. If there is any play in the bearing, the distributor shaft will wriggle and upset the timing. Also, if the distributor has a helical drive gear shaft, end float should preferably be 0.003in, and not more than 0.006in. Excessive end float will allow the shaft to ride up and down and give erratic timing so fit a shim of the required thickness between the drive gear and distributor body to bring the end float down to that required. A drive gear which moves on the shaft will also upset the timing. When play is evident peen the pin to tighten the gear on the shaft.

The simplest and most accurate way to check if the standard rate of advance, called the advance curve, is suitable is to run the engine on a dyno and check power at various engine rpm. If the spark is under or over advanced at any engine speed, this will be indicated by a loss in power at that particular rpm. When the required rate of advance is plotted on a graph like that illustrated, the distributor should be removed from the engine and fitted to a distributor test stand. The standard rate of advance can then be checked and plotted on the same graph. In this example it can be seen that the

Distributor centrifugal advance curves. Curve A – advance rate required as indicated by dyno testing. Curve B – stock centrifugal advance rate. Curve C – rate when two heavy governor springs were fitted.

standard springs were allowing the distributor to advance too quickly. Two slightly heavier advance springs were fitted to slow the rate of advance, but now the rate was too slow. Next one of the heavy springs was replaced by one of the standard springs, and this combination gave the advance curve which dyno tests had shown previously to give the best performance.

Plotting the advance curve without the aid of a dyno is more time consuming, and usually prone to a slight degree of error, but with patience and practice performance superior to that possible if the stock advance curve was retained is achievable. Begin testing by blocking the vacuum advance and giving the engine 5° more initial advance than stock, up to a maximum of 20° before TDC. If the engine pings when accelerating hard from 1000rpm to 1500rpm in 4th gear, back the initial timing off until it stops, and record the firing angle. On the other hand if there is no trace of ping with an additional 5° initial advance you can try up to another 3°. Very few engines require more than 8° over stock. Next, test for ping when accelerating in 4th gear from 1700rpm to 2300rpm. Again, if the engine pings, back the timing off until   135 it stops, and then back it off another 2°. Conversely, if there wasn't any pinging increase the timing until the engine just pings and then back it off 2°. Without altering the timing, record the timing angle at 1500rpm, 1750rpm, 2000rpm and finally 2250rpm. Obviously to do this accurately you will require some additional timing marks on the harmonic balancer, plus an assistant to keep the rpm steady. With that done, test for pinging in 4th gear, accelerating between 2500rpm and 3000rpm. Again back the timing off 2° from the angle where ping was noted and with the aid of your assistant record the firing angle at 2500rpm, 2750rpm and 3000rpm. From all of these angles you can now plot an advance curve, but before pulling the distributor to change the springs one further test should be done: a test to find the required total advance.

The total advance for best performance is determined by timing the acceleration from 50 to 100mph in 4th gear. The amount of advance that produces the quickest time will also give best power. Begin testing with the timing retarded 5° from the stock initial timing angle, then repeat the test backed off another 2°. If the time improves, keep retarding the timing in 2° steps until the car begins slowing down. Conversely, if at 7° retard from stock the car is slower than at 5°, take your testing the other way; 3° retarded, 1° retarded, 1° advanced from stock, and so on.

Many enthusiasts have a tendency to over-advance the timing, but my advice is to use the least amount of advance conducive to peak performance. Usually you will find that once you reach a certain point, the engine will not perform any better with just a couple of degrees more advance. Instead, it may respond only to an extra 4° or 5°. When you have reached the stage that the engine becomes insensitive to a small amount of additional advance, you have gone far enough, so back the timing off a couple of degrees out of consideration for today's poor fuel.

With the total advance determined from testing, next plot the timing angle at 3500rpm, 4000rpm and 4500rpm. As illustrated, the distributor may have a very slow advance curve which is still advancing way past 3500rpm. Many tuners like to see the

Ignition total advance curves measured at the crankshaft. Curve A – advance rate required as indicated by road testing. Curve B – stock distributor advance rate with initial timing bumped up to 12°.

distributor reach full advance between 2800 and 3200rpm, yet I have not found it to be any disadvantage in road engines to have full centrifugal advance reached at 3800 to 4000rpm. In fact this often allows more vacuum advance at cruise to improve the economy.

To determine what distributor modifications are required it is necessary to plot the stock advance curve, so set the initial timing at the angle which you found kept the engine from pinging during the 1000rpm and 1500rpm 4th gear acceleration test. Run the engine and record the timing angle on the graph at 500rpm increments, from 1500rpm to 4500rpm. Comparing the two advance curves it is clear that the stock distributor is advancing too quickly, and because the initial advance has been increased from 6° to 12° before TDC, the total advance is excessive. Probably if the engine was to be run with the stock distributor the initial timing would have to be reduced to stop the engine pinging when accelerating at cruise engine speeds. This in turn would reduce power at other rpm levels. To rectify the problem, stiffer advance springs are needed in this example, and the centrifugal advance has to be reduced by 8°.

After the distributor has been recurved and advance limited, the vacuum advance can be sorted out. If emissions devices, particularly the exhaust gas recirculation (EGR) valve, are left operative, the stock vacuum canister will probably give the correct amount of additional advance under cruise conditions. However, if the EGR has been disconnected, the standard vacuum canister may give too much advance at certain vacuum levels. This would be indicated by the engine pinging under light acceleration or when pulling over gradual hills with the throttle just open. To correct this, a canister with a lower rate of advance should be fitted.

Testing to get the right cruise advance is quite simple, but it may take some time to find a vacuum canister which gives the desired amount of advance at various vacuum levels. The best place to test is on the dyno with the engine lightly loaded to produce vacuum levels of 13in of Hg, 10in of Hg and 7in of Hg at 1500rpm, then 2000rpm, 2500rpm, 3000rpm and finally 3500rpm. In all tests the vacuum hose is disconnected from the distributor. For example, at 1500rpm the engine would be loaded to give a vacuum of 13in of Hg. The distributor would then be unclamped and gradually advanced by hand to give the best power reading. The amount of advance would be checked with a timing light and recorded. The test would be repeated at 10in of Hg and 7in of Hg. Next, the engine would be run at 2000rpm; first at 13in of Hg, then 10in and 7in. At the end of the 3500rpm test it be quite clear just how much extra advance the engine needs to give best cruise power, and hence best cruise economy at various vacuum levels.

For example, if the engine responded as shown in Table 9.1 we would require a vacuum canister which gave 12° or 13° advance at 13in of Hg, 5° or 6° at 10in, and 2° or 3° at 7in. The additional advance required at the 3000 and 3500rpm, 10in and 7in vacuum levels had to be disregarded so as to avoid over-advancing the timing at lower engine speeds. The graph shows the vacuum advance curves of three canisters available for this particular type of distributor. Clearly canisters "A" and "B" have too much advance at the 7in and 10in vacuum levels while canister "C" is in the range required.

Cruise vacuum testing without the aid of a dyno is not so accurate, but is often much quicker. Apart from a strobe light, an accurate vacuum gauge and a 6 to 8ft

TABLE 9.1 Vacuum Advance Test

rpm	Initial timing + centrifugal advance	Best power advance			Increased Advance Requirement		
		13in Hg	10in Hg	7in Hg	13in Hg	10in Hg	7in Hg
1500	14°	26°	20°	16°	12°	6°	2°
2000	22°	35°	27°	25°	13°	5°	3°
2500	24°	36°	32°	27°	12°	6°	3°
3000	26°	39°	36°	33°	13°	10°	7°
3500	28°	42°	39°	34°	14°	11°	6°

length of rubber vacuum hose are the only tools required. Place the gauge somewhere in the car where you, or preferably an observer, can keep an eye on it fairly constantly. Run the vacuum hose through any spare hole in the firewall and connect it to the distributor vacuum source after disconnecting the distributor vacuum hose. For the first test increase the initial advance by another 12° to 15° and then gently accelerate from 1500rpm to 2500rpm, keeping the vacuum level at 13 to 15in of Hg. If the engine doesn't ping, try climbing a few gentle hills at least a ¼ mile long with the vacuum at 13 to 15in. Pinging would indicate that 2° or 3° less advance is desirable at this vacuum level. On the other hand if no pinging is noted, repeat the test with the initial advance increased by 18° to 20°. The second test is similar to the first, but this time the initial advance is 8° to 10° more than stock and the acceleration and hill work is done at 9 to 11in of Hg. Again, pinging would indicate that the test should be repeated with 2° or 3° less initial advance. Then when all traces of ping are eliminated, record how much extra advance the engine liked at this vacuum level. The third test is done at 5 to 7in vacuum and 3° to 5° extra initial advance.

Advance curves of three vacuum advance canisters.

If at the conclusion of these three tests it was clear that the engine responded well to 3° extra advance at 7in vacuum, 8° extra at 10in and 15° more at 13in of Hg, a vacuum advance canister with a curve close to this should be fitted. Finding such a canister may not be easy. The place to start looking is in your workshop manual or an extensive tune-up book to see what canisters are fitted to various engines with the same distributor. If the advance curves for the different canisters are graphed,

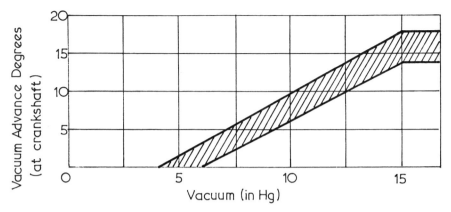

A vacuum canister which the manufacturer states starts to advance at 4 to 6in Hg with full advance of 14° to 18° at 15in Hg will have an advance rate in the range shown.

selecting the correct unit is fairly straight forward. Often though, numbers which at first may appear irrelevant may be all that is given. It could be stated that vacuum advance starts at 4 to 6in Hg and full advance is 14° to 18° at 15in Hg. From these figures we must draw a graph as shown to determine how much the canister advances the timing at various vacuum levels.

When a canister is found which appears to be suitable, install it, but do not assume that it will advance exactly at the rate specified as errors do occur in manufacture. If you are equipped with a vacuum pump it is quite simple to check if the canister is advancing correctly. Connect the vacuum pump to the distributor and with the engine idling note how many degrees the timing advances at 7in, 10in and 13in of Hg. If the figures tally with your graph, the canister is okay, but if they do not correspond get another canister after you have checked to be sure that the graph that you drew up is accurate.

Those who do not possess, or cannot borrow, a vacuum pump need not despair. With a vacuum gauge, a "T" piece, a length of vacuum hose and some vigorous sucking the same thing can be accomplished. Connect the gauge and "sucking" hose to two branches of the "T" and connect the third branch to the distributor canister. Suck on the hose to register 7in of vacuum, pinch or clamp the hose to prevent loss of vacuum, then see how far the timing advances at idle. Repeat the test at 10in and also 13in of Hg.

Getting the vacuum advance right is very important from the aspect of economy. I have seen engines show a 25% reduction in fuel usage with the correct vacuum canister and the vacuum source modified as outlined in a later chapter on emission controls. On the other hand with the wrong vacuum canister the engine can lose performance or ping under light engine loads. If the engine pings with gentle acceleration or cruising over hills don't assume that the engine should have the distributor retarded to reduce the amount of initial advance. The problem could be too much vacuum advance, so disconnect the vacuum line from the distributor and check if the pinging goes away. If it ceases, the canister must be advancing either too quickly or too much. A canister with less total advance or a slower advance rate is needed. However, if the pinging continues with the vacuum hose disconnected and 139 plugged, the centrifugal advance is excessive, so fit stronger springs to slow the advance rate.

Computer-controlled ignition systems cannot be easily modified to change the advance rate or the total advance. However, as a knock sensor is usually incorporated with this type of ignition, the initial timing can be advanced by several degrees to take care of a camshaft which is hotter than stock. Technically, the engine may be over-advanced at engine speeds above 1500rpm, but the knock sensor will relay a signal to the ECM to retard the spark until the knocking ceases.

Engines which utilise a pulse-type distributor can have the initial advance angle increased fairly simply, but unclamping the distributor and advancing it may not have any effect on some cars because the ECM may keep the original initial advance timing angle in its memory. What must be done is to unplug the connector which links the distributor to the computer; the low tension wires which join the distributor to the coil must remain connected. Start the engine and in the usual manner, using a strobe light, advance the initial timing by moving the distributor. Next, stop the engine and disconnect the positive (+) cable on the battery for a minute or two so that the ECM loses its previously programmed timing information. Reconnect the battery cable and the connector which links the distributor and ECM. Start the engine and check the timing. The computer should have moved the timing around but if it hasn't, repeat the procedure a few times. Take care though not to disconnect or reconnect the distributor to the ECM with the engine running as this could cause electrical surges in the system and do damage. Note that it is normal for the engine to run strangely after the battery is disconnected as it takes some time and a little driving for the computer to get its act together. Also, it is normal for the engine check light to come on. This doesn't mean that you have blown the electronics; it means that the ECM is receiving input outside its normal parameters and thinks there is a problem.

Computerised ignitions which receive their triggering pulses from firing pins embedded in the flywheel, the harmonic balancer or the crankshaft, also may not allow the initial timing to be easily adjusted. If it is possible, the best solution is to move the pick-up sensor into a more advanced position. When this is not feasible, all the firing pins have to be advanced. After these changes it may still be necessary to disconnect the battery and then after a minute reconnect it and start the engine, so that the ECM learns the new firing angle.

Just as electronic fuel injection systems can be fooled by false input from the various sensors, so too can computerised ignitions. For example, the Ford EEC4 system relies on the distributor to send a stream of PIP pulses (profile ignition pulses) to the ECM. If the distributor is set at $7°$ before TDC the ECM then fires the electronic ignition module at all engine speeds and operating conditions relative to the $7°$ before TDC reference point. As we have seen previously, moving the distributor body so that the PIP pulses occur at $20°$ before TDC effectively advances the ignition timing by $13°$ at all points in the ignition curve. Obviously this is way too much extra advance except at idle, so what is required is an electronic delay between the distributor and ECM. With $13°$ delay the timing returns to normal, so by varying the delay the ignition is effectively advanced or retarded. Hence with $8°$ delay the timing is advanced $5°$ ($13 - 8 = 5$), with $15°$ delay the timing is retarded $2°$ ($13 - 15 = -2$), and so on.

The electronic delay is usually made a part of an auxiliary ECM which alters the fuel injection curve. It has its own ROM chip into which new ignition timing information is "burnt". With the car on a chassis dyno an ignition delay curve is set by means of an external computer which is capable of altering the timing to suit engine rpm, engine load, turbo boost etc. while the engine is operating. Once this ignition advance/retard delay map is finalised, the ROM chip is "burnt in" so that it becomes a permanent memory in the auxiliary ECM.

Because of today's poor fuel quality, detonation and pre-ignition damage are both being seen in modified new generation road engines, whereas in the past only race engines were seriously affected. Detonation occurs when a portion of the fuel/air mixture, usually the "end gases", begins to burn spontaneously after normal ignition takes place. The flame front created by this condition eventually collides with the flame initiated by the spark plug. This causes a violent and rapid burning, almost an explosion, of any remaining fuel which hammers the engine's internal components with such force that the cylinder wall and piston crown actually vibrate, producing a pinging sound. Pre-ignition is ignition of the fuel/air charge by a "hot spot" before the spark plug fires to initiate normal combustion. Typically, in its early stages, this leads to a loss in performance much like excessive ignition advance. If allowed to continue it can destroy an engine.

When engine damage results from either type of abnormal combustion, the culprit can usually be identified after an examination of the pistons and spark plugs. Pre-ignition damage is caused by the extreme combustion temperature which results, melting the piston and also possibly the ring lands. If a hole is present in a piston crown, it will appear to have been burned through with a welding torch. The metal around the hole will be fused and have a melted appearance. A spark plug out of the same cylinder may have the centre electrode melted away and in extreme cases the insulator nose and earth electrode will also be fused.

A piston damaged by detonation will show signs of pitting on the crown. The edge will be gray and eroded, as if sandblasted. In the very early stages, gray ash-like deposits form on the most exposed areas of the crown. In extreme examples the piston will be holed. The hole will appear to have been punched through, with radial cracks and a depressed area around the hole. A spark plug subjected to fairly severe detonation will usually show signs of cracking at the insulator nose.

Pre-ignition can frequently be traced to deposits in the combustion chamber, or on the piston crown or the exhaust valve becoming incandescent. Since these deposits do not conduct heat well, very high temperatures can be reached within such accumulations. Spark plug heat range can also affect pre-ignition. If the electrodes retain too much heat from previous combustion cycles, they will glow and pre-ignite the fuel.

The conditions which lead to detonation are high fuel/air mixture density, high compression ratio, high boost pressure, high inlet charge temperature, best power fuel/air ratio, and excessive spark advance. Additionally, a piston crown or combustion chamber overheated by pre-ignition can initiate detonation by excessively heating the "end gases". Driving style can also bring on detonation, as when accelerating hard in a high gear.

Because of increased combustion temperatures in a modified engine, consideration must be given to finding spark plugs with the correct heat range. A hot plug transfers combustion heat slowly and is used to avoid fouling in engines with relatively low combustion temperatures, or in engines which are operated at lower speeds in city driving. On the other hand a cold plug transfers heat rapidly from the firing end. It is used to avoid overheating of the insulator and electrodes where temperatures are high, as in a high performance engine being driven at constant high speed.

The length of the insulator nose and the composition of the electrode alloys are the primary factors in establishing the heat ratings of a particular plug. As shown, hot plugs have long insulator noses, and hence a long heat transfer path. Cold plugs have

The heat rating of a spark plug is dependent on the length of the insulator nose and the electrode alloys. Basically a hot plug has a long heat path from the firing end of the plug and a cold plug has a short heat transfer path.

TABLE 9.2 Spark plug reading for correct heat range and other conditions

Spark plug condition	Indications
Normal – correct heat range.	Insulator nose white or very light tan to rust brown. Little or no cement boil where the centre electrode protrudes through the insulator nose. The electrodes are not discoloured or eroded.
Too cold – use hotter plug.	Insulator nose dark grey or black. Steel plug shell end covered with dry, black soot deposit that will rub off easily.
Too hot – use colder plug.	Insulator nose chalky white or may have a satin sheen. Excessive cement boil where centre electrode protrudes through the insulator nose. Cement may be milk white or meringue-like.

	Centre electrode may 'blue' and be rounded off at the edges. Earth electrode may be badly eroded or have a molten appearance.
Pre-ignition – use colder plug and remove combustion chamber deposits.	Insulator nose blistered. Centre electrode and side electrode burned or melted away.
Detonation – retard ignition and richen mixture.	Fractured insulator nose in sustained or extreme cases. Insulator nose covered in tiny pepper specks or even tiny beads of aluminum leaving the piston. Excessive cement boil where centre electrode protrudes through insulator nose. Specks on plug shell end.
Insulator glazing – replace with plugs of same heat range. If condition reoccurs fit plugs one grade colder.	Shiny yellow, green or tan deposits on the insulator nose, particularly close to the centre electrode.
Ash fouled – clean or replace with plugs of the same heat range.	Thick yellow, white or light brown deposit on insulator, centre and side electrode.

shorter nose lengths to transfer heat more rapidly from the insulator tip to the cylinder head. Road engines usually require a standard heat range plug or one not more than a couple of grades colder than standard. The only way to determine the correct heat range is to do some testing and then check the insulator nose, the electrodes and the plug shell, for the conditions listed in Table 9.2. As I pointed out in an earlier chapter, the most accurate way to get a plug reading is to use new plugs and drive for at least 600, and preferably 1000 miles. Then when you check them take the car for a good hard run of 5 or 6 miles to burn off idling and low speed deposits. If you can't get home without sitting in traffic, pull the plugs while you are out along the road, so as not to distort the reading.

The big problem is trying to find a plug which resists low speed fouling under city driving conditions and yet allows hours of high speed running on the freeways. There is no easy answer to the problem especially in emissions engines which in particular require a plug with a very wide heat range. The plug type which I prefer to use in non-turbo engines is of the projecting core design with a copper-cored centre electrode. It has a very wide heat range and is able to resist low speed fouling and high speed pre-ignition in all but a few engines. At low speeds the long insulator tip, longer than an equivalent standard projecting nose plug with the same heat range, runs hotter to burn off low speed combustion deposits. Then at high speeds the long insulator nose is cooled by the incoming fuel charge, and the copper-cored centre electrode conducts more heat away, to increase the plug's cold heat range. The only plugs with a wider heat range are also of the projecting nose design, but these have a platinum centre electrode which increases their price fourfold.

143

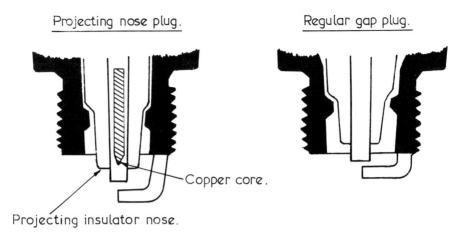

Projecting nose plug.   Regular gap plug.

Copper core.

Projecting insulator nose.

Copper-cored projecting nose plugs are preferred for non-turbo performance/economy engines. For turbo applications a regular gap plug with a copper-cored centre electrode is more resistant to plug tip burning and detonation.

For turbo engines I recommend a conventional plug with a copper-cored centre electrode. The shorter nose is necessary to avoid high speed insulator glazing and electrode melt-down. Unfortunately this type of plug does not offer the low speed fouling resistance of the projecting nose design. There are a number of solutions to this problem; the first is to put up with a misfire when accelerating on fouled plugs, which I feel is less than satisfactory. Secondly, you can risk using projecting nose plugs but initially, until you accurately assess them, limit full throttle bursts to less than 60 seconds. Thirdly, you can use projecting nose plugs in the city and swap to regular short-nosed plugs for highway running.

The width of the spark plug gap for best performance depends primarily on the compression pressure of the fuel/air charge, the engine rpm and the high speed electrical intensity of the coil. Obviously increasing the first two factors without an increase in the latter calls for a decrease in the gap width. Therefore, it is fairly safe to say that many modified performance/economy engines will require a gap narrower than that recommended by the manufacturer.

Manufacturers generally stipulate a relatively wide gap of 0.040in to 0.060in as this improves performance at lower rpm and reduces the risk of the gap being bridged by whiskers of carbon, or beads of lead or petrol. As there is much less turbulence in the combustion chamber at low engine speeds, it is very easy for a blob of carbon or fuel to settle between the electrodes, shorting the plug out. With a wider gap the odds are better because the speck of carbon or fuel may not be large enough to bridge the gap. Later, when the engine is given a few more revs, the increased turbulence will blow the electrodes clean. Also, because the spark generated in a wide gap is larger than in a narrow gap, an important consideration in lean burn emissions engines which have the inlet charge diluted to exhaust gas recirculation, a more sizeable initial flame is produced. This improves flame propagation through the fuel mixture and allows for a more complete burn.

As the engine speed and compression pressures increase, the coil is not able to

supply electrical energy of sufficient voltage or duration to jump a wide spark gap and keep the air between the electrodes ionised for a period long enough to initiate combustion. What happens is that the coil has enough energy reserve to electrically bridge the spark plug electrodes but, before the spark generated can get a combustion flame started, turbulence within the combustion chamber will actually blow out the spark. This was a big problem with early electronic and particularly capacitor discharge ignitions, as the spark was produced for only a short duration. When a narrow gap is used, the magnetic field within the gap is much more intense, as it is confined to a much smaller space. Hence the spark holds together for long enough to effect ignition, in spite of receiving severe buffeting from the turbulent gases within the combustion chamber.

From experience, I would recommend that any modified engine using a conventional points-type ignition should not use a plug gap exceeding 0.028in. If it has breakerless high energy ignition, the gap can be as wide as 0.040in. A gap wider than this just encourages high speed misfire and crossfire particularly in V8 engines, and in many engines there are problems with high voltage flashover within the distributor cap or leakage through the rotor button to the distributor shaft. In some engines with high energy ignitions this later problem can actually wreck the advance mechanism.

In addition to using narrower plug gaps there are a number of other steps which should be taken to ensure an intense spark of long duration, even at high rpm and high cylinder pressures. The life of a spark plug is 8,000 to 12,000 miles, but it should be filed, regapped and tested every 3,000 miles. Filing the electrodes lowers the voltage required to fire the plug, firstly because electricity prefers to jump across sharp edges, and secondly because the electrical conductivity of the electrodes is improved. Combustion heat and pressure tend to break up and oxidise the electrode firing surfaces, increasing the electrical resistance. Filing removes this "dead" material and exposes new, highly-conductive metal. To avoid damaging the plugs, bend the earth electrode back just far enough to permit filing of the firing surfaces. As shown, a points file should be used to file a flat surface with sharp edges on both the centre and side electrode.

File end of earth electrode.

File centre electrode flat.

Filing the side and centre electrode square to expose new metal and produce sharp corners reduces the voltage required to fire the plug.

Spark plugs should never be cleaned with a wire brush, as metallic deposits will impregnate the insulator nose and short out the plug. I also do not recommend cleaning in an abrasive blast plug cleaner as some abrasive material always seems to become wedged between the insulator and plug shell. If this cannot be probed out with a scriber, it will later drop into the cylinder and possibly cause damage. However, if you choose to have your plugs abrasive blasted, be sure to remove all abrasive grit inside the plug nose and around the threads and gasket.

Because of their design, electronic ignition systems require some extra attention to ensure good service and high spark output. To avoid overloading any of the electronic components the engine must never be cranked over if any of the spark plug leads or the coil lead is disconnected. For example, when carrying out a compression check, the low voltage positive (+) ignition wire at the coil should be disconnected.

As with any ignition system the coil polarity must be correct for good firing performance. A coil with reversed polarity loses the equivalent of 40% energy because when connected in this manner the spark has to jump from what would normally be the earth electrode to the centre electrode. The side electrode is many hundred degrees cooler than the centre electrode, hence there is much more restrained electron activity on the metal surface. This considerably increases the voltage required to cause the electrons to leave one electrode and jump to the other, thus ionising the gap and creating a spark. Cold engines are more difficult to get started for this very reason. The plug electrodes are cold therefore a very high voltage is necessary to tear the electrons from one surface and have them jump the gap to the other electrode. As illustrated, a dished spark plug earth electrode indicates reversed polarity. The dish is caused by metal leaving the electrode each time a spark jumps across to the centre electrode.

Dished earth electrode.

Reversed polarity increases the voltage requirement necessary to fire the plug and initiate combustion. A dished side electrode indicates reversed polarity.

The polarity is correct when the wire from the coil to the distributor is connected to the coil terminal with the same polarity as the earth terminal of the battery. Therefore, if the negative (−) battery terminal is earthed, the wire running between the coil and distributor should be connected to the negative coil terminal. To avoid incorrect electrical connections it is wise always to tag wires before they are disconnected. A diagram is also an aid in ensuring that all wires are reconnected to the correct terminals.

Most stock electronic ignition system coils work well in road engines, even at high rpm, providing the spark plug gap is not too wide. There are exceptions, however, where the standard ignition coil just isn't up to the task. For example, the ignition output of the General Motors Delco HEI system weakens at about 5000rpm in V8 engines; with the same ignition 6 cylinder engines run fine with 0.040in plug gaps to nearly 7000rpm because fewer sparks per minute are required. Hence if your GM V8 is required to make good power at engine speeds higher than 5000rpm, an ignition booster kit will be required, or alternatively the plug gaps should be reduced to 0.032in. Whenever it is necessary to uprate an electronic ignition it is necessary to use components, preferably in a kit, which have been tailored to work with the standard system. If the incorrect type of coil is fitted it could damage the electronic devices, and the replacement coil's output will probably be inferior to the stock coil anyway. Never swap coils which appear similar unless they have the same part number. It is not unusual for coils from the same manufacturer to appear similar, but to be quite different internally. Some electronic systems, while basically alike through a whole family of engines, may use coils that look to be identical; however, the internal windings and the core could be different for 4, 6 and 8 cylinder engines.

The high tension leads provide the electrical connection between the coil and distributor cap and the spark plugs. Usually in road cars radio suppression cables, with a powdered carbon impregnated rayon cord to conduct the high voltage current, are fitted. With age the electrical resistance of this type of "wire" increases, which reduces spark intensity and increases the probability of misfire under load or at higher rpm. To avoid this problem only the best quality silicone-jacketed leads should be used, and replaced every three years. Also, when removing the leads from the plugs or from the distributor cap do not jerk them off as this also can reduce their conductivity. Firmly grip the rubber boot, give it a half turn, and then while holding the boot and metal connector remove the cable. An alternative to carbon core leads is leads with a metal core. These leads have a very long life if the insulation is not damaged. Two types are available: common copper-cored leads which require the use of a resistor at each spark plug, and induction-type suppression leads which use an induction spiral within the lead to give suppression.

The ignition cables must have good boots, without any cracks or holes, fitted at each end to prevent high voltage trackover or arcing. Many misfires under load can be attributed to the spark jumping from an exposed spark plug top to a nearby earth, or from the coil tower to one of the low voltage terminals on the coil.

Apart from the plug leads, the distributor cap and rotor button and the coil tower can also be high voltage leakage areas. Obviously these parts must be free of dust, moisture, cracks and carbon tracks if a good strong ignition surge is to reach the plugs. Periodically check to ensure that none of these conditions exist. In particular, when high voltage HEI type systems are in use, attention must be paid to keeping all the insulating mediums clean, otherwise the system will actually be performing more poorly than a conventional type ignition because of electrical flashover or leakage. With these systems only the best quality distributor caps and rotors made of alkyd material should be fitted.

Unwittingly, some enthusiasts bring ignition troubles upon themselves when removing build-up on the distributor cap terminals and the rotor button contact. Quite often the knife or screwdriver being used to remove the unwanted material slips and scratches the glaze inside the cap. This drastically reduces the dielectric strength and can lead to a carbon track developing during wet conditions. Similarly, when a piece of abrasive paper is used to polish the rotor button contact, the insulating glaze is cut, allowing electrical leakage to earth through the distributor shaft. Carbon on the rotor button contact does no harm, so just wipe off the powdery stuff and leave the rest there.

In high compression V8 engines cross fire can occur whenever high voltage ignition leads are grouped closely together, or allowed to run in parallel for any distance. Cross fire causes the engine to run roughly, and in high load or high rpm situations may give rise to serious pre-ignition or detonation. The problem is not due to poor insulation, but rather is a product of magnetic induction. A magnetic field surrounds any high tension conductor, and the lead which is carrying high voltage at any instance induces voltage into an adjacent plug lead. A cross fire that will give trouble is most likely to occur between consecutive firing cylinders when these are located alongside each other in the engine. Hence if the engine has the common V8 firing order of 1-8-4-3-6-5-7-2, cylinders 5 and 7 are most likely to give trouble. With the Ford firing order of 1-5-4-2-6-3-7-8, cylinders 7 and 8 are most likely to experience cross fire problems. The easiest way around the difficulty is to route the leads in such a manner so that the offending leads cross over once. Hence with the first firing order, leads 5 and 7 would be crossed to invert the magnetic field and effectively cut out any induction. Note that one lead must pass over the other head just once; never tape any leads together or run them through steel clips or other metal fittings.

Chapter 10
Turbocharging and Intercooling

The first wave of engines given the "hot-up" treatment by tuners simply bolting on a turbocharger were a real disappointment. When the throttle was pressed down at speeds below 3000 to 4000rpm nothing happened: it seemed as if the engine was running with all of the plugs fouled. Then, after gaining some boost, the vehicle would rocket off with an incredible surge of power which was most disconcerting and intimidating. Controlling a turbo car on a twisting slippery road was a nightmare. That was 20 years ago when turbocharging first became fashionable on race cars. Tuners didn't know much about this new technology and tried to apply what little knowledge had been gained on the race circuit to the road. It didn't work. At about the same time a number of car makers were involved in their own development projects which eventually led to the design of smaller, lighter turbos and compatible engine management systems that have virtually eliminated the dreaded "turbo lag". The majority of new generation turbo cars are pleasant to drive, but with a few ill-conceived modifications they can be quickly transformed into the volatile beasts of former times. Therefore before undertaking any modifications on a factory turbo car a thorough knowledge of the subject is an asset if driveability problems are to be avoided.

There is nothing magical or hard to comprehend about why a turbo greatly increases the potency of an internal combustion engine. Basically, the power an engine produces is a product of the amount of fuel/air mixture it is able to breathe in and then burn. A turbocharger is a type of supercharger or compressor that forcibly crams into the cylinders far more mixture than the engine could draw in in naturally-aspirated form. At 100% volumetric efficiency and a manifold vacuum level of zero, a 500cc cylinder will be filled with 500cc of fuel mixture due to the effect of normal air pressure, 14.7 psi at sea level. Theoretically, if the inlet boost is 7.4 psi above atmospheric the cylinder will fill with about 750cc of mixture, so the engine will perform as if it were 50% larger. Hence at cruise a lightweight 2 litre engine will perform with a fuel efficiency just a little less than that of an ordinary 2 litre engine, mainly due to the reduced compression ratio, but at full boost of, say, 7.4 psi, it will perform as a super-lightweight 3 litre unit.

The turbo is made up of a centrifugal compressor, which is part of the induction system, connected by a common shaft to a turbine which is joined to the exhaust system. The engine's exhaust gases thus drive the turbine, utilising energy that would otherwise go to waste. The turbine in turn spins the impeller to force fuel/air mixture into the engine. Certainly the concept is very simple, but things become a lot more complex when translated into the real world. Firstly, the turbocharger itself is an expensive, highly-engineered, precision item. On the exhaust side it has to be able to withstand enormous stresses due to operating temperatures which may exceed 1000°C, while at the same time the turbine is spinning at 100,000rpm and more. Additionally, the precise shape and dimensions of the turbine and impeller, and their separate housings, need carefully to be tailored to give the required throttle response, driveability and power.

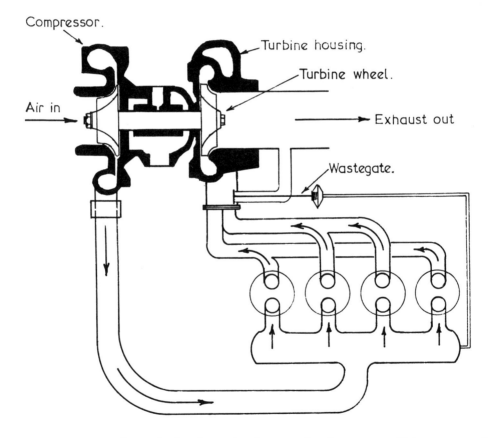

The turbocharger turbine wheel is driven by the engine's exhaust gases. Being connected to a common shaft, the compressor impeller forces the air charge into the cylinders under pressure. When full boost is reached, the wastegate opens, bypassing some of the exhaust gas away from the turbine. Note that the turbine illustrated is a split pulse type with divided exhaust inlets, used to improve low speed boost.

This tiny turbocharger adds about 30% to the engine's power output. The centrifugal compressor, on the right, pressurises the induction system. The turbine side of the turbo is hidden away under a heat shield. Lubricating oil is fed to the turbo bearings through the oil feed pipe visible in the centre of the turbo.

Aside from this there are the problems arising out of a fundamental characteristic of a centrifugal type compressor; namely that flow through it rises in proportion to the square of its rotational speed. Hence at lower engine rpm there is little or no boost, and at higher rpm and full throttle, boost is excessive. It is in the resolving of this dilemma of how to get low speed performance up without unduly restricting high rpm power, and perhaps causing excessive high speed fuel consumption, in which the real science of turbocharging lies.

Looking firstly at the low speed component of this problem it should be obvious that modifications which reduce the low rpm performance of a naturally-aspirated engine will have a like effect on a turbo engine. In fact the decline in performance and economy will be greater in the turbo engine due to the compression ratio being 1 to 1.5 points lower. Therefore big ports and cams are definitely not for road turbo cars. If the engine is 2.3 litres or larger and the car isn't too heavy, a Phase III cam is about as wild as you would want to go. Personally, in engines of this size I prefer a Phase II grind if the car sees a lot of running on the highway, and a Phase I grind if the majority of driving is done in the city. For engines smaller than 2 litres a Phase I cam is a good compromise for highway/city use, but if most running is done in the city you will probably be happiest with the standard factory cam or the standard factory cam out of a non-turbo model.

The other factor in low speed performance is the actual boost of the turbo at lower rpm. Here the size of the exhaust turbine and the dimensions of its housing play a major role. Naturally a large diameter turbine, which will flow a lot of exhaust gas without causing much restriction at high rpm, is very heavy so it will need a large exhaust flow to get it spinning up to speed to create boost. Because the exhaust flow is low at lower rpm with the throttle closed, the turbine will be rotating slowly. Opening the throttle increases flow but it takes time to accelerate the heavy turbine up to speed to produce boost. It is this time lag between opening the throttle and actually getting response which is called "turbo lag". A small turbine, on the other hand, has less inertia so it spools up to speed to produce boost more quickly. However, if it is too small it plugs up the exhaust at higher rpm, and by restricting exhaust flow reduces power and increases fuel consumption. Clearly a compromise must be struck, with the majority of manufacturers choosing comparatively small turbines to enhance performance, particularly from 1800 to 4000rpm.

When it comes to the exhaust turbine housing the critical dimension is what is called the A/R ratio. As illustrated, this refers to the ratio between the area of the

Turbine housing nozzle area.

Turbine wheel.

The turbine housing A/R ratio is determined by dividing the area of the turbine nozzle A by the radius R from the centre of the turbine axle to the centroid of the housing throat.

turbine nozzle A, and the radius from the centre of the turbine axle to the centroid of the housing throat R. The smaller the A/R, the smaller the passage and the faster the turbo spins for a given exhaust flow. This is good for low speed boost but a housing which is too small causes excessive back pressure and heat. A large turbine housing A/R flows the exhaust gas without causing so much restriction at higher rpm; however, due to the turbine speed being reduced at lower revs, low speed boost may be

Small A/R turbine housings make more boost at lower engine speeds but reduce maximum power and economy because of exhaust flow restriction.

poor. Again a compromise is necessary, with car manufacturers generally opting to get either low speed or mid range boost up at the expense of maximum power and economy.

On the inlet or compressor side of the turbo unit selecting the correct impeller and housing is considerably easier. Manufacturers match the compressor to a given engine by calculating the anticipated inlet air flow and then plotting the flow against the pressure ratio on a series of compressor performance maps. A compressor is chosen which gives the required flow and pressure in a good efficiency zone, without running into surge.

Many enthusiasts think of improving the performance of their turbo car simply in terms of increasing the boost pressure. This should not be a primary consideration for a number of reasons. For example, if the mufflers are restrictive and the exhaust pipe is too small, bumping the boost from say 6 psi to 9 psi will not give the 15 to 20% power increase that many would expect, simply because the engine cannot breathe. Additionally, the extra boost will add heat to the inlet change temperature which by itself will reduce power as well as bringing the engine closer to detonation. In total, the power increase will be no better than about 10%.

Consider the engines used in CART races in the USA, of which the Indianapolis 500 is the most famous. The purpose-built race engines are restricted to a capacity of 2.6 litres and a turbo boost of 9 psi, and yet they produce around 700hp. Why? Not because of massive boost pressures, but because the inlet and exhaust systems and cylinder heads flow efficiently thus encouraging good flow in and out of the cylinders. Therefore the very first modifications should be directed toward improving the breathing of the engine. Get the exhaust size right and the system completely free of leaks. The original Ford Pinto 2.3 turbo, for example, required nearly 10 psi exhaust pressure to make just over 5 psi boost with the standard exhaust. By re-routing the crossover pipe from the exhaust manifold to the turbo, and fitting a 2½in system down-stream of the turbo, the engine made full boost earlier and with only 6 psi exhaust back pressure. With reduced back pressure the cylinders were better scavenged of hot exhaust gases, which lowers the risk of detonation and improves fuel economy by several percent. When exhaust gases are left unscavenged, they add a considerable amount of heat to the inlet charge, raising the charge temperature and increasing the danger of detonation. Apart from causing sluggish performance, exhaust leaks are to be avoided because of their danger to personal health. I've seen minor exhaust leaks which were almost undectable cost up to 2 psi in lost boost.

Next, clean up the cylinder head by unshrouding the valves and reprofiling their underhead shape, and rework the port bowl area on both the inlet and exhaust side. If you plan on fitting a modified cam that too should be carried out before altering the boost. After that, tune the injection and ignition systems as outlined in previous chapters. Pay a lot of attention to getting the ignition right. Turbo engines which are a bit sluggish at lower speeds can be transformed by a little more low rpm ignition advance. However, be careful to take advance off the top end otherwise piston damage is likely. Next, give consideration to lowering the gearing by changing the rear axle ratio. With lower gearing the vehicle will be much more spirited in traffic and when cruising on the highway. As discussed in a later chapter, with the proper gearing the vehicle's performance can be transformed. In particular, all 4 cylinder cars, and cars with 6 cylinder engines smaller than about 2.5 litres, require relatively low gearing.

Finally compare the boost pressure, using an accurate gauge, with what is stated in the specifications. If it is lower than specified this could be due to the modified cam or perhaps the wastegate is opening prematurely; at this point I assume that exhaust leaks ahead of the turbo have been rectified. To test the wastegate disconnect the hoses leading to it and run the engine at full load, being careful not to let the turbo overboost. If the boost comes up to specification, the wastegate should be adjusted to open at the factory boost level. On the other hand if the boost level doesn't rise, the wastegate must be leaking or jammed partly open. Note in a very few cases lack of boost could be due to an over-small turbine or small A/R housing.

If after making the above modifications you desire still more boost, some steps must be taken before changing the wastegate opening pressure. This action is not as straightforward as many enthusiasts and some tuners believe, as an increase in boost may cause the turbo to overspeed or send the compressor into surge conditions. To ascertain the probability of either situation arising we have to go through a series of calculations and plot the results on the turbo manufacturer's compressor map. This may appear to be a lot of bother, but because car makers are tending to use smaller turbos there is some risk of turbo reliability-related problems at high rpm and/or above sea level operation.

The first calculation is to determine the compressor pressure ratio, using the formula:

$$Pr = \frac{Bp + Ap}{Ap}$$

where Bp = boost pressure psi

Ap = air pressure psi (14.7 psi at sea level; subtract 0.5 psi for each 1000ft above sea level.)

For example we may want to increase the boost pressure to 11.5 psi and operate at 5000ft altitude.

$$Bp = 11.5 \text{ psi}$$

$$Ap = 14.7 - 2.5 \text{ psi}$$

$$\text{Therefore } Pr = \frac{11.5 + 12.2}{12.2}$$

$$= 1.94$$

The next step is to find the density ratio and this involves a number of calculations due to the fact that the inlet air is heated as it is compressed; the less efficient the compressor the more heat that is passed to the inlet air.

First calculate the compressor outlet air temperature rise assuming a perfect compressor using the formula:

$$It = F \times (At + 460)$$

where It = ideal temperature rise °F

At = ambient temperature °F

F = factor from Table 10.1.

Hence if the air temperature outside the car is 80°F then:

$$It = 0.208 \times (80 + 460)$$

$$= 0.208 \times 540$$

$$= 112.3°F.$$

However, because the compressor doesn't have a 100% adiabatic efficiency we then have to calculate the actual air temperature rise with the formula:

$$Rt = \frac{It \times 100}{E}$$

where Rt = real compressor temperature rise °F

E = compressor efficiency
(assume 60% efficiency)

$$\text{Therefore } Rt = \frac{112.3 \times 100}{60}$$

$$= 187.2°F$$

The compressor discharge air temperature will be the outside air temperature, 80°F, plus the real compressor temperature rise:

$$Dt = At + Rt$$

$$= 80 + 187.2$$

$$= 267.2°F.$$

Having found the compressor air discharge temperature and with the pressure ratio previously calculated, the compressor density ratio can then be figured out using the formula:

$$DR = \frac{(At + 460) \times Pr}{(Dt + 460)}$$

where DR = compressor density ratio

At = ambient temperature °F

Dt = compressor discharge temperature °F

Pr = compressor pressure ratio

$$\text{Therefore } DR = \frac{(80 + 460) \times 1.94}{267.2 + 460}$$

$$= \frac{540 \times 1.94}{727.2}$$

$$= 1.44$$

The final calculation is to determine the compressor inlet flow so that this figure can be plotted on the map to find if the compressor will overspeed or surge at our desired boost of 11.5 psi and an altitude of 5000ft. The formula is:

$$CF = \frac{L \times RPM \times VE \times DR}{56.6}$$

where CF = compressor inlet flow cubic feet
per minute

$$L = \text{engine capacity in litres}$$

$$RPM = \text{maximum engine speed}$$

$$VE = \text{engine volumetric efficiency (usually about 0.9 for an engine with a mild cam)}$$

$$DR = \text{compressor density ratio}$$

Assuming that the engine capacity is 2 litres and the maximum rpm is 6200, then the compressor inlet air flow will be:

$$CF = \frac{2 \times 6200 \times 0.9 \times 1.44}{56.6}$$

$$= 284 \text{ cubic feet per minute (CFM)}$$

When the compressor map is scaled in lbs/min air flow rather than CFM it is necessary to multiply the above flow figure by 0.07. Hence in this example the flow is 19.9 lbs/min.

Plotting this in the compressor map opposite the 1.94 pressure ratio we find that the compressor will be operating well away from the surge line at maximum engine rpm and the turbo speed for this type of turbo is within reliable limits at about 114,000rpm. However, to be certain that the compressor will not run into surge at other engine speeds and boost levels the above calculations would have to be repeated. For example, if this engine made full boost of 11.5 psi at 5000ft altitude and at an engine speed of 3000rpm, the compressor would be just into the surge range.

To increase the boost pressure the wastegate will require adjustment or modification. The integral wastegate on turbochargers like the AiResearch T–03 is easily adjusted as the actuator is usually connected to the wastegate via a threaded rod. Simply altering the length of the actuator rod will change the boost pressure at which the wastegate opens to bypass some exhaust flow away from the turbo. If the actuator rod isn't threaded it is a simple matter to unbolt the actuator, saw the rod in half and thread it with a suitable thread such as ¼in NC. Using an internally threaded coupling sleeve and a jam nut the actuator then can be adjusted. When sawing and threading the actuator rod care must be taken to hold the rod securely to avoid damaging the actuator diaphragm.

TABLE 10.1 – Factors for calculating inlet air temperature

Pr	F	Pr	F	Pr	F	Pr	F
1.35	0.089	1.8	0.181	2.25	0.258	2.7	0.325
1.4	0.100	1.85	0.192	2.3	0.266	2.75	0.331
1.45	0.110	1.9	0.199	2.35	0.274	2.8	0.338
1.50	0.120	1.95	0.208	2.4	0.281	2.85	0.345
1.55	0.130	2.0	0.217	2.45	0.289	2.9	0.352
1.6	0.142	2.05	0.225	2.5	0.296	2.95	0.358
1.65	0.152	2.1	0.234	2.55	0.303	3.0	0.365
1.7	0.162	2.15	0.242	2.6	0.311	3.1	0.377
1.75	0.172	2.2	0.250	2.65	0.318	3.2	0.390

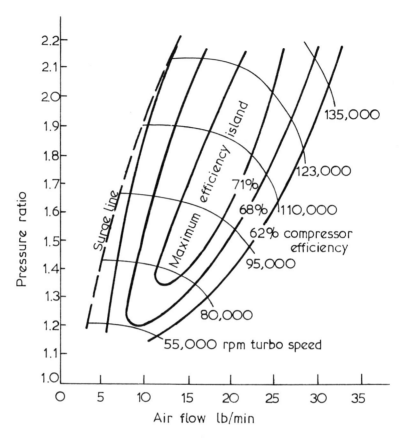

Compressor maps are used for determining compressor suitability for specific engine specifications and operating criteria.

Since this type of actuator is controlled by inlet boost pressure, an alternative method of adjusting the boost pressure is to fit a hard plastic tube in the pressure line which runs from the compressor to the wastegate and perforate it with a number of bleed holes. By bleeding off some boost pressure signal the actuator is tricked into allowing boost pressure to rise above the pre-set factory level before opening the wastegate. Since only tiny holes are needed it is best to perforate the tube using a 0.040in needle which has been heated so as to melt a hole in the plastic. Commence with just one hole and add additional holes, as needed, to raise the boost level. Note that this method of boost control must not be used on engines which add fuel into the air stream ahead of the turbocharger.

When a poppet valve wastegate is utilised, the perforated tube trick can also be used, although there are a number of alternatives. Simply placing a spacer under the diaphragm pre-load spring will raise the boost pressure at which the diaphragm rises to by-pass exhaust gas away from the turbine. Replacing the spring with a stiffer item has the same effect. A more sophisticated control is to fit a spring pre-load seat that is attached to a threaded rod which passes through to the outside of the actuator

Adjustable spring seat.

Atmospheric pressure.

Diaphragm.

Boost pressure.

Poppet valve.

When a poppet valve type wastegate is used, the boost pressure can be easily changed by installing an adjustable pre-load spring seat.

chamber to provide pre-load adjustment. Screwing the rod down increases spring pre-load, thus raising the boost level.

Just how much power increase can be realised honestly with increased boost can be easily figured reasonably accurately using the formula:

$$PG\% = (DR - 1) \times 100$$

$$\text{where PG\%} = \text{percentage power gain}$$

$$DR = \text{compressor density ratio}$$

I won't go through the calculations. If you refer back a few pages you will see how we arrive at the density ratio. For example, an engine operating at sea level, with 80°F ambient temperature and 7 psi boost, will have a DR of 1.23, assuming 60% compressor efficiency. Therefore its power gain over a naturally aspirated engine will be about 23%. Now if that same engine has the boost raised to 11 psi, the DR becomes 1.36; a 36% power gain over a naturally-aspirated engine but only a 13% gain over an engine boosted to 7 psi, and that is assuming the engine would handle the extra boost without running into detonation. Why so small a gain you ask? The answer is quite simple – heat. At 7 psi boost the inlet air temperature (Dt) will be 188°F and at 11 psi this rises to 235°F. Obviously anything that can be done to get rid of heat out of the inlet charge will result in significant power gains.

An air-to-air intercooler gives off heat from the compressed inlet charge to the cooling air passing by its core fins and tubes.

This is exactly what intercooling aims to achieve. As illustrated, an air-to-air intercooler is really just like a cooling system radiator through which flows the inlet charge after it leaves the turbo. It is called an air-to-air intercooler because the charge air which is within the "radiator" gives off its heat to the outside air. With an air-to-water intercooler, common in boat and truck applications, the heat exchanger is enclosed within a water jacket through which water flows to take away inlet charge heat. Because of the possibility of fuel condensation and a subsequent backfire blowing the core of the intercooler or the ducting apart, intercoolers should not be used in applications where fuel enters the inlet system ahead of it.

Basically, an intercooler's ability to reduce inlet charge air temperature will depend on the size of the heat exchanger, the ambient air temperature and the flow rate of cooling air through the heat exchanger. The actual size of the heat exchanger is obviously limited by the amount of space available to locate it and by the cost. As with coolant system radiators, the more the area of cooling tubes and fins, the greater the expense. The ambient temperature isn't something over which we have any control, but the flow rate of this air through the heat exchanger can be improved at lower vehicle speeds by the use of a good electric fan. Even so, the intercooler will be more effective at removing charge air heat at higher vehicle speeds.

Realistic intercooler efficiency, temperature-wise, is about 80%. Temperature efficiency or effectiveness is defined as the ratio between the actual charge air temperature decrease and the possible decrease. Hence a heat exchanger which is

100% effective would reduce the charge air temperature to the same level as the ambient temperature. Except in race applications, such a large intercooler would not be practical. Conversely, an intercooler which is less than about 60% efficient is basically of little value. If the intercooler is 80% effective, it will draw off 80% of the heat rise generated in the charge air by the turbo. Hence if the ambient temperature is 85°F and the charge leaving the compressor is at 235°F, a heat rise of 150° (235 − 85 = 150), it will remove 120° of the heat rise (150 x 0.8 = 120), resulting in a charge air temperature of 115°F (150 − 120 + 85 = 115) leaving the intercooler.

There are drawbacks which make intercooling of limited value in turbo systems operating at boost levels lower than about 7 psi. Obviously there is some flow resistance due to turbulence in the intercooler and ducting. In a poorly-designed cooling system with a number of tight bends, this alone can reduce the boost pressure actually entering the engine by 2 psi. Additionally, there is a natural pressure drop due to the charge air being cooled. In a well-designed intercooler system the total pressure drop should not be more than 10% of the boost pressure as measured at the compressor outlet. Hence a system that is regulated to 13 psi should deliver 11.7 psi at the inlet manifold. Of course this boost loss could be compensated for by adjusting the wastegate to a higher boost. If the wastegate is a solenoid-operated unit controlled by the vehicle's computer, and hence not adjustable, the pressure loss can be overcome by relocating the pressure sensor from the compressor outlet to the inlet manifold.

Just how effective intercooling can be purely from the performance viewpoint can be seen by referring to our previous example, where raising the boost from 7 psi to 11 psi resulted in a power increase of only 13% at the very most. With an 80% efficient intercooler and an overall boost loss of 1 psi, the charge air temperature will fall from 235°F to 111°F and the power will rise by 46% over the stock 7 psi boost level and by 23% over the non-intercooled 11 psi boost. Clearly, very efficient intercooling is an effective means of obtaining large performance increases without adding additional stress to the engine.

However, to realise this potential increase the intercooler must actually work as efficiently as it does on paper. Consequently it is necessary to carefully check out your potential intercooler supplier. Ask him to produce test figures to prove how much temperature drop occurs across the intercooler. Then get him to calculate how efficient the intercooler is at your proposed boost pressure. If he can't work it out he probably doesn't know very much about intercooling, so shop elsewhere. If he does the calculation go home and check if his figures tally. This caution is necessary because there are not too many people who actually test their intercoolers to find out how efficient they really are. The more common approach is to build an intercooler to fit a particular vehicle and then draw some numbers out of the air to persuade potential customers that the product works marvellously.

Finding a home for the intercooler is quite a challenge. The common solution is to mount the unit in front of the radiator, but in hot climates, particularly if the vehicle is air conditioned, this is less than successful because of reduced engine cooling efficiency. Additionally, the length of ducting required increases turbo lag and sluggishness at lower rpm. An alternative is to mount the intercooler at the side of the radiator. This may not be possible because of space limitations in which case a narrower custom-built radiator with an extra row or two of tubes can be used with space left for a narrow intercooler alongside. The position chosen by Ford for the Mustang SVO was to mount the intercooler up high alongside the engine, with cooling air being admitted through a bonnet-scoop. This in many ways is an excellent location as the amount of ducting is greatly reduced, so turbo lag isn't affected and because of the intercooler location engine cooling is not impaired. However, at lower speeds the intercooler will not be very effective, due to lack of cooling air flow, unless a small electric fan is mounted beneath the core.

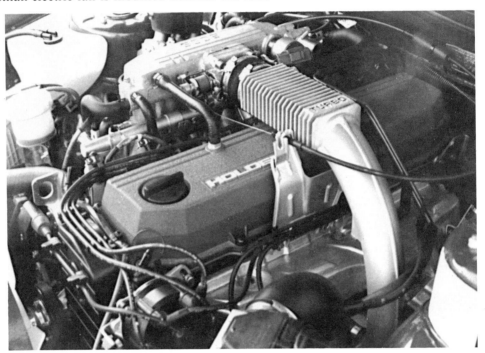

A finned inlet duct will help reduce the charge air temperature. For maximum efficiency the duct should be finned over its entire length. Leave the fins rough cast and paint the duct matt black to increase radiating efficiency. Cooling air is directed over the inlet duct via a bonnet scoop or trunking.

Where direct intercooling is not desirable some intercooling affect can be achieved by directing cool air onto the inlet duct which carries the air charge to the inlet manifold. Preferably the duct should be cast with fins on the external surface to increase the heat radiating area, and it should be left rough cast and painted matt black. The cooling air could be admitted through a bonnet-scoop or it may be ducted from the front of the vehicle through a flexible pipe about 4in in diameter. Whatever method is used, the cooling air must be diffused over as much area of the charge air duct as possible to gain the maximum cooling effect. Shield the duct from engine and exhaust heat. Also ensure that cooling air doesn't blow over the exhaust manifold or the turbine side of the turbo as this could take too much heat out of the exhaust gases and reduce boost.

Apart from the performance aspect there is another beneficial side to intercooling; namely reliability of the engine and turbocharger. A rule of thumb is that for every 100 degrees the intake charge temperature is reduced there is a 100 degree drop in exhaust temperature. This makes life easier for the exhaust valves and seats, the turbine and housing, the exhaust manifold, and the engine cooling system. As you should appreciate by now, turbocharging puts a lot of heat into the inlet air and increasing the boost just worsens the situation. Many tuners shrug this off; in fact I know of some who have doubled the standard boost pressure from 8 psi to 17 psi with the only engine modifications being the addition of forged pistons and a lowering of the compression ratio by 0.5. They figured that the engine won't detonate due to electronic controls, and as high boost pressures are good for business from the aspect of advertising and it is what the customer wants, go ahead and use high boost. It is true that many turbo engines have a knock sensor to detect detonation. The system which I prefer has the wastegate controlled to open when detonation is detected. Thus boost is always kept below detonation level. The more common system retards the ignition timing at the onset of detonation, and this is less than satisfactory. In effect it is the easy way around the problem, without really getting right to the problem itself. Retarding the spark severely increases the turbine and housing temperature, so much so that at sustained high boost the housing warps and eventually the turbine wheel contacts it and the turbo blows. The other possibility occurs because the retarded timing greatly increases the temperature of the piston crown, combustion chamber and in particular the exhaust valve. With all of this additional heat being added to an already overheated inlet charge, the engine pre-ignites. If initially this is not intense enough to melt the pistons, the knock sensor reads the shock as detonation and further retards the ignition timing. With more retard more heat is added to the turbo, combustion chambers, pistons and exhaust valves, until eventually either the turbo lets go or the pistons are holed by pre-ignition. Not a good scenario at all; obviously only more restrained levels of boost, together with an intercooler of sufficient capacity, can avoid this type of outcome.

Of course intercooling and/or higher boost levels only result in more power if there is a corresponding increase in fuel flow to keep step with the additional inlet air flow. Some injection and electronic engine management systems will compensate for the extra flow resulting from a boost increase of about 4 psi and 80% effective intercooling, while others have just enough reserve capacity to cope with either intercooling alone or a boost increase of 3 to 4 psi. If the fuel system cannot maintain flow at the desired level, action as outlined in the earlier chapter on fuel injection will be necessary. The problem is not always insuffient flow, but lack of fuel pressure to give the required flow at the injectors at elevated boost pressure. This can be overcome by the use of a high pressure, high flow fuel pump.

For example, when a Ford Cosworth Sierra was modified, the fuel system was found to be just adequate for the standard engine. As shown in Table 10.2 the standard engine produced 200hp without any bother at 6000rpm, although the mixture leaned at higher rpm. It was reasoned that this was probably due to the electronics interrupting fuel flow 500rpm prematurely. Because the management system was going to be modified to raise the boost 40% to 13 psi it was decided to carry out some additional electronic trickery to change the fuel curve and allow full power up to 6800rpm. Out of regard for the increased turbo boost the intercooler size was doubled. Test 2 shows what effect these changes had on power output. Maximum power was up 10% which wasn't too impressive considering the work involved. The next step was to   163

TABLE 10.2 – Comparison testing of Cosworth Sierra 2 litre turbo

rpm	Test 1 hp	Test 1 Torque	Test 2 hp	Test 2 Torque	Test 3 hp	Test 3 Torque
2000	46	121	51	135	51	133
2500	85	179	93	196	95	200
3000	110	193	118	206	122	214
3500	127	191	139	208	141	212
4000	143	188	163	214	167	219
4500	171	199	190	222	196	229
5000	188	197	202	212	211	222
5500	195	186	213	203	219	209
6000	200	175	220	193	227	199
6500			216	175	235	190
6800					242	187

Test 1 – standard engine.

Test 2 – electronics modified to give 13 psi boost and richen fuel curve, intercooler size doubled.

Test 3 – as above plus auxiliary injector added and turbine housing changed.

fit an auxiliary injector nozzle to get more fuel into the engine at higher rpm. In addition, the turbine housing was changed to free up exhaust flow. As can be seen in Test 3, these modifications really paid off. The engine was now more responsive at all engine speeds and it ran easily to 6800rpm, where it now produced 242hp. With the bottom end strengthened to allow 7500rpm in safety, the output would probably have climbed to in excess of 250hp at 7000 to 7250rpm.

Another approach to more power and better fuel economy is to use a turbine housing with a larger A/R ratio than stock. In general, manufacturers fit small A/R turbine housings to their engines to get good low speed boost. The small nozzle increases turbine speed so that even at lower engine speeds there is sufficient exhaust gas flow to spin the compressor fast enough to make boost. The trade-off is that as the engine speed increases, the small turbine housing nozzle restricts exhaust flow out of the engine in the same way as would a small diameter exhaust pipe. Maximum power is thus limited by restricted exhaust flow and fuel consumption increases because the pistons consume power, forcing the exhaust gas out of the cylinders and through the turbo. Even at cruise many turbos cost up around 5% to 8% fuel economy loss due to increased back pressure.

In the most mildly tuned turbo engines the turbine housing chosen should give full boost on wide open throttle at the engine's peak torque rpm. Fitting a housing smaller than this usually does very little to improve low rpm performance and it will, as a rule, result in excessive higher rpm power losses and a significant drop in economy at cruise and on boost. Ideally, the exhaust back pressure, as measured at the turbine inlet and with a 2ft long open exhaust connected to the outlet, should not be more than about 25% higher than the boost pressure at maximum hp rpm. Therefore if maximum boost is 10 psi, the exhaust pressure at the turbine inlet should not be more than 12.5 psi at maximum power revs.

With performance/economy engines a higher level of performance and reduced fuel consumption is desired so in this instance a turbine housing is selected which achieves peak boost at about 500 to 700rpm higher than the stock turbo engine's peak torque revs. A turbine housing of this A/R ratio will reduce considerably the exhaust back pressure so that at maximum power rpm the exhaust pressure at the turbine inlet will be about the same as the maximum boost pressure. Thus when a full exhaust is added, the total exhaust pressure should not be more than about 3 to 4 psi higher than the boost pressure at maximum revs. Table 10.3 shows a comparison of the inlet and exhaust pressures for a full emissions Porche 911 turbo with the stock exhaust system in place. At peak power rpm back pressure in the standard exhaust is 4.7 psi higher than the boost pressure, but with an open exhaust the exhaust pressure was just over 1 psi higher than the boost.

TABLE 10.3 – Comparison of inlet and exhaust pressures in Porsche 911 Turbo

rpm	Boost pressure	Exhaust back pressure
1500	1.5 psi	1.1 psi
2000	4.0 psi	2.6 psi
2500	9.6 psi	6.0 psi
3000	10.9 psi	7.6 psi
3500	11.0 psi	8.7 psi
4000	11.0 psi	10.3 psi
4500	11.2 psi	13.0 psi
5000	11.4 psi	14.7 psi
5500	11.6 psi	16.3 psi
6000	11.6 psi	17.2 psi

Note: peak power occurs at 5500rpm; peak torque at 3000rpm.

When a larger A/R housing is used, the effect is similar to fitting a warm cam. The engine makes less power at lower rpm because the turbine spins the compressor more slowly, hence the boost level is reduced. However, at higher engine speeds the engine makes more power, not because of more boost, but because the energy which was previously being consumed forcing the exhaust gases out past the turbine wheel is now doing the more useful work of increasing the twisting force being applied to the engine's crankshaft. Therefore more maximum power can be produced at lower maximum boost pressures, as shown in Table 10.4.

Table 10.4 also shows clearly the massive increase in fuel consumption which occurred when a smaller turbine housing was tried on this twin cam 2.8 litre Toyota in an attempt to improve the performance below 3500rpm. BSFC stands for brake specific fuel consumption. This figure is assessed during engine development work on the dyno as one of the factors to indicate just how well the engine is performing. It is calculated by dividing the engine's fuel flow, lb of fuel per hour, by the power output. If   165

TABLE 10.4 – Comparison testing of turbine housing on Toyota 2.8 litre

| | Test 1 | | | Test 2 | | |
rpm	hp	Torque	BSFC	hp	Torque	BSFC
1500	52	182	0.502	57	199	0.512
2000	73	192	0.496	81	212	0.514
2500	104	219	0.498	127	266	0.514
3000	150	263	0.493	159	278	0.511
3500	190	285	0.496	179	269	0.519
4000	225	295	0.500	208	273	0.525
4500	248	289	0.502	237	277	0.537
5000	264	277	0.511	255	268	0.552
5500	274	262	0.516	265	253	0.556
6000	283	248	0.529	260	228	0.599
6500	268	217	0.554	231	187	0.631

Test 1 – large A/R ratio turbine housing, 11.5 psi boost with intercooling.

Test 2 – smaller A/R ratio turbine housing, 13 psi boost with intercooling.

the engine was consuming 100lb of fuel per hour to make 200hp at 5500rpm, then the BSFC would be 0.500lb/hp hr (100 ÷ 200 = 0.500). Obviously the less fuel the engine is using for each hp produced, the more efficiently it must be working. With the large turbine housing the engine made 283hp and showed a fuel flow of 149.7lb per hour, but when the smaller housing was tested, power fell to 265hp and the fuel flow was 147.4lb per hour. This means that the small A/R housing cost 18hp and from 4500rpm to 6500rpm it cost 7 to 14% in economy at full throttle.

It was apparent from these initial tests that the longer A/R turbine housing should be retained to give the best economy. During subsequent testing a final package was developed to overcome the lack of performance below 3500rpm. It included an exhaust cam with shorter duration, increased compression ratio and a reduction in boost to 10 psi, and a further refinement of the ignition and fuel curves. Maximum power fell by only 7hp and the engine picked up just over 20hp at 2500rpm, and 12 to 15hp more from 3000 to 4000rpm. Also the BSFC fell to around 0.485, indicating an improvement in efficiency.

The use of larger A/R turbine housings should not generally be considered for engines smaller than about 2.0 litres, and then only if the vehicle is correctly geared, has a manual gearbox, and is not over-weight, otherwise around town performance may be a little sluggish unless extensive developmental work is undertaken. To some extent intercooling will help because even though the boost pressure with a larger A/R housing will be reduced at lower rpm with intercooling added, the compression ratio may be raised, providing the stock boost pressure is maintained, and this will pick up low speed performance quite considerably.

When power increases 15% over stock are desired some turbo engines may require an extensive rework to maintain reliability. The areas where problems can occur vary from engine to engine. It could be blown head gaskets. For some engines this may be simply overcome by fitting a different head gasket of better design and/or materials; others may require stronger head studs which do not stretch at higher pressures. The problem could be with the pistons. Perhaps they need to be stronger forgings, with wider areas between the ring lands, or with thicker crowns to increase their durability at elevated temperature. Maybe the ring placement is wrong, allowing the top ring to overheat and lose its tension after a minute or two of full boost. For some engines the problem area could be with the exhaust valves and seats. Some valve seat materials become as soft as putty at high temperature, allowing them to pound out or perhaps drop out of the head. Naturally these potential difficulties must be given due consideration when higher power levels are desired.

Everyone who has much to do with turbochargers regularly hears horror stories of turbo failures. Mostly the enthusiast blames his turbo or his oil for such early failure, often at less than 10,000 miles service. More often than not the driver is to blame, although there is some truth to oil-related failures which is why I recommend only the use of oils which are produced to provide turbo protection. Using a turbo oil and changing it along with the filter at the intervals outlined in a later chapter is good insurance, but in essence this is just the start of turbo care.

Today, many turbos have a water-cooled bearing arrangement to increase the reliability and life of the bearings. Unfortunately this has lulled many into a false sense of security as they feel the turbo no longer needs to "idle down" before the engine is stopped. This just isn't so; after a run which has put a fair amount of heat into the turbo it must be allowed time to cool for a period of about 3 minutes. Actually I don't advocate allowing the engine to idle for that period. I would rather see it run at about 1500rpm or a little higher to promote a good flow of oil through the turbo bearings. At idle the oil flow will not be sufficient, which could allow the heat in the turbine to carbonise the oil. If the oil becomes carbonised it blocks the minute clearance between the shaft and bearings. When the engine is next operated oil flow through the bearings is reduced; without adequate lubrication the bearings soon fail. However, this may not be the limit of the problem as the shaft may also be wrecked; the turbine and impeller wheels may touch their respective housings, damaging the turbo beyond economical repair.

Some enthusiasts do the right thing in allowing the turbo to cool before stopping the engine, but just before switch-off they give the throttle a few quick jabs to, in their words, "clear the plugs!". Such action may spin the turbo up to 30,000rpm and then with oil flow cut, when the engine is stopped, the bearings soon run dry and suffer premature wear.

A similar problem occurs right after starting the engine. It can take up to 30 seconds for oil to flow to the turbo so don't quickly rev the engine as this spins the turbine to high speed at a time when the bearings have only minimal lubricant in reserve. In similar vein when a turbo is refitted after being off the engine for any time, or if a reconditioned unit is being fitted, do prime it with engine oil before attaching the oil feed line. When this isn't done the bearings are damaged from the time the engine is fired up. Likewise, if the engine has not been started for some time, as during winter, it is wise if the turbo or oil line can be reached easily to prime it with oil before starting the engine.

Whenever a turbocharger is removed from the engine place it in a plastic bag so as to prevent foreign matter entering the turbine or compressor, or the oilway. Also cover the inlet and exhaust ducts on the engine so that no nuts or washers etc. can get into them and later find their way into the turbo. By following these simple precautions expensive damage is easily avoided.

In normal usage a turbocharger should require servicing only about every 30,000 to 50,000 miles. If the vehicle spends a good deal of time idling at lights or at high speed, the service interval could be more frequent. Usually, a service kit is available containing the necessary bearings, seals, bolts etc. Turbos are of very simple construction and quite easy to service if approached with proper consideration for cleanliness of oilways and bearing surfaces, and if it is remembered that the rotating assembly has to spin at speeds in excess of 100,000rpm. Some manufacturers do not recommend that servicing be done except by authorised agents with the necessary, expensive, service equipment to rebalance the turbine/impeller assembly as imbalance may cause undue noise. However, I have never experienced any problems when the compressor wheel and turbine wheel/shaft is undamaged, and thus reusable. Simply marking the position of the impeller on the shaft with a dab of paint during disassembly and then on reassembly accurately lining up the paint mark on the impeller with the paint mark on the end of the shaft overcomes any imbalance/ noise problems. Obviously if either the impeller or the turbine wheel/shaft are replaced because of damage or wear, the complete assembly will require balancing.

During disassembly carefully hold the centre housing/bearing assembly in a vice by the irregularly-shaped nut on the turbine end of the shaft. By the way, the nut is ground that shape to balance the assembly. Because there isn't much area for the vice to grip onto be very careful when removing the other nut which holds the impeller onto the shaft. If the assembly slips you will wreck the turbine blades. When the blades are bent don't attempt to straighten them otherwise they will eventually break off. If it is an impeller blade that goes it could finish up inside the engine and do damage, or the impeller may explode and come through the compressor housing. Expert opinion should be sought when the blades are bent. When minor, the assembly may be reusable, but it is best to have this determined by someone experienced.

There are two other points of which to be mindful. Before dismantling the turbo, mark the positions of the compressor housing and the turbine housing on the centre core assembly. This will save you a lot of assembly hassles later. Also, take care to follow carefully the torque settings recommended by the manufacturer when reassembling the unit. If the manufacturer says that a particular nut is to be tensioned to what may appear to be a small value, such as 10ft/lb, follow the instructions and do not rely upon your own judgement. Possibly you will not have a tension wrench which is accurate at anything less than about 30ft/lb, so borrow or buy a suitable wrench.

Chapter 11
The Bottom End

In the main, new generation engines are quite robust and will give reliable service with very little attention to the bottom end when tuned for performance and economy. Unless the engine is regularly worked at high rpm or is turbocharged, the stock crankshaft, connecting rods, pistons and bearings should be up to the task and the manufacturer's recommended rebuild clearances and procedure will be satisfactory.

The weak link in many engines is the pistons. Unless the stock piston is an unslotted semi-competition type it will not take sustained high engine speeds or constant turbo boost. The problem isn't that manufacturers can't make better pistons, but as in all other areas of engine design a compromise is necessary to accommodate a number of conflicting requirements. The majority of drivers demand that an engine be quiet at idle and cruise, and consume a minimum of oil at ordinary speeds. A piston with two long slots cut in the oil ring groove best meets those requirements, at the expense of sustained high rpm reliability. The long slots effectively divide the piston crown from the skirt. This keeps the high temperature prevalent in the crown isolated from the piston skirt, thus allowing tight piston to cylinder clearances of 0.001 to 0.0015in. Such tight clearances reduce the tendency of the pistons to rock in the bore and emit noise. Also the skirt does much to scrape oil from the cylinder walls, reducing the load on the rings to control oil consumption. Hence even when the engine has seen a long service life and the rings are shot, oil consumption will still be reasonable at normal engine speeds.

These benefits come at a price; reduced reliability. When the engine is new there should not be any problems providing the manufacturer's rpm limit is observed. However, as the pistons age constant flexing of the skirt causes cracks to appear. A piece of the skirt may break away or the entire skirt may part company with the crown. Needless to say an expensive blow up could result.

169

To avoid this type of problem, high performance engines usually come from the factory with unslotted pistons. Specialty piston manufacturers can supply this type of piston to suit just about any engine. With this design the piston is solid with just a few small holes drilled in the oil ring groove to provide oil drain-back. The disadvantage is that these pistons need four to six times as much clearance as slotted pistons, because a lot of heat will transfer to the skirt at high engine loads. However, at idle and cruise, when the piston crown is relatively cool, there won't be much heat getting to the skirt to expand it out to the cylinder wall. Hence the pistons rock about more and produce noise. Additionally, this rocking increases ring and groove wear, necessitating more frequent overhauls.

Pistons are ground tapered and oval to allow for expansion caused by additional heat in the piston crown and around the pin boss areas.

There has been a good deal of discussion among engine tuners as to whether forged or cast pistons are better. For road engines I have no personal preference; if the piston manufacturer produces a good product either type will work equally well. Therefore if forged pistons are more expensive and heavier I would not hesitate to use a good cast piston. The exception would be in high output road turbo engines where the higher material density of forged pistons may give an added margin of reliability. Being denser, thermal conductivity from the piston crown is superior, reducing crown temperature by about 100°F. Also forged pistons are capable of withstanding higher pressures and heat loads.

Care is necessary whenever pistons are being handled. Accidentally dropping a piston could distort the skirt and eventually lead to seizure. Belting the piston pin out with a hammer and drift can also push the skirt out of shape. If the pin will not push out easily, heat the piston in boiling water or oil and then gently tap it out. Where the pin is a press fit in the connecting rod it must be removed and installed using special tools to avoid piston damage.

No matter how carefully pistons are handled they can still be easily wrecked in service if the connecting rod is misaligned. Therefore when the engine is being reconditioned the rod alignment should be checked to ensure that the rods are not bent, twisted or incorrectly offset.

If it is decided that stronger unslotted pistons are necessary because sustained high rpm usage is contemplated, a decision has then to be made whether the bore will remain within the range of the manufacturer's standard rebore sizes or whether a massive overbore will be sought. Many new generation engines use light thin-wall castings which will not successfully rebore more than 0.030in over stock. Quite frankly I do not like to see road engines which are expected to see a long and reliable life taken to the limit. I usually do not recommend more than 0.060 to 0.080in oversize, even for very thick-wall blocks, which are frequently taken 0.120in oversize. I'm not prepared to trade long term reliability for a few extra cc.

When an engine is taken 0.060 to 0.080 oversize have the boring bar operator take the metal out in two cuts. It will cost more because of the time involved but the cylinders will be easier to hone accurately because the boring tool marks will not be so deep and rough. Finely machined cylinders with parallel walls are a necessity. Any leakage past the rings reduces performance, wastes fuel and increases oil consumption. Hence only reputable operators with the best equipment should be given the job. The hone must leave the cylinders perfectly round and parallel with a 45° cross-hatch pattern and a surface finish of 10 to 12 micro-inches. A finish like this makes it necessary to run the rings in, but they will last for a long time and not leak. After honing, the bores must be thoroughly scrubbed out with hot, soapy water to remove all honing grit.

For ease of bedding in I prefer moly-filled nodular cast iron piston rings. Nodular iron has almost three times the strength of conventional grey cast iron and because it is ductile rather than brittle, it can be bent without breaking. Molybdenum belongs to the same family as chrome but is superior as it has a lower coefficient of friction and higher resistance to abrasion. Its thermal conductivity is several times greater than chrome plated cast iron and because of its porous nature it acts like an oil reservoir, reducing ring wear and cylinder scuffing and wear.

Chrome plated rings are harder to bed-in than any other type of ring, but they offer a long service life and seem to be less affected by detonation then moly-filled rings. I have never experienced any problems with moly rings although a few reputable tuners maintain that they will not hold up under heavy detonation as well as chrome plated rings.

Apart from a perfect seal being necessary between the ring face and cylinder wall an equally important consideration is a perfect seal between the bottom of the ring and the piston ring groove. If the bottom of the groove is worn or scratched, leakage will occur. I like very tight groove to ring clearances of 0.001 to 0.0015in. Certainly with new pistons and rings the clearance should not be more than 0.002in. The wider the clearance the more the rings can flop about and accelerate groove and ring wear. Eventually the ring will move about so savagely that it breaks. If the clearance is over 0.0045in with new rings fitted, the pistons should be replaced or reconditioned.

Another cause of ring breakage is insufficient ring gap, allowing the ring ends to crash together. The minimum gap per inch of bore is as follows: turbo engines 0.005in for the top ring and 0.0035in for the second ring, naturally-aspirated 0.004in for the top ring and 0.003in for the second ring.

When rings are being fitted, care is needed to avoid fitting them the wrong way up and to prevent damage by incorrect installation practices. Compression rings can be permanently twisted or distorted out of round if they are stretched open too far or if 171

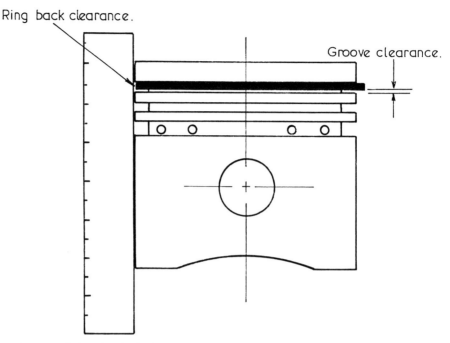

Ring back clearance.

Groove clearance.

When rings are being fitted, the back clearance and groove clearance should be checked. With used pistons carbon may build up in the groove, reducing back clearance and causing ring breakage. Likewise, excessive groove clearance leads to breakage by allowing the rings to flop about.

they are fitted in the piston ring groove at one end and then screwed around until the ring is in place. Rings should only be expanded sufficiently to just fit over the piston, and then be allowed to drop into the groove. Special expander tools are available for this purpose but I prefer to use two 0.015in feeler blades placed between the ring and the piston. The blades provide a bearing surface and prevent the ring from digging into the piston.

To obtain a good gas seal and control oil consumption, the compression rings must be fitted the correct way up. Taper face rings are either "dimpled" near the ring end or marked TOP, and should be fitted with this side up. The more common unbalanced section or torsional twist ring is fitted with the inner chamfered edge, or inner stepped edge, uppermost. The inverted torsional taper face ring looks similar but it is used in the second ring position and is fitted with the inner step downwards. The more common second compression rings are all scraper types, either stepped or scalloped on the outer edge. These should be fitted with the step downwards.

There are many designs of oil control rings around and all should be fitted in accordance with the manufacturers packaged instructions. When multi-piece rings are fitted, always double-check that the ends of the expander ring have not been lapped over.

When fitting the assembled pistons in the block, dip each piston in engine oil.
The cylinder walls should already be well oiled from the time that they were scrubbed

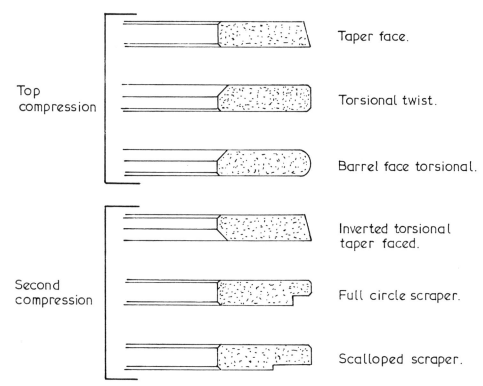

Top compression
- Taper face.
- Torsional twist.
- Barrel face torsional.

Second compression
- Inverted torsional taper faced.
- Full circle scraper.
- Scalloped scraper.

These are the more commonly fitted rings for car engines. If any are installed the wrong way up, power is lost, fuel and oil consumption increases.

clean of honing residue. Do not coat the piston rings or cylinders with anything other than straight engine oil. I know some people paint oil additives onto these surfaces but this is an incorrect practice. It slows down bedding-in and can result in glazed rings and bores.

In addition to proper machining and assembly practices, proper ring seal demands correct bed-in procedure. To achieve this do not allow the engine to idle on the first start-up after being rebuilt. Rather keep the engine running at about 2000rpm to ensure adequate oil throw-off to the rings, pistons and cylinder walls. When the engine is up to normal operating temperature drive off, keeping the engine speed above 1500rpm. Then in top gear give the car a near full throttle burst to accelerate it from 35 to 45mph. On reaching 45mph snap the throttle shut and coast down to 35mph. Hold that speed for a minute or two and again accelerate up to 45mph. Repeat this about twelve times. By giving the engine nearly full throttle high combustion pressures are attained, forcing the rings out against the cylinder wall. Snapping the throttle closed causes a high vacuum within the cylinder which draws up extra oil. This and low engine speeds minimise the risk of glazing and allow the ring face to cool between acceleration bursts.

After the rings are initially bedded-in the engine can be operated at up to 60% of its rev/power potential for the next 250 to 400 miles. However, the speed must be constantly varied, coasting for a while and then accelerating. If this is not done the rings may still glaze. At around the 500 to 700 mile mark up to 80% of the rev/power potential can be used, but do avoid constant high speed running until the engine has clocked 1500 miles. At 2000 miles the engine's full potential can be unleashed.

Because the majority of new generation engines have semi-hemi heads with canted valves, some thought must be given to providing adequate valve to piston clearance. The check involves quite a deal of work but it must be carried out if expensive damage is to be avoided. The check is necessary whenever a modified cam or larger valves are fitted or whenever the head or block is skimmed on an engine with a canted valve head, a wedge chamber head, or a flat head (bowl in the piston combustion chamber design).

There should be a minimum of 0.060in vertical clearance between valve and piston; 0.080in for the inlet and 0.100in for the exhaust is safer. Additionally, the valve cut out diameter should be 0.120in greater than the valve head diameter.

There are two basic ways to go about the clearance check, but either way the engine has to be almost totally assembled with the cam accurately timed to the angle that it is going to be used in the engine, and a head gasket of the appropriate thickness used.

The first method involves the use of a piece of modelling clay pressed down on the piston top. After the clay has been smoothed out, spray it and the valves with something like WD-40 to help prevent the clay sticking to the valves. With the head tensioned and valve clearances adjusted, very carefully turn the crankshaft through two complete revolutions. If the crank resists turning at any point, stop turning immediately, open the valve clearances up 0.050in and try again. After the crank has been turned through two revolutions remove the head and measure the clay thickness over both valve cut outs and around their periphery. Where the clearance is less than required, the pistons will have to be removed and machined.

The other method is accurate only if the valve cut outs are central under the valves, as there is no provision for a check to be made on the clearance between the edge of the valve and the edge of the cut out. In this instance light checking springs are fitted instead of valve springs. As with the previous method the head is tensioned and the valve clearances adjusted. Next, set up a dial gauge on the inlet valve and turn the crank until the valve is fully open. Now zero the gauge and push the valve until it contacts the piston. The dial gauge reading indicates the clearance. The exhaust valve clearance is measured in a similar way.

The majority of engines use cast nodular iron crankshafts which normally give long reliable service if sensible rpm limits are observed. Even high performance engines like the 16 valve 2.3 litre Mercedes are using cast cranks without any problems. If the standard cast crankshaft is tested and found to be free of cracks and the bearing journals are true, there is no reason to discard it in favour of a forged steel item.

When measuring the main bearing and crankpin journals remember that the journals wear oval. Hence it is necessary to measure the diameter at several angles around each journal. Also measure at each end of every journal as wear can vary along the length of the journal. Ovality and taper should be less than 0.0007in. If the wear is greater than this, grinding the journals undersize will be necessary. When the
174   crankshaft is machined, instruct the operator to pay close attention to maintaining the

fillet radius specified by the manufacturer as any reduction in the radius will weaken the crank.

To assist in the smooth operation of the engine and reduce bearing inertia loading, the crank may be accurately dynamically balanced. Balancing will increase the life of the crankshaft as a result of a reduction in the shock loading and vibration to which any imbalance would give rise. Most manufacturers do a reasonably good job balancing their cranks so I personally feel that unless the engine is to run at sustained peak rpm it is not worth the expense. Likewise in performance/economy engines crankshaft oilway modifications and Tuftriding or any other type of heat treatment are unnecessary.

With some engines a useful increase in capacity and low speed torque can be gained fairly inexpensively by using a long stroke crank out of another engine from the same basic family of engines. For example, swapping the long stroke crank out of the 400cu in small block Chev will give smaller Chevs a capacity increase of about 30cu in. The only drawback is the main bearing journals have to be ground down by 0.200in so that it will fit. Technically, this weakens the part but in practice the crank is plenty strong enough and gives no trouble even in engines approaching 450hp.

There are, however, crankshaft modifications of which I do not approve. The first one involves the welding up of the crankpins and then grinding them on a new centre to increase the stroke. This should not be done as the welding process causes a change in the crystalline structure of the underlying metal. The affected area then becomes a stress point likely to fail as the crank ages. Another practice is commonly applied to "A" series British Leyland engines and involves grinding the crankpins undersize on a new centre to increase the stroke. This modification reduces the crank beam strength and increases bearing loads; low mileage big end bearing failures are common.

If you have a surplus of money you may be tempted to purchase a specially-manufactured long stroke forged crank. These cranks are very strong, and expensive; however, they tend to make some engines run a lot more harshly at certain engine speeds.

When a long stroke crank is fitted, some grinding may be necessary inside the block for connecting rod clearance. There could be engine mount bolt bosses which need just a touch with the grinder and a few of the clearance slots at the bottom of the bores will probably require enlarging. The camshaft or jackshaft may also need clearance slots, but do not machine the cam all the way around as this will weaken the shaft excessively and lead to flexing and inaccurate valve timing. The sump pan may have to be dimpled in places with a hammer to provide rod clearance.

The connecting rods fitted to new generation engines are reasonably strong and as such do not require any special preparation techniques apart from standard reconditioning procedures when used in performance/economy applications. If the rods have a little end designed for press fit piston pins it is important that the bore finish is smooth and free of deep grooves, and it must be of the correct diameter to give the necessary interference to properly retain the pin. Some reconditioners do not pay adequate attention to this aspect of rod preparation, with the result that the pin moves and badly scores the cylinder wall. Where the little end is bushed for a floating-type piston pin, the bush should be replaced when worn to bring the pin to bush clearance down to 0.0008 to 0.0015in. With age, the big end may move out of shape so to avoid pinched or spun bearings the inside diameter should be checked for size and concentricity with the bolts torqued to specification. Standard connecting rod preparation must always include a check, using a special jig, to ensure that the rod is not twisted or bent. Either condition will in time wreck the piston and/or big end bearings.

The only additional work which I like to see performed on rods for midly tuned applications is to lightly radius the sharp corners which are formed by the flat machined for the rod bolt and nut seat. These sharp corners can cause stress concentration and eventual cracking.

Connecting rods which are regularly worked hard may crack through at the corners of the flats machined for the rod bolt and nut seat. To relieve the stress concentration the rod cap is radiused in the corners and the rod is notched, as shown. Note that rods which use bolts without nuts do not require relief notching.

Whenever an engine is dismantled, new connecting rod bolts must always be fitted; the old bolts should never be reused. Apart from piston breakages, rod bolt stretch or breakage is probably the most common cause of serious internal damage in modern engines. Where special bolts of higher grade steel are available these should be utilised in preference to the standard item.

Unless the engine is going to be operated at sustained engine speeds significantly higher than the manufacturers recommended rpm limit, don't waste your time and money polishing the rods. The tough skin formed on the rod by forging actually gives the rod much of its strength and fatigue resistance. Therefore rods should never be polished unless this is followed up with shot peening to form a new work-toughened and compressed skin. It is quite pointless polishing the entire rod because the main area of weakness is, in fact, along the edges of the rod. If you take the time to inspect a rod you will see a rough ridge of metal along the edges where the metal appears to have been sawn away. This is where excess metal called flash was squeezed from the forging dies when the rod was being made. Later, most of the flash is trimmed off, leaving behind a rough ridge. There is no hard forging skin along this ridge; actually its roughness is a stress raiser. If it is decided that the rods are to be polished it is this ridge which has to be removed, using a belt sander. After rough sanding the entire beam should be polished using fine emery cloth and then buffed. Finally the polished areas should be shot peened to add strength to the rod and increase its fatigue resistance.

The shot peening process has a very useful place in the preparation of connecting rods which are to be fitted in fast reving engines. Fatigue failure most often starts at the surface because under usual forms of loading maximum stress is at the surface and it is here that surface imperfections and irregularities, which are in actuality stress raisers, are to be found. By bombarding the part with steel shot the surface layer is compressed and unified. Consequently when the component is under load any tensile stresses at the surface will be lessened, while compressive stresses will be increased. Because shot peening can seal over surface cracks, all crack testing must be carried out prior to peening. Additionally, any straightening or aligning should be done before peening, as either operation will diminish the effect of shot peening. After being peened, the part should be checked dimensionally as there will be some growth, and also check for bending as this may occur if the peening has been done incorrectly.

Cylinder block preparation is very basic and simple. First knock out all the welch plugs (freeze or core plugs) and inspect the coolant passages for rust or scale. Any sediment or flaky material can be dislodged with a screwdriver and then flushed out. If an inhibitor has not been used and advanced corrosion is evident, it will be necessary to boil the block in a chemical bath. When this is done the oil gallery plugs must be removed and all oilways carefully cleaned and flushed to ensure that any rubbish present in the boiling tank which could have found its way into the oilways is expelled. Next, all stud holes should be cleaned, with particular attention being paid to the head stud holes and the main bearing cap stud holes. The standard two bolt cast iron main bearing caps will be quite adequate for mildly tuned performance/economy engines so don't throw away any money on steel caps.

After being bored, or any other machining work has been done, the block must again be thoroughly cleaned. Initially, scrub it out using a bristle scrubbing brush and plenty of hot soapy water. Scrub inside every cylinder and every place within the crankcase. Then give the block a blast of high pressure hot water to remove every trace of machining dust or honing grit. Give the oilways a final flush with hot water, quickly dry the block using compressed air and immediately spray all machined surfaces with a water dispersant such as WD-40 to stop rust. After this oil the cylinder walls and in the case of pushrod engines also the lifter bores. If the engine is not to be immediately assembled place the block in a heavy duty plastic bag (a garbage bag is excellent), force as much air out of the bag as possible, and then seal it.

The manufacturer's standard engine bearings can be used, or if preferred tri-metal bearings may be fitted for the mains and big ends in engines which leave the factory with bi-metal copper lead or aluminium tin bearings. Both F770 specification and F77 specification tri-metal bearing have a higher load endurance factor and fatigue strength than either bi-metal bearings which makes them the favoured bearing types for performance engines. The F770 and F77 bearings use a 24% lead, 75% copper intermediate layer that imparts the superior characteristics of good fatigue strength and load carrying capacity, as well as resistance to hydraulic break out. The running surface is a 0.001in thick lead-based overlay which imparts good embedability characteristics. All engines have some dirt circulating in the lubrication oil no matter how carefully the engine has been cleaned and assembled. Bi-metal bearings lack this soft overlay so any minute dirt particles act as a grinding agent between the bearing and crankshaft journals, wearing away at the bearing. Tri-metal bearings on the other hand allow this dirt or wear debris to embed in the soft overlay. In effect the lead alloy overlay absorbs or digests the foreign material, without undue damage to the bearing itself. Of course as the overlay wears thinner after, say, 50,000 to 70,000 miles of driving, its ability to digest dirt particles is reduced. Naturally when dirt is embedded in the bearing surface some additional abrasive wear of the crank journals does occur.

F770 and F77 specification bearings have identical bearing materials; their differences lie in the manner that they are manufactured. With F770 bearings a copper lead alloy powder is sintered onto the steel backing whereas the F77 bearings have the copper lead alloy cast onto the steel backing strip. At this stage of development cast copper lead F77 bearings offer a slight advantage over the cheaper to produce F770 type. In race engines I wouldn't use anything but F77 bearings made by such companies as Vandervell, TRW (Clevite CL-77) and Sealed Power, but for road engines F770 bearings are more than adequate.

Correct bearing clearance is an obvious necessity. Excessive clearance promotes knocking and pounding, and causes excessive oil throw off into the cylinders. This produces higher frictional losses and increases fuel consumption as the pistons and rings drag the surplus oil off the bore walls. In addition, oil control past the rings is reduced. Oil consumption increases, as does the risk of detonation because oil in the combustion chamber dramatically lowers the fuel's effective octane rating. Excessive clearance at the big end bearings starves the main bearings of needed lubricant and gives rise to rapid wear, or even bearing failure. In a similar vein excessive con rod side clearance or float on the crankpin is to be avoided for the same reasons. This problem most frequently occurs when the crankpin is accidently widened during crankshaft reconditioning work. Insufficient bearing clearance leads to rapid bearing deterioration as a result of the elevated temperatures that come about due to reduced oil flow or a thin oil film. To avoid this type of problem I prefer to see performance/economy engines assembled with bearing clearances close to the manufacturer's specified upper limit. Hence if the specifications called for clearances of 0.0008 to 0.0018in I would try to keep the clearance up around 0.0015 to 0.002in.

Bearing clearance is checked by accurately measuring the inside diameter of every main bearing and big end bearing housing, correctly tensioned and without the bearing shells fitted. Measurements should be made perpendicular to the joint line of the bearing housings taking care to keep the micrometer square to the housing bore. From these measurements subtract the respective crank journal diameters and then subtract the bearing insert thickness multiplied by two. The final figures give the bearing clearances.

Before being fitted, the bearings should be carefully washed in clean solvent to remove the protective film, and then dried and covered so that they do not collect any dust. The bearing housings need to be cleaned with a kitchen scouring pad like Scotchbrite which has been moistened with solvent. This is done to remove any varnish deposits which could retard heat transfer from the bearing shell. After being scoured, the housings must be wiped clean and then washed with solvent. It should be noted that careful cleaning of the bearing shells and housings is essential. The presence of oil or varnish either on the back of the bearing shell or on the bore of the housing will cut heat transfer. The presence of any dirt particles on either surface will reduce bearing clearances, and in severe cases leads to early bearing failure.

After ensuring that the shells and housings are perfectly clean and dry, the main bearing shells may be fitted. This sounds simple enough but I have seen engines damaged because someone got it wrong. Some bearings have identical oil grooves and oil holes in both halves, allowing them to be fitted in either the upper or lower position. However, many engines require that the big end bearing shells and sometimes also the main bearing shells only be installed in one position otherwise oil flow will be cut off. Hence when bearing inserts are being fitted take care to ensure that the insert with the oil hole is matched to the oil hole in the cylinder block or connecting rod. Also check that the oil holes correctly align; if they do not, rectify the misalignment using a small round key file. After filing, carefully dress the back of the bearing shell to remove any metal fraze. Once fitted in their respective housings give the bearing surfaces a liberal coating of straight engine oil: don't add anything to the oil. Lower the crankshaft into the block and fit the main bearing caps in their correct numbered locations and with the arrows facing the front of the block. Tighten the caps to about 30ft lb and then with the aid of a lever force the crank backward and forward a couple of times to make the flanges of the thrust bearing line up. After this tap the crankshaft from side to side with a soft hammer and in turn tap the main bearing caps to improve the alignment of the bearings. Finally, progressively tighten each cap bolt to its specified tension. At this point the crankshaft end float can be measured. With a cast iron block preferably it should be within 0.004 to 0.006in. If it is more than this, thicker thrust bearings will be required.

Big end bearings are fitted following the same basic steps. The main exception is that the bolts should initially be tensioned to about 15ft lb before tapping the caps to align the bearing inserts. Also I like to use Loctite on the bolt threads to avoid engine damage from the bolts later loosening off. Note that when piston/rod assemblies are being installed, protruding connecting rod bolts must be covered with plastic or rubber sleeves to prevent the threads digging into the crankpin.

Most enthusiasts pay little attention to the pulley or harmonic balancer attached to the nose of the crankshaft. However, they have their part to play in the durability of the engine and in keeping the under-bonnet environment safe. A number of engines use a pressed metal drive pulley which is spot welded or riveted. When the manufacturer's recommended rev limit is regularly exceeded, a pulley of this construction is liable to fly apart, wrecking anything in its path. If the engine is to be extended above the recommended engine speed either a cast pulley, or a pulley machined from solid stock, should be used.

Five, six and eight cylinder engines and a few four cylinder engines are fitted with a harmonic balancer to dampen crankshaft torsional vibrations which if not controlled could wreck the crankshaft and bearings. Harmonic balancers are made of three parts bonded together. A rubber belt is bonded between the hub and the outer inertia ring which in some engines also serves as a pulley. Failure is caused by this outer ring losing its bond with the rubber. When this takes place it can fly off at any time, often with spectacular and expensive results. The only way to avoid that from occurring is to inspect the harmonic dampener on a regular basis. To assist in your inspection paint a common line across the face of the harmonic balancer from the outer ring across to the hub. If the line moves apart it indicates that the rubber bond has broken, allowing the inertia ring to move around on the hub. Fit a new or reconditioned harmonic balancer, do not try to repair it by screwing the outer ring to the hub. The inertia ring has to be able to move, within limits, to dampen crank vibration. Locking it up solid will eventually wreck the bearings and the crankshaft.

Before fitting the crankshaft pulley to the engine paint it black and then after fitting it accurately find top dead centre (TDC) and file a good groove into it to align with the TDC mark on the engine timing case. Paint the filed groove and the timing marks on the timing case either white or silver. Taking the time to do this will make it easier to adjust the ignition timing accurately. Stock timing marks are notoriously inaccurate, and they are often difficult to see clearly so anything that you can do to rectify these problems will help.

The stock flywheel gives little trouble in the majority of road engines. If the crank flange and flywheel mating surfaces are clean and the flywheel is correctly mounted with the retaining bolts coated with Loctite and properly torqued, there should be few problems at normal engine speeds. However, at higher rpm some engines do display a tendency to loosen the flywheel bolts. If your engine type is prone to this sort of trouble it can be overcome either by fitting two ⅜in dowels and/or additional retaining bolts.

From the aspect of performance the flywheel does have an affect. Removing metal from the outer edges of the flywheel improves acceleration. Because the amount of power required to overcome the flywheel's inertia is reduced, this power is then available to accelerate the vehicle more rapidly. Lightening should only be done near the outside as weight close to the centre has virtually no inertia effect. Actually it is a very dangerous practice to remove metal from the centre. Flywheels are none too strong and taking metal from the centre could lead to an explosion. Taking a lot of weight off the flywheel is undesirable for a road car as it can give rise to a lumpy engine idle and jerky slow speed driving. Manufacturers fit a relatively heavy flywheel to absorb the uneven torsional pulses coming through the crankshaft, and to keep the engine turning fairly smoothly at lower engine speeds.

Chapter 12
Lubrication

Because modern engines are so reliable and maintenance-free, lubrication tends basically to be forgotten. Hence the oil is changed only when it turns to a black goo or perhaps an oil company advertisement prods us to act. On the other hand there are still a few who suffer "lubrication paranoia", changing the lubricant frequently and fortifying it with expensive additives which supposedly make engines last forever. As is usually the case, the prudent course is somewhere between these extremes. Obviously to obtain the best service life from an engine the correct oil must be used and it must be replaced regularly.

Engine oil has to perform a number of basic tasks: lubricate and prevent wear by minimising friction, seal combustion pressure, cool vital engine parts, permit easy starting, keep the engine clean of sludge, minimise combustion chamber deposits, provide rust and corrosion protection and resist foaming. To indicate just how well an oil performs, the American Petroleum Institute (API) assigns oil a service rating such as SD, SE and SF. Currently the toughest API rating is SG, and to carry that rating an oil must, in theory, pass a series of dyno tests. One test monitors the oil's ability to prevent valve train wear in an overhead cam 2.3 litre American Ford. Like its 2 litre European cousin this engine is notorious for valve train problems, in its early life being subject to a recall for abnormal cam lobe wear. Another test monitors the oil's capacity to prevent wear and resist oxidation in a 350cu in Oldsmobile run for 64 hours with the oil at 149°C sump temperature. The big oil companies do test their oils honestly according to the prescribed API test schedule but it is not unknown for some unscrupulous businesses to fudge the test results or even rate their oils without carrying out any of the API tests. I will only recommend the use of SF-rated oil from reputable oil companies, and for turbo engines I use only those oils which are actually rated by the oil company as suitable for use in turbo engines as I have found that ordinary SF-rated oils can cause excessive varnish and carbon deposits in the turbo bearings.

The viscosity of oil is a measure of its ability to flow through a graduated hole at an established temperature; $-18°C$ for W (winter) rating and $99°C$ for SAE rating. High viscosity oils are thicker and offer more resistance to flow while low viscosity oils flow more easily. Obviously in a highly stressed performance engine we need a high viscosity oil to keep metal parts from contacting one another at higher temperatures. However, such a thick oil would fail to get between closely fitting parts in sufficient quantities after engine start up when the oil is cold. Additionally, the starter motor would not be able to turn the engine over in winter due to the friction caused by the thick oil. The solution is to use a multi-grade oil suitable for your climate as indicated in Table 12.1.

TABLE 12.1 – Recommended oil viscosity

Temperature °C	Temperature °F	Oil Viscosity
0 to 45	32 to 113	20W–50
0 to 30	32 to 86	20W–40, 20W–50
−8 to 30	18 to 86	15W–40
−18 to 15	0 to 60	10W–40
−18 to 3	0 to 37	10W–30
−38 to −6	−36 to 21	5W–20

An oil with a rating of 20W–50 is basically made of 20W refined stock with viscosity index (VI) improvers added to give it a 50 SAE rating at $99°C$. The VI improvers, polymers, are long-chain plastic molecules which expand to thicken the oil as the oil temperature increases, and reduce in size as the oil cools. Unfortunately these polymers are not completely shear stable so under certain conditions they will be chopped up, allowing the oil to thin. The prime chopping agent is transmission gears, but as very few cars (unlike motorcycles) have a common engine/transmission oil supply this is usually not a great problem. Age will weather these long-chain plastic molecules so that in time a 20W–50 oil will break down to a 20W–30. You have probably noticed that with fresh oil in the engine, oil consumption may be only a half pint in a thousand miles but after a couple of thousand miles the consumption dramatically increases to two pints per thousand miles. The reason is that the polymers shear with age, allowing the oil to thin and increase consumption.

Adding polymers is not the only way to improve the viscosity index of an oil. Another way is to blend synthetic base stocks with petroleum base stocks to produce a blended synthetic, or to use only synthetic base stocks to produce a so-called one hundred per cent synthetic.

What makes synthetics different from normal mineral oils is the refining process that produces the oil. Everyone knows that ordinary mineral oils are distilled from crude oil. Such things as tars, petrol, diesel, kerosene are removed to leave an engine oil base stock. To produce a synthetic, the refining process continues much further until very basic components of the crude are separated. These basic substances are then combined into new molecular structures to form synthetic base stock. Some synthetics use only petroleum derived base stock, but other hydrocarbon molecules from refined coal, natural gas, animal fat and bone marrow may also be added to produce specific characteristics.

All synthetics have two benefits over ordinary mineral oils. They have excellent low temperature characteristics with a winter rating often as low as 5W and with the addition of polymers, the 99°C rating is usually 50 SAE, so the oil can be used in extreme climatic conditions. Because it is so thin, cold start engine wear is considerably reduced. Additionally, synthetics are more oxidation resistant and so in theory, less frequent oil changes are required. However, as a number of synthetics contain polymers which shear and break down with age, this is open to debate. Personally I would use a synthetic in a cooler climate where the temperature is regularly below 5°C and then only if the engine was subjected to frequent short drives of less than 15 minutes duration at least twice each day. Also, if I was having trouble with turbo bearing failures, I would give a synthetic such as Mobil 1 a try.

Any oil gets contaminated with combustion by-products and the various additives eventually stop working, so the oil must be changed. For a few years now oil companies and some car makers have been advocating very long oil change periods but I am not at all in favour of this practice. After all about the cheapest maintenance is an oil change. Table 12.2 sets out my recommended oil change periods to keep combustion chamber deposits to a minimum and reduce engine wear. To make the oil change really effective, take your car for a good run to bring it to normal operating temperature. This ensures that any sediment and sludge will be well stirred and will drain out with the oil. Take care though to avoid burns as the oil will be quite hot.

TABLE 12.2 – Recommended oil change periods

Driving Conditions	Temperature conditions during daytime	
	Below 10°C/50°F	Above 15°C/59°F
Regularly driven less than 15 min from cold start	1000 miles/30 days	1500 miles/45 days
Stop-start city driving	1000 miles/30 days	1500 miles/45 days
Regular high speed above 80mph	2000 miles/45 days	3000 miles/60 days
Regular high speed above 80mph turbo or common engine/gearbox sump	2000 miles/45 days	2000 miles/45 days
Regularly driven at least 1 hour from cold start usually at less than 70mph	2500 miles/60 days	4000 miles/90 days

Note: change oil at mileage stated or number of days, whichever comes first. The recommended change periods are for engines in good condition – engines with excessive blow-by will require more frequent oil changes.

Some feel that there is something to be gained by the use of oil additives or oil produced for diesel engines. I do not use additives and I do not recommend their use. Today's road oils are well able to cope with the stresses imposed by race engines so additives are completely unnecessary. In fact some additives are reputed to cause turbo problems due to oil orifice blockages. Many manufacturer's warranties are nullified by the use of additives. Diesel engine oil is formulated to combat the combustion by-products of diesel fuel. Most oil companies have diesel oil with a petrol engine SF rating, but these oils do not provide the protection of high performance oils which usually far exceed the minimum requirements for an SF classification.

Some enthusiasts also wonder if the use of racing oils would afford some additional engine protection benefits. The answer is no and yes. No, oils like Castrol R30 and R40 (castor bean vegetable oil) and BP Corse 30, 40 or 50 (mineral oil) should not be used as they do not contain additives necessary to combat sludge build-up and resist oxidation. While being excellent for competition they are definitely not to be used in road engines. However, there are some so-called race oils which may be suitable. Look for the API service rating on the container. If it is rated SF and is produced by a well-known oil company there should not be any problem. Some American oil companies call their high performance oils "race oil". This usually means that the oil contains more detergent and more zinc anti-wear additives than the company's more humble standard road oils.

Maximum engine protection is afforded by the use of the correct grade premium SF rated engine oil and a large capacity oil filter. Change both oil and filter regularly.

Another question which I am frequently asked is "Is there a difference between the cheapest SF oil at a discount parts shop and the most expensive SF oil?". Perhaps the most expensive oil may be better but a high price is no guarantee of quality. Obviously there is a cost difference between a very good oil which far exceeds the SF tests and one that just passes. Better additives and a larger total volume of additives, plus the best high quality shear-resistant polymers add to the cost of producing a good oil. On the other hand not all costs are related to producing a high quality product. Making a small quantity of oil dramatically increases its cost per litre which is why some oils made by small companies are so expensive.

No matter how good the oil it must be maintained at the correct temperature to lubricate effectively. A good deal of engine wear takes place when engines are operated with cold oil. An engine should never be driven hard until the oil reaches 50°C. The ideal oil temperature is 90°C – 120°C. It can go as high as 150°C but oil breakdown and excessive oxidation will take place above this temperature.

Years ago, an early modification was to fit an oil cooler but with advances in oil technology this usually is no longer necessary. During full throttle 24 hour track endurance testing, manufacturers regularly record sump oil temperatures of 150°C and as high as 180°C for the entire test period with SE and SF oil. Subsequent engine teardowns revealed that such high temperatures were not presenting any problems. This is not to say that such high oil temperatures are acceptable indefinitely but these tests do indicate that a new engine with little blow-by past the rings can be operated at 120–130°C sump oil temperature and as high as 150°C for short periods when SF oil or the latest SG oil changed as recommended in Table 12.2 is used. I would only recommend an oil cooler if under normal driving conditions the oil temperature is regularly in excess of 140°C.

If an oil cooler is necessary there are several "musts" which should be kept in mind. Cold oil wrecks engines and deteriorates quickly so either an oil thermostat will be required or else the oil cooler should have a shutter or blind fitted in front of it which can be opened or removed when driving at constant high speed. The oil lines connecting the cooler into the system should be of at least ½in bore so as not to restrict flow. Additionally, the take-off sandwich block which usually fits between the oil pump and filter, or between the engine block and filter, must be of good design. Many cause severe restriction to flow by requiring the oil to travel through two 90° bends. In good designs oil passages are cast into the sandwich block, not machined, as this results in 90° bends. Oil coolers are impossible to clean out so do not purchase a used oil cooler as it could be full of dirt or bearing material. Also, if your engine or turbo suffers a bearing failure, the cooler will require replacement, otherwise this material will eventually cause another bearing failure.

By-pass closed.   Filtered particles.   By-pass open.

Unless the oil filter is of sufficient size, the by-pass will be open when the oil is cold or the engine is operating at higher rpm. Unfiltered oil is allowed through to the bearings, causing premature wear and possibly failure.

The next requirement of an efficient lubrication system is adequately filtered oil. Any solid material in the oil acts as an abrasive, wearing bearings, turbo shafts and crank journals, tappets and cam lobes. Also it can quickly block turbo oilways and cause bearing failure. Most engines have an oil filter, but some are less than adequate, being only about the size of a tea cup. In almost all cases, the oil systems on modern cars are of the full-flow type. This means that all the engine oil is supposed to pass through the filter. The truth is that small filters are incapable of handling full oil flow at anything over about 2000rpm, and then only when the oil is at full operating temperature. The rest of the time the by-pass opens, allowing unfiltered oil to circulate through the engine. Worse still, a lot of sediment material collects below where the by-pass is located so that when it opens much of this rubbish is flushed through the engine.

The simplest way around the problem, if there is sufficient clearance, is to fit a large filter preferably 5in long by 3½in diameter. Do carefully check that the gasket size and depth is correct to effect a good seal. If such a larger filter cannot physically be accommodated on the engine it should be possible to find room to mount a remote filter somewhere under the bonnet (hood). Adapters are available that can be installed in place of the stock filter which will route oil lines to the new remote filter. As with oil coolers, these lines should be ½in minimum bore, and keep away from 90° fittings or adapter blocks with 90° passages.

Just how often the filter should be changed will depend on its size and on driving conditions/style. Any filter smaller than 5in by 3¼in should be replaced at least every time the oil is changed. If it is of a good size it should be replaced at least every second oil change or 6,000 miles, whichever comes first. In the case of turbo engines and those regularly driven above 80mph, the filter should be replaced at every oil change.

For engines tuned for performance and economy the standard oil pump will usually suffice, providing gear clearances etc. are within the manufacturer's specifications. Oil pumps do wear out so do not assume that the pump is in good condition because it looks to be all right. Many pumps are none too efficient at idle so do check clearances to ensure good oil flow through the engine at lower rpm. This is most important in turbo engines. Most standard pumps can flow sufficient oil at higher rpm. Usually a relief valve is incorporated within the pump to bleed-off some flow at higher engine speeds. Hence if more flow is needed at high rpm it is a simple matter to increase flow either by fitting a stiffer relief valve spring, or inserting a spacer to increase spring tension. Instead of breaking open at, say, 30 psi the relief valve will not open until oil pressure reaches 40 psi, thus increasing oil flow through the engine. Remember that it takes power and consumes fuel pushing oil through an engine so unless the engine is known to suffer an oil flow problem be content to run with stock oil pressure and flow. Most engines have 40–50 psi oil pressure standard, few require more than 70 psi in full race trim. For road cars I would advise against anything over 60 psi, unless it is higher than this stock, as such high pressures can rupture the oil filter element when the oil is cold as well as unnecessarily consuming power. Even manufacturers have on occasions used oil pumps with excessive pressure. The Pontiac 455–SD engine, for example, has 75–80 psi; most tuners replace this with a 455–HO engine oil pump which has less flow and 60 psi.

As road tyres become more grippy and road suspension designs advance, new

generation cars are generating higher cornering G-forces which causes oil surge problems. Any vehicle with a wet sump (ie. oil reservoir in the sump) will be a candidate for oil surge unless the manufacturer has taken measures with the standard oil pan to prevent surge. Oil surge can occur during violent braking, cornering and acceleration, when the oil can be forced away from the oil pickup, allowing air to be pumped to the engine and turbo bearings. If allowed to go unchecked, bearing failure will result.

Some sump pans are made with vertical baffles, but these have little effect as the oil will rise over them, particularly under hard braking and cornering. For example, at 1 G the oil will be almost vertical, pushing up the side of the sump pan and into the crankcase. A simple solution is to fit a flat, horizontal baffle, as illustrated. It should be no more than a ½in and preferably closer to a ¼in above the full oil level. Ensure that the rods and crank counterweights have sufficient clearance. The baffle should cover the entire oil reservoir area of the oil pan, without any gaps around the edges or in the

Horizontal baffle.

Turned down lip.

A horizontal baffle will prevent oil starvation during vigorous cornering, braking and acceleration manoeuvers. The pickup must be in the centre of the oil reservoir and ¼in off the floor.

corners. A hole large enough for the oil pickup to fit through should be cut as close to the centre of the baffle as possible. This, however, will to some extent be determined by the location and shape of the pickup suction pipe. Around this hole, which also takes care of oil drain back into the reservoir, a ¾in turned down lip is required to discourage oil surging up through the hole. As well, make another small hole large enough for the dipstick to fit through.

To help eliminate oil surge in some engines the oil pickup may also require modification. The actual pickup should be in the centre of the oil reservoir and exactly ¼in off the floor of the pan, taking into consideration the thickness of the sump pan gaskets. If the pickup is closer than ¼in, oil flow into the engine will be restricted, and if it is more than ⅜in air will be sucked in during hard driving with G forces approaching 0.8.

Some people advocate adding on an extra litre of oil to eliminate oil surge, but this is quite wrong. With an overfull sump you are sure to have the crank and rods dipping into the oil every revolution. This consumes power and aerates the oil which can also lead to bearing failure in extreme cases. As well, a lot of oil is thrown up into the cylinders. The rings have to drag it off the bore walls consuming more power and fuel. Then if the rings can't cope with the additional oil it ends up in the combustion chamber, so you will have combustion problems as oil effectively lowers the fuel octane rating. Additionally, the plugs may oil and misfire.

Remember, no matter how good your lubrication most engine wear occurs in the first few minutes after start up so keep the revs down and your foot off the power until the engine is up to operating temperature. Fuel injected engines run very smoothly, even when cold, and unfortunately this can encourage spirited driving at a time when lubrication is quite marginal. If the engine has a carburettor with a manual choke, use as little choke as possible once the vehicle is moving, otherwise a lot of raw fuel will end up down the cylinders, washing away critically needed lubricant. Carburettors with an automatic choke require careful adjustment to ensure that the minimum of choke is used and that it opens fully within about 2 to 3 minutes after starting.

Chapter 13
Cooling

The water, or more correctly called liquid cooling system, is very simple; a radiator, a water pump and a couple of hoses along with a thermostat comprise the system's components. However, the efficiency of the cooling system is dependent on much more than these basic bits. The major deterrent to effective engine cooling is poor heat transfer from the combustion chamber and cylinder due to deposits or air in the cooling system.

Metallic oxides twelve thousandths of an inch thick formed in the water passages will cut heat transfer by up to 40%. In order to maintain optimum heat transfer, the cooling system must contain an inhibitor that will stop corrosion of the water jacket surfaces and the radiator cooling tubes. If the engine has been run for any time without an inhibitor, the cooling system may require chemical cleaning and a high pressure flush to remove deposits.

There are two basic families of inhibitors; chromates and non-chromates. Sodium chromate and potassium dichromate are two of the best and most commonly used water-cooling system inhibitors. Both are highly toxic so handle them with care. Non-chromate inhibitors (borates, nitrates, nitrites) provide anti-corrosion protection in either straight water or water/anti-freeze mixtures. Chromates must not be used in a system containing anti-freeze. Mixed in the correct proportions inhibitors will protect the system for up to one year.

When freeze protection is required, a permanent type anti-freeze must be used. Ethylene glycol is preferred as methyl alcohol-based anti-freeze has a very low boiling point, and it has an adverse effect on radiator hoses and the water pump seals. A 10% glycol/90% water mixture gives freeze protection down to $-3°C$ ($27°F$), a 25% concentration down to $-12°C$ ($10°F$), and a 50% glycol mix down to $-34°C$ ($-29°F$). Cooling solutions composed of more than two-thirds ethylene glycol should not be used as heat transfer is adversely affected. When ethylene glycol anti-freeze is used in concentrations above 30%, additional inhibitor protection against corrosion is not

In colder climates an anti-freeze must be added to the coolant to avoid ruptured radiators and cracked heads and blocks. Concentrations of above 30% anti-freeze also provide cooling system corrosion protection. When anti-freeze isn't used, or if the concentration is lower than 30%, an inhibitor must be added to the coolant to prevent corrosion.   13/1

required. To maintain the correct level of corrosion resistance the cooling solution should be replaced annually.

Anti-freeze containing cooling system sealer additives should not be used, as the sealer may plug the radiator core tubes and possibly even narrow coolant passages in the engine. Stop leak or sealer of any description is not to be recommended, except in an emergency to get you home. Then, as soon as possible, have it cleaned out by a cooling system specialist with a high pressure air and water flusher.

Petroleum-derived products such as soluble oil, often used as a water pump lubricant and corrosion inhibitor, must never be used. A 2% concentration of soluble oil can raise the cylinder head deck temperature by up to 10%, due to reduced heat transfer efficiency of the coolant. New generation engines already run close to detonation, so do not increase this risk by using soluble oil. One popular radiator stop leak contains a high proportion of soluble oil, which is an added reason for staying clear of radiator sealers. Soluble oil turns water milky when added.

The presence of air bubbles in the coolant reduces the heat transfer capacity of the coolant by acting as an insulator. Water pump pumping efficiency is also reduced. Air can be sucked into the cooling system through a leaking hose and gas bubbles can form due to localised boiling around the combustion chamber. In the first case, air can be kept out of the cooling system by ensuring that there are no air or water leaks, and by keeping the coolant at the proper level. When fitted for the first time, new radiator hoses seldom leak at the connections. However, with subsequent re-use there is often some weepage, with the possibility of water loss or air being introduced into the system. To prevent this, thoroughly dry the hoses and clean the internal connecting surface of scale or corrosion particles. Then coat the connecting surface with Permatex No 3 sealer and leave to dry a little for 15 minutes. In the meantime carefully scrape all scale from off the water pump, thermostat and radiator tank hose connection areas. This done, the hoses can be fitted and the clamps tensioned.

Gas bubbles or steam pockets are prevented by pressurising the system to the degree necessary to prevent the coolant boiling. Many wonder why it is necessary to pressurise the cooling system at all as the boiling point of water, at sea level, is 100°C and most cars operate at about 88–95°C. Firstly, the system is pressurised to prevent boiling after the engine is switched off. Once the coolant stops circulating its temperature climbs rapidly to something like 110°C, way past the boiling point of water at normal sea level air pressure of 14.7 psi. If the water boiled each time the engine of every car was stopped we would all be driven crazy by the noise, and cars without a coolant overflow/recovery system would suffer considerable coolant loss.

Secondly, regardless of what the temperature gauge is reading, the coolant temperature is very high in the water passage around the combustion chamber and in particular close to the exhaust valve. The temperature gauge is only giving a reading of the circulating water temperature, which is an average reading. The spot temperature around the exhaust valve seat is well above the boiling point of water, so to prevent this water from boiling and forming a steam pocket, the cooling system has to be pressurised. If the coolant were allowed to boil here, no coolant would contact the combustion chamber and carry heat away. Localised heating would occur, creating thermal stress points that would lead to cracking of the metal. Worse still, the overheated combustion chamber could induce detonation and wreck the pistons. By pressurising the system to 15 psi (105 kPa) the boiling point is raised to approximately 122°C at sea level. Normally, the coolant around the combustion chamber should not reach this temperature, but this allows a margin of safety to permit operation at altitudes above sea level, where the boiling point is reduced. Obviously to maintain the cooling system at the required pressure it will be necessary regularly to inspect the radiator pressure cap for deterioration of the seal and also check the "blow-off" pressure.

As the actual heat exchange between the cooling medium and the air takes place at the radiator, it is important that it is free of bugs or other debris that would restrict air flow, and hence reduce cooling efficiency.

Another deterrent to good air flow through the radiator is a flow path blocked by such things as the licence plate and auxiliary lights. A number of new generation cars have only a relatively small under-bumper air inlet so do not restrict air flow to the radiator by partially blocking that air inlet with a pair of fog lights. The radiating efficiency will be maintained if the radiator is regularly re-painted with matt black paint. This will serve to increase the life of the core as well, by reducing external corrosion.

A high temperature thermostat which maintains coolant temperature at 88–95°C is usually fitted to production cars. Such a thermostat is fine if you want good heater efficiency in winter, but a thermostat rated at about 74°C will usually better serve the interests of power and economy. The inlet charge will remain cooler, because the inlet port is cooler, permitting a little more compression and/or spark advance before running into detonation. Some engines, though, will not show a drop in coolant temperature when a cooler thermostat is fitted. This occurs when the manufacturer fits a radiator just large enough to maintain the coolant at 90°C in summer. The only way around this problem is to fit a radiator with more cooling tubes. Never run a road engine without a thermostat. The engine will take too long to warm up, and except in summer it will not reach normal operating temperature. As a result engine wear is accelerated, and on carburated engines there will be less power and diluted engine oil due to reduced fuel vaporisation.

A big clutch type fan can consume up to 10hp and reduce fuel economy. Such a fan is best replaced by one or two electric fans.

The cooling fan consumes a good deal of power which can be used beneficially to reduce fuel consumption and improve performance. At 2500rpm a big fan, even a flex blade or silicone slip clutch type, can drain up to 10hp. Unless the engine is working under a heavy load, a road speed of about 30mph will provide sufficient moving air to cool the engine without the aid of a fan. Naturally if you engage in peak hour city driving, a cooling fan will be required. Preferably, in the interests of power and economy, an electric fan should be fitted. Alternatively, if the car is equipped with an air conditioner it may already have a small auxiliary fan fitted in front of the condenser which is large enough to cool the engine in traffic. Usually these fans are preset to switch on when the coolant reaches 100°C, but if the thermostatically-controlled switch is by-passed by a dash-mounted toggle switch, the fan can be manually activated at any time. I've used this system on my cars for years without any problems. At times in very heavy traffic in hot weather I've had to switch off the air conditioner for short periods otherwise the engine would overheat. This could be rectified by fitting another small electric fan, but I never seem to get around to doing it.

If you wish to retain a standard slip clutch-type fan, in spite of the power which it consumes and the noise which it makes, do ensure that it is working correctly. This type of fan will not function correctly for ever; the clutch unit and bearings wear, allowing the fan to lock up at higher rpm when it should be slipping to reduce power loss. Usually, if this type of fan is still roaring at 2500rpm and higher, the clutch assembly is locked up due to an internal failure. This is not a positive test, but it usually indicates that further investigation should be made, so consult the workshop manual.

One problem which I see from time to time is that of head gaskets with enlarged water passages. I've seen gaskets with larger holes punched into them by tuners who should know better and I've also seen high performance and race head gaskets which have been manufactured with water passages much larger than stock. Apparently these people reasoned that as there is, say, a ½in coolant hole in the block and a corresponding ½in hole in the head then you must get better water flow, and hence

The six small white holes in this head gasket are vent holes. Opening them out to the size of the corresponding large holes in the head and block upsets coolant flow and reduces cooling efficiency.

better cooling, by enlarging the coolant passage in the head gasket to ½in also. This is totally wrong reasoning; with the exception of the coolant holes at the extreme rear of the engine, all of the holes in the block deck and the head are made large to make it easier to get the core sand out at the end of the casting process. To vent air which would otherwise be trapped in the block small vent holes, usually 0.060 to 0.125in diameter, are punched in the head gasket to correspond with these large core holes. Note that these small holes are primarily intended to vent air trapped in the top of the block; they are not coolant flow holes, although naturally there is some coolant flow through them.

Enlarging these head gasket vent holes just upsets the flow path of coolant through the engine with the result that the front cylinders run too cool and the rear cylinders run too hot, with the risk of detonation. The flow path of water through the engine is simple enough to follow. Coolant from the radiator is fed to the water pump and is forced into the front of the cylinder block. Then the coolant flows toward the rear of the block, picking up heat as it goes. When it reaches the rear of the block, the water moves up into the head through the large water passages interconnecting the block and head. From here it flows forward past the combustion chambers and ports, out through the thermostat and into the top of the radiator. From this description you will understand that any coolant passages at the front of the block just upset the flow path by allowing water to flow up into the head before it reaches the rear of the block. With reduced flow past the rear cylinders and combustion chambers these run too hot; the compression ratio and spark timing have to be cut back to avoid detonation. Conversely, the front cylinders are overcooled and lose power. Hence it should be obvious that we want only minimal water flow from the front of the block into the head if we are aiming for performance and economy.

Unfortunately some car manufacturers don't care too much about the coolant flow path with the result that their head gaskets are all stamped with large vent holes right from the front to the rear. There are two ways around this problem; the solution which I prefer is to tap the large core holes in the block, except at the rear, and screw in aluminum pipe plugs into which I have drilled a 2mm vent hole. The other solution is quite effective, in fact it can be used in conjunction with the first solution, but can only be applied to cars with a continuous flow heater system ie. a heater system which has water flowing through it even when the heater is turned off. In this case the rear of the cylinder head is tapped to accept a heater hose fitting. By connecting the heater inlet to this fitting a constant flow of coolant passes over the rear combustion chambers, bringing their temperature closer to those at the front of the engine.

To some people all of this concern over coolant flow may appear to be a lot of effort, but if you are really serious about economy and power you have to be able to equalise, as much as practicable, combustion chamber temperatures so as to run maximum compression ratio and spark advance.

Chapter 14
Pollution Control and the Law

Many enthusiasts feel that the motor car has been singled out, perhaps unjustly, as a major contributor to the pollution problem of our industrialised world. Because this is perceived to be discriminatory, car enthusiasts and a number of motoring journalists have adopted an anti-establishment attitude toward pollution laws. They figure that anything which the government has to force upon us is no good, and as a consequence all pollution controls tend to be viewed in the same light. To back up their conviction they point to the nasty engines which the people of the USA had to put up with during the 1970s. Emissions engines have come a long way since then so it is foolish to develop opinions based on outmoded data. Good performance and economy can be realised working within the constraints imposed by pollution laws. In some localities these laws are rigidly enforced; in other places there is virtually no enforcement. Whatever the situation locally, enthusiasts have an obligation to modify their vehicles with due regard to the spirit of the law so as to not unnecessarily foul our environment.

The major pollutants are: carbon monoxide (CO), hydrocarbons (HC), nitrogen oxides (NOx), ozone (O_3), sulphur dioxide (SO_2), lead and particulates. Petrol fueled engines emit CO, HC and NOx primarily, plus some particulate matter, and lead if leaded fuel is used. Diesels produce CO and HC at lower levels, but emit much more particulate matter and NOx. In certain sizes particulates, tiny solid particles of soot, can lodge in the lungs and cause long-term damage. They also discolour the sky. Coal-fired furnaces are primarily responsible for SO_2 emissions, which appear to cause acid rain, plus the release of NOx.

Hydrocarbons are any of a number of compounds containing hydrogen and carbon, usually derived from petroleum. Just the vapours released when tanks are being refilled with petrol releases a large amount of HC into the atmosphere. Carbon monoxide is a poisonous gas that is both odourless and colourless. This is the gas which kills if the engine is run for a period in a closed up garage so obviously we don't want much of it in the air we breathe. The nitrogen oxides are composed of about 10% nitrogen dioxide (NO_2) and the rest is nitric oxide (NO). NO_2 is a toxic gas with a pungent smell and brown colour that is a by-product of any combustion process. In the air it may combine with hydroxyl (OH) to produce nitric acid (HNO_3). Obviously in either form it is not good for us or the environment. Nitric oxide on the other hand is non-toxic, colourless and odourless. However, it too has an undesirable side. The initial reaction in the atmosphere is for NO to reduce ozone (O_3) into oxygen (O_2) and the spare O atom combines with the NO to form NO_2, nitrogen dioxide. The reaction continues beyond this under the influence of sunlight which breaks the NO_2 down into NO and O. The O combines with oxygen in the atmosphere to make more ozone. Ozone is the stuff which makes your lungs hurt on smoggy days and it kills crops. It also wrecks the exterior of cars, in particular chrome and rubber.

To reduce these pollutants governments around the world have enacted, or are in the process of enacting, clean air regulations which require vehicle emissions to be below a certain maximum level. The standard varies from country to country and even from state to state according to the perceived degree of the problem. In some cities in California, for example, the smog problem is very serious. Accordingly, that state has much tougher emissions laws than the rest of the USA, and the laws are more rigidly enforced.

The actual test procedures vary in different countries and as it is the manufacturer that certifies new models before they are released onto the market I won't describe in detail exactly what is involved in obtaining certification. The basic test takes place with the vehicle on a chassis dyno which is loaded to a prescribed schedule to simulate certain city driving conditions. The test usually involves one cold start and a hot start, plus a number of idle, acceleration, cruise and deceleration phases over a 20 to 30 minute drive. The test fuel type is specified for uniformity.

During the dyno "drive" the exhaust gas is mixed with atmospheric air and routed through a constant volume pump which mixes and measures the flow. A specified proportion of the mixture is collected in a bag and after the test the contents are analysed for HC, CO and NOx concentrations. To avoid errors, air in the test cell is constantly sampled in a "background" bag so that pollutants in the atmospheric air can be ascertained and subtracted from the tailpipe sample.

The test to which enthusiasts cars may be subjected is much simpler. It is often referred to as a "sniff" test. In the few places where this test is carried out to determine the legality or otherwise of a car, it may be performed at random by the roadside or at specified intervals of 1 or 2 years as part of the vehicle licence registration inspection. For the sniffer test a probe is placed in the tailpipe and a CO and HC reading is taken with the engine idling. The test instrument is of the non-dispersive infra red type which considering its relative low cost gives fairly accurate readings. Note that with this type of testing NOx levels are not checked, so it is not too difficult to get a modified engine to pass if it is in good mechanical condition and correctly tuned.

A much more difficult inspection for enthusiasts is the 'visual' which in some places complements the sniff test. The problem for a number of enthusiasts is that their cars can have the appearance of being illegal. If the vehicle looks like a street racer with excessively wide wheels, gaudy decorations and loud exhaust, it will be given "special" treatment come inspection time. Engine/chassis numbers will be checked and charts consulted to find what size engine should be fitted; what number

196

of carby venturis there should be; what transmission should be fitted etc. In addition, a careful check will be made to ensure that all pollution equipment listed for that particular model is in place and actually working. If it isn't, the vehicle will fail even though it may have passed the sniff test.

On the other hand a tastefully modified car is generally treated as for a standard model. Engine/chassis numbers may be compared with those appearing on the owner's registration papers and then a quick underbonnet visual will be carried out, usually without any check being made that the emissions parts are working. If what appears to be a standard air filter is in place, the carburettor probably won't be scrutinized either.

Obviously it is up to the individual enthusiast to become informed of just what the emission laws are in his area and then personally investigate their interpretation and enforcement at the local level as there can be wide variance in this from one area to another. It is beyond the scope of this book to define how emissions laws will be applied from city to city, from province to province, from state to state or from country to country. Rather the purpose of this book is primarily to inform the enthusiast just how to modify new generation engines for power and economy. In addition, in this chapter I have set out how the engine can be tuned to pass emission inspections; however, it should be noted that such procedures could be illegal according to the strictest interpretation of the law in some places.

There are three major types of car emissions which governments have attempted to address: crankcase emissions, evaporative emissions and exhaust emissions.

The PCV valve was the first emissions device added to engines, about 30 years ago.

Almost thirty years ago crankcase emissions began to be legislated against. Prior to this, engines had a simple open road-draught vent tube to release blow-by vapours from the sump into the atmosphere. These vapours contain unburned hydrocarbons and carbon monoxide at very high levels. In fact the experts say about one third of all vehicular pollution was in the form of crankcase emissions. To overcome the problem what today is called the PCV system (Positive Crankcase Ventilation) was devised. Air from the air filter case enters the engine via a tube connected to the rocker cover. This air mixes with the crankcase vapours and exits the engine through a PCV valve and tube connected to the inlet manifold to be burned as part of the inlet charge. The PCV system works very effectively and does not contribute to power or economy losses. The PCV valve is quite reliable but should be periodically checked as it will at times become gummed up and stick. This allows an excess of air to flow into the inlet manifold, upsetting the fuel/air ratio at idle and cruise in particular.

About ten years later the problem of evaporative emissions was tackled. As the term suggests, evaporative emissions are emissions due to the evaporation of hydrocarbon fuel. All of the vapour haze which you see being vented from your car's filler neck when refueling is, in fact, a part of our pollution problem. Additional to this, vapours escape from the carburettor, particularly when the fuel percolates in the bowl from underbonnet heat after the engine is stopped. To lessen these problems a number of measures have been taken by manufacturers which in no way reduce performance or economy; with the exception of one modification that is applied to only a smaller number of carburated engines.

The heart of the evaporative emission system is the charcoal canister. It has a volume of about 2 litres and is filled with charcoal granules. To this canister are

The charcoal canister collects vapours from the fuel tank and carburettor which would otherwise be released into the atmosphere.

connected vent lines from the carb fuel bowl and the fuel tank. During refueling a large volume of vapour is trapped inside a bell within the fuel tank. This is then transferred to the charcoal canister to be absorbed onto the surfaces of the granules. When the car is restarted, the vapours are sucked, via a line connecting the canister to the inlet manifold, into the engine to be burnt. Vapours from the carburettor are handled in the same manner and subsequently made part of the combustion process. The most basic evaporative emissions systems purge the canister of vapours whenever the engine is running, although this can lead to unacceptably high exhaust emissions at start-up and idle, so many systems now incorporate a valve to permit purging only when the engine is up to temperature and running at above idle rpm.

Some engines have excessively high emissions at start and idle because of being equipped with a carburettor having large volume fuel bowls. Naturally enough big bowls such as on Holley carbs contain a lot of fuel which can be converted to vapour during hot soak conditions. To reduce such vapour emissions stuffers are at times inserted in the fuel bowl and also the metering block, purely to reduce their volume. These stuffers can cause hot start problems and slower full throttle acceleration because of insufficient fuel volume being available to meet the engine's needs. The stuffers may have to be removed to avoid fuel starvation under such conditions.

Exhaust emissions systems are quite complex when compared with those which control crankcase and evaporative emissions. Basically, there are three exhaust pollutants which have to be kept in check: carbon monoxide (CO), unburned hydrocarbons (HC) and nitrogen oxides (NOx).

CO is produced when there isn't enough oxygen to complete the combustion process. In general terms it is correct to say the richer the mixture, the higher the levels of CO. However, even when the air/fuel mix is at the stoichiometric or chemically correct ratio of 14.7:1, carbon monoxide will be formed due to non-uniform fuel droplet sizes, cylinder to cylinder distribution differences, scavenging differences, and combustion differences.

Unburned hydrocarbons, as the name suggests, arise from fuel which hasn't burned on its way through the engine. Obviously a rich mixture will increase HC emissions but one of the more common causes of high HC levels is a misfire in one or more cylinders. Just one cylinder misfiring can increase HC levels by 500% so obviously the plugs and the rest of the ignition system must be in perfect order. Apart from ignition deficiencies, a weak mixture will also cause a misfire, so this too has to be avoided. As is explained later, additional spark advance and the high vacuum produced under deceleration conditions up the HC.

Nitrogen oxides are produced in the engine under conditions of high temperature and high pressure, hence engine modifications which increase the temperature and pressure of combustion raise the level of NOx. The tendency to form this pollutant is increased with engine loadings – raise the engine load and up goes the NOx. Also with increased availability of oxygen, as with a lean mixture, NOx concentrations rise.

To lower the levels of these pollutants vehicle manufacturers have resorted to a number of controls and engine modifications. Some of these changes have been beneficial, improving economy and cold driveability, others have reduced performance and economy while lowering emissions.

Carburettors are jetted to provide leaner mixtures, particularly in the part 199 throttle range, and other devices such as dashpots and throttle retarders have been added to reduce emissions, particularly of HC, during deceleration. The high manifold vacuums produced under closed throttle over-run conditions can indirectly lead to misfiring, with a resultant increase in HC. To eliminate this barely perceptible misfiring, manufacturers have resorted to a number of controls, either in combination or singly. One device shuts off fuel flow at high vacuum. With no fuel entering the engine there aren't any unburned hydrocarbons and as a bonus economy improves. However, there is a jerk when the vacuum level drops and fuel flow recommences. A more common device is the throttle retarder which initially holds the throttle partly open and then allows it to close slowly. It doesn't have any effect on performance or economy but I personally don't like it because it seriously reduces the engine braking effect normally associated with lifting off the throttle. I find it quite an unnerving experience to crest a hill at speed and find the rear of a slow moving 18 wheeler just ahead which you imagine you may soon be under as you lift off the throttle and feel the car accelerate as the retarder holds the throttle open.

The other problem time for a carburated engine is at cold start. If the choke is held open for some time to give smooth performance, emissions are excessive; when it is closed quickly to lower emissions, cold driveabilitity is poor. To improve cold performance two systems are usually employed, one is dubbed APH (Air Pre-Heat) and the other EFE (Early Fuel Evaporation). The APH system uses heat from the

Vacuum diaphragm and air direction valve.

Thermostatic valve.

Manifold vacuum.

Cold air enters stove.

Exhaust manifold.

In colder climates the APH system aids driveability when the engine is cold by using exhaust manifold heat to warm the inlet air and improve fuel vaporisation and distribution. The disadvantage is that the standard air filter restricts high speed air flow.

exhaust manifold to heat the inlet air, improving vaporisation and cylinder to cylinder distribution. As illustrated, a thermostatic vacuum valve in the air filter case regulates the temperature of air entering the carburettor by means of an air control valve and diaphragm in the air filter snorkel. Below about 30°C underhood, the valve admits only pre-heated air. Above this temperature the valve allows in some cool air until at 50°C it fully closes off and admits only cool air. The system functions very reliably and greatly improves cold driveability. The main problem is reduced performance due to air flow being restricted by the standard air filter case.

The EFE system is more commonly found on V8 and inline 6 cylinder engines. It uses hot exhaust gases to heat the inlet manifold and improve fuel vaporisation and distribution. The EFE system should not be confused with the earlier manifold heating systems which basically operate full time. Being unregulated, such systems reduce maximum performance by adding heat to the inlet charge even when a cool mixture for good power is required. A modification of this early system is found on some inline 6 cylinder engines. Rather than having exhaust gas directed at the base of the inlet manifold full time it has a weighted flap in the hot box to regulate the flow of hot gas to the inlet manifold. Under full power conditions the high volume of exhaust flow overcomes the influence of the weighted flap and closes off the hot box, thus preventing the hot gas flowing directly under the inlet manifold. This system too is most unsatisfactory from a performance viewpoint. Because the inlet and exhaust manifolds are bolted together as a common unit a lot of heat still got into the inlet charge, even when the hot box was closed off. Worse, the flap often seized with time, allowing heat to the manifold full time, and because of the two-way design of the flap, it blocked off half the flow area of the exhaust manifold, further reducing performance.

To overcome these problems and still get the benefits of exhaust heat to the inlet

Diaphragm actuator and exhaust direction valves.

Thermo - vacuum valve.

Inlet manifold heat passage.

Manifold vacuum.

The EFE system allows quicker choke opening times by using exhaust gas heat to warm the base of the inlet manifold, thus keeping the fuel vaporised. When the coolant temperature reaches 70°C, the diaphragm actuator is denied vacuum. It then opens the exhaust manifold valve and closes the heat passage valve, restoring normal exhaust flow.

manifold from cold starts, the EFE system was developed. As illustrated, a thermo-vacuum valve permits inlet vacuum to draw on a diaphragm actuator when the engine is cold. With inline 6 cylinder engines the actuator closes a butterfly in one exhaust outlet, for cylinders 1, 2 and 3, completely blocking it off, and opens another butterfly

The EFE actuator which operates butterfly valves to divert exhaust flow to heat the inlet manifold.

which allows the hot exhaust gas to flow at the base of the inlet manifold and exit through the exhaust outlet for cylinders 4, 5 and 6. When the coolant temperature reaches about 70°C, the thermo-vacuum valve closes, blocking vacuum to the diaphragm actuator. The actuator then opens the exhaust outlet butterfly and closes the butterfly at the base of the inlet manifold, preventing any further heating of the inlet charge. The system functions very reliably and effectively reduces emissions while improving cold driveability. About the only problem which does regularly arise is that of vacuum lines being connected to the wrong ports of the thermo-vacuum valve. When this is done, the actuator cannot vent through the valve and so stays in the heat-on mode. To check for this problem bring the engine up to temperature while watching to see the actuator actually move to the heat-off position. If it doesn't move, pull the vacuum hose off the actuator. If it moves with the hose disconnected and there is no vacuum sensed when you put a finger over the end of the hose, the hoses are connected to the wrong thermo-vacuum valve ports. Vacuum at the hose would indicate that the thermo-vacuum valve has failed if the coolant is above 85°C.

With Vee-type engines the EFE system works in a similar way. A butterfly partially or completely blocks the exhaust outlet on one side of the engine, forcing the hot gas through the heat passage of the inlet manifold and then out the other exhaust manifold when the engine is cold. When up to temperature the actuator opens the butterfly, allowing normal exhaust flow. The problem, however, is that the inlet manifold heat passage is not blocked by a butterfly as with inline 6 cylinder engines so some exhaust flow continues to heat the inlet mixture at all times. This is good for economy but it reduces maximum power, so what I recommend for those living in warmer climates is to block off the actuator vacuum hose with a ball bearing to render it inoperative. Next, fit a heavy-duty inlet manifold gasket with a blocked heat passage to one cylinder head to prevent exhaust flow through the inlet manifold. Use a normal gasket on the other head so that some heat is available to warm the manifold when the engine is cold.

Retarded ignition timing is an effective means of reducing unburned HC emissions because exhaust gas temperatures increase significantly with retarded spark. The hot gases ignite the hydrocarbons on their passage through the exhaust so that they are more completely burned, thus lowering HC emissions. Unfortunately, retarded timing also reduces power and economy, so action is needed to get the spark advance back up to the necessary angle. Basically, in non-computerised systems the manufacturers retard the spark at idle and part throttle cruise by various switches and thermo-vacuum valves, and by using ported rather than manifold vacuum to activate the distributor vacuum advance mechanism.

The basic components of the system are a Transmission Controlled Spark (TCS) solenoid, cold feed switch, thermo-vacuum valve, transmission switch and a maze of vacuum hoses. The illustration sets out how the system functions. Basically, unless the transmission is in top gear and the head temperature is above 68°C, no ported vacuum is permitted past the thermo-vacuum valve or the TCS solenoid to the distributor. Only at idle with the coolant temperature above 104°C is full manifold vacuum permitted in the interests of lowering the coolant temperature. To restore full manifold vacuum advance to the distributor, disconnect the vacuum hose from the canister and insert a ball bearing or plug it with silicone sealant and then discreetly route another

Ported vacuum above throttle plate.

Manifold vacuum below throttle plate.

Vacuum connections below the throttle plate or into the inlet manifold are called manifold vacuum. Connections before the throttle plate are a ported vacuum source.

vacuum hose directly from the inlet manifold to the distributor. This ensures that full manifold vacuum, not ported vacuum, is reaching the distributor at all times.

Some tuners prefer to route ported vacuum rather than manifold vacuum to the canister. As Table 14.1 indicates, the amount of vacuum available from either source is

TABLE 14.1 Vacuum comparison test

	Ported vacuum	Manifold vacuum
Cruise on level road at 50 to 70mph	14–20in Hg	13–14in Hg
Cruise up long steady gradient at 50 to 60mph	8–9in Hg	7–8in Hg
Maximum acceleration	0in Hg	0in Hg
Moderate acceleration	10in Hg	9in Hg
Idle	0in Hg	18in Hg
Deceleration from 70mph	7in Hg	25in Hg

similar under most engine operating conditions, except idle and over-run deceleration at 70mph. The high manifold vacuum under over-run conditions will give maximum vacuum advance, about 16° on this particular test engine, while ported vacuum will give no advance (Table 14.2). Less advance under these conditions is obviously good for emissions. However, at idle there isn't any vacuum with ported connections, but with manifold vacuum connected there is 18in Hg because of the mild Phase 1 cam. This will provide an additional 16° advance to smooth out the idle and allow a leaner idle mixture. In normal highway driving this won't contribute much to economy but around town, stopped at the lights or with the air conditioner on, fuel economy could improve by 10% with manifold vacuum connected. With one of my cars this simple modification lifted city economy with the air on to within 6% of what was being achieved on the highway.

TABLE 14.2 Vacuum advance canister specifications on test engine

Vacuum (in Hg)	Canister advance
5	0°
7.5	0°
10	6.5°
12.5	13°
15 plus	16°

The other problem when ported vacuum is connected to modified engines is that a little too much vacuum is created under cruise conditions. This in turn gives more advance and may lead to pinging unless the distributor is recurved or a different advance canister is fitted. This additional expense can often be avoided by connecting manifold vacuum to the distributor.

The EGR valve meters exhaust gases into the inlet system to lower NOx emissions.

The main modification added to reduce NOx emissions is exhaust gas recirculation (EGR). By metering up to 4% of the exhaust back into the inlet manifold to be mixed with the fuel/air charge, peak combustion temperatures are lowered, thus reducing the formation of NOx. The system is very simple comprising a thermo-vacuum valve, an EGR valve and sometimes a signal amplifier to modify the vacuum signal. When the engine reaches operating temperature the thermo-vacuum valve opens, permitting ported vacuum to control the EGR valve. Below about 4in Hg the valve is closed, and it is usually fully open at 9in Hg.

Obviously the inclusion of exhaust gas in the inlet charge is good for neither power nor economy. The gas is non-combustable and gets between the oxygen molecules and the fuel particles, slowing the rate of combustion. The other problem is that exhaust gas is hot so it adds heat to the inlet charge, causing it to expand and thus reduces cylinder filling.

To stop the EGR valve from operating, a ball bearing can be inserted in the vacuum hose. However, when this is done, the car may no longer pass careful "visuals" so a more discreet modification may be called for which still permits EGR operation. Remove the EGR valve and plug either the inlet manifold exhaust outlet port, the inlet manifold exhaust inlet port or the EGR valve outlet. I prefer to plug the inlet manifold exhaust outlet as it is usually round and a suitable size brass welch plug (freeze plug) is easy to fit. With the port plugged the EGR valve will operate normally but no exhaust gas will be allowed through. Note that if the vacuum line is blocked with a ball bearing the EGR valve should be removed and checked to ensure that it is closing fully as a jammed or eroded pintle will allow exhaust leakage to the inlet manifold.

EGR flow is easily prevented by inserting a welch plug into this round hole in the inlet manifold.

With no EGR some engines have a tendency to ping when climbing gentle hills at part throttle. This can be overcome by using a vacuum advance canister which commences advancing at vacuum levels above about 9 to 11in Hg. Alternatively, the distributor advance rate may be slowed.

The air injection reactor (AIR) system accomplishes additional burning in the exhaust manifold to lower both CO and HC emissions. A belt-driven air pump and an air manifold deliver air to each exhaust port. The extra air along with the very high exhaust temperatures caused by retarding the spark oxidise the carbon monoxide and the unburned hydrocarbons.

In itself the actual AIR system doesn't cut power or economy to any significant degree. Actually, in turbo engines the additional heat and gas volume assists the turbo spool up boost more quickly at lower rpm. What does reduce power in naturally-aspirated engines is the fact that a large area of exhaust port is blocked off by the reactor nozzle and support boss when these are located in the cylinder head. (With a small number of engines the nozzle is inserted in the exhaust manifold).

Except in turbo installations, good power and economy are not really possible if the reactor nozzles and attendant bosses in the exhaust ports are left in place. The air manifold has to be removed and the bosses ground out of the exhaust ports. When the standard cast iron exhaust manifold is left in place enough heat will be retained in the exhaust gas to give some afterburn and cut HC and CO concentrations.

Naturally those vehicles which are subject to "visuals" will have to retain the AIR equipment. What must be done is to cut the nozzle off flush with the bosses, or shorter if possible. Weld their ends closed and drill a couple of holes in the underside

of the air manifold where they cannot be seen. This will allow air from the pump to be exhausted without building up pressure. With this done, screw the nozzles into the head and grind away as much of the bosses as is practical, giving consideration to the metal thickness in the top of the exhaust ports and the need to adequately support the air manifold.

The greatest advancement in the reduction of exhaust emissions came with the introduction of the catalytic converter. A catalyst is an element or compound that helps promote a chemical reaction without actively taking part in it. These catalysts are of the oxidising type, helping oxidise CO and HC into water (H_2O) and carbon dioxide (CO_2) in the case of the early two-way converters. The latest three-way converters also convert NOx emissions into harmless nitrogen (N).

With CAT-equipped cars it is usual for the fuel/air mixture to be a little richer at part throttle to ensure that a reaction takes place. The ignition is also often advanced a little more and this, along with the more combustable inlet mix, improves driveability and economy. Some of the latest three-way converters have air injection at the converter for a more effective reaction.

Within the converter canister is a fine ceramic honeycomb with a surface area estimated to be the size of several football fields. This huge area is coated with a microscopically thin layer of a mixture of the noble metals platinum, palladium and rhodium. As the exhaust gases flow over the surface, the exhaust heat and the excess oxygen present in the exhaust from the air pump trigger an oxidisation process. The honeycomb is very fine but there is no appreciable back pressure when the converter is new and internally clean. With time, however, combustion by-products from the burning fuel and engine oil do reduce the flow area available. Although not to be recommended, when this occurs a number of enthusiasts and tuners convert the CAT to a straight-through type by knocking a bar with a 2in cutter attached through the honeycomb.

The flow problem with catalytic converters is much more serious in vehicles with engines over about 3 litres. Therefore a twin exhaust with dual converters should be fitted if enough underfloor space exists. However, this action could mean failing the "visual" in some areas so before investing the large amount of money involved in new CATs and a dual system it would be wise to check on this point.

In modern CATs a good deal of the flow problem is due to turbulence at the entry and exit. (The older pellet-filled converters are very restrictive and should be replaced by a honeycomb type.) Sometimes the restriction is due to very sharp bends at the entry or exit, which are necessary to fit the CAT in the space available up near the front of the car. If you can reposition the converter so as to eliminate tight exhaust bends, flow will improve a good deal. Even when there are no tight bends, flow through the converter is still relatively poor because the CAT causes the exhaust gases to diverge and then converge too quickly. Frequently the exhaust diverges into the converter honeycomb section at an angle of 35° to 60°. Because the gases are travelling very fast, they break away from the tapered converter walls, causing severe turbulence, and flow loss results. Similarly, when the gases pass from the honeycomb, they are forced to converge at an angle that is too great, and more flow turbulence is produced. To overcome this, the tapered ends of the CAT should be cut off and megaphone-like sections added to give a gentle entry and exit taper. As illustrated, the inlet walls ideally should diverge at a fairly shallow angle of only 5° to 8°. However, when space is a problem, up to 12° is acceptable. For the exit the taper can be much more severe; 207

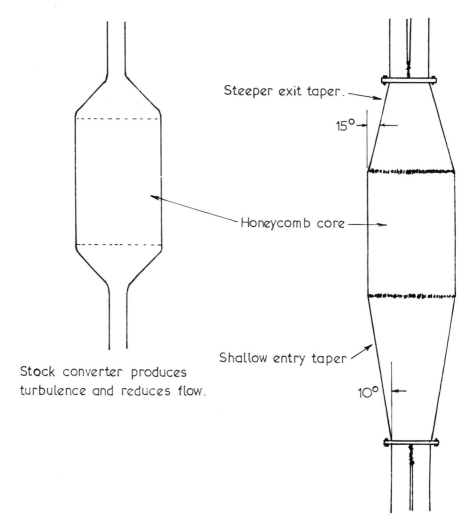

Steeper exit taper.

15°

Honeycomb core

Shallow entry taper

10°

Stock converter produces
turbulence and reduces flow.

Turbulence in the entry and exit of catalytic converters cause a considerable restriction to exhaust flow. If it is not illegal to modify the CAT, megaphone-like sections should be welded on after the standard entry and exit have been cut away.

10° to 12° is ideal but up to 15° is okay. Modified in this way the converter flow rate is doubled.

When it is necessary to use a single CAT in dual exhaust applications, the twin pipes should enter and exit the megaphone extensions side by side as shown, rather than first joining into a single large diameter pipe. This increases exhaust flow and allows fairly short megaphone extensions which are much easier to accommodate under the average car.

Another way around the flow problem if you are not subject to a visual is to move the CAT from the usual location at the front of the floorpan to the rear just in front of the back axle. With more distance for the exhaust gases to cool down and contract, the flow restriction won't be so great. Because there is less heat in the system, the CAT will not work so effectively, but with some of the tricks that are covered later, the car should be able to clear the "sniff" test. Note that when the CAT is moved, the muffler should be placed at the rear of the car.

All cars equipped with CATs must not use leaded petrol or any fuel additive which will "poison" the catalyst. The experts claim that a tank of leaded is enough to seriously impair the converter's effectiveness. Because you probably want to get rid of some of the other emissions devices you may need a functioning CAT to pass sniffer testing. Hence if you are going to run leaded for weekend competition, remove the CAT and insert a length of exhaust tube in its place.

When a vehicle fails the sniff test or if a fail is probable, there are a number of steps which can be taken to get through. Obviously a full tune-up is a necessity. Fit new spark plugs at least one grade hotter than standard and open the gap up to the manufacturer's specifications. Remove these "test" plugs as soon as the inspection is over, and don't be tempted to do any hard driving either to or from the test station. Before the plugs are packed away, oil their threads. If the air filter element is dirty now is the time to replace it. Check the carburettor float level and ensure that the needle and seat is not weeping. Remember that it only takes a little excess fuel to push the HC and CO readings way up. To get extra heat into the exhaust for an afterburn of HC and CO, insert a ball bearing into the distributor vacuum hose. This will take out anything from 10° to 20° advance at idle so the engine idle speed will drop right back. Turn the idle speed screw in a half turn or more to bring the idle speed up around 850 to 950rpm. Now lean the mixture by adjusting the mixture screws about a quarter turn. Ensure that the choke is opening right off. Getting the coolant temperature up will improve fuel vaporisation and distribution at idle as well as raising the exhaust temperature, so place the piece of cardboard in front of the radiator which is large enough to bring the coolant up around 95 to 100°C. Table 14.3 sets out a few things to check for according to the HC and CO test readings.

TABLE 14.3 Check list for failed sniff test

Meter Reading	Check for
High HC and high CO	Rich fuel/air mixture, incorrect float setting or leaky needle valve, leaky power valve or gasket, restricted PCV valve, choke not fully off.
High HC and low CO	Air leak in induction system, cracked vacuum hoses, worn throttle spindles, broken manifold gasket or carb base gasket.
High HC and normal CO	Low compression because of worn rings or valves, fouled spark plugs, pitted points, faulty condenser, cracked distributor cap, advanced timing or sometimes excessively retarded timing.

Correctly-tuned engines which have been modified with economy in mind as well as performance should not normally have too much difficulty passing either the idle or high speed (2500rpm) sniff test in ordinary tune. If you have to resort to the standard tricks mentioned above, the engine probably has some of the problems listed   209 in Table 14.3. Naturally if the engine has been radically modified, even more radical tricks may be called for. Inline 6 cylinder engines can easily have more heat put into both the inlet and exhaust system by switching the EFE system vacuum lines at the thermo-vacuum valve. The switch must be made just prior to testing, when the engine is still cold, otherwise the actuator will not lock into the heat-on position. With more heat in the inlet system, fuel vaporisation and cylinder to cylinder distribution is better, thus reducing both HC and CO readings. The EFE butterfly blocking off one manifold outlet increases exhaust flow resistance, decreases exhaust heat loss and improves exhaust afterburn to further reduce emission levels.

Another approach is to run a special "test" fuel. Alcohol, either ethanol or methanol, burns significantly lower emissions of both HC and CO than petrol. The NOx levels are higher but at present only the manufacturers are subjected to NOx testing. By blending 15 to 25% alcohol into your petrol, the tailpipe readings will go down because the alcohol will lean out the mixture as well as burn cleaner. When purchasing the alcohol, buy a sealed 5 gallon drum from a distributor who has a high turnover of racing fuel. This should ensure that it hasn't absorbed any moisture from the atmosphere. Any water contamination makes it very difficult to blend. If you are going to use a 20/80 mix, pour 1 gallon of alcohol into a 5 gallon drum containing 4 gallons of petrol and give it a good shake. Pour a sample into a clear glass jar and check for separation or layering after a couple of hours. If its okay, drain your fuel tank and refill with the blend. Some carb adjustment may be necessary to bring the idle speed to that required. When there is a problem with fuel separation due to water in the alcohol, 3 to 4% acetone added will assist in blending. Note that alcohol is a very effective paint stripper so if any spillage occurs; wash it off, don't wipe, immediately.

Some people no doubt feel that performance tuning and/or the modification of emissions equipment is not compatible with our need for clean air. However, a closer look will show that this is generally not the case. There are many, many cars running on our roads today which if sniff tested would fail simply because of poor maintenance. Just one misfiring plug or a bad ignition lead will push up HC emissions 500%, yet how many people do you know who drive cars with a misfire. Enthusiasts tune their cars often and replace parts as required so they do not contribute to pollution in this way. The same principle applies with regard to engine wear. Worn rings and valves significantly increase HC concentrations, but as enthusiasts are seeking performance they keep the engines in their cars "freshened up". Irregular oil change periods allow the oil to breakdown, increasing blow-by. This too raises tailpipe emmisions, but few enthusiasts are guilty because they care about engines and know how important is new oil.

It may be true that the ordinary motorist has left the pollution gear on his car. However, again due to lack of maintenance and/or care, a lot of it isn't working anyway and to compound the problem the automatic choke is probably sticking half on. No doubt you have followed many cars in the city through a number of sets of lights, belching black smoke because the choke is still on. All that smoke shows that the HC and CO is very high.

When an engine is modified, a number of changes actually lower, rather than increase emissions. Increasing the compression ratio, for example, pushes the NOx levels up. However, if the increase has been achieved by milling the block to reduce the piston deck clearance, HC concentrations will fall because there is less area between the piston and head squish areas for the fuel to hide and escape combustion. Fitting a camshaft with more duration and overlap lowers NOx emissions in two ways. First, there is less trapped inlet charge at lower rpm so there is less compression which in turn keeps peak combustion pressures lower. Secondly, a modified cam will allow more exhaust reversion back into the cylinder. This dilutes the inlet charge, slows combustion and reduces peak pressures. In effect it does the same thing as EGR. Additionally, because of the increased overlap, some fuel/air mixture will pass from the inlet tract straight into the exhaust, giving an afterburn effect that lowers both HC and CO levels. Naturally both of these outcomes are more pronounced when the standard cast iron exhaust manifold is retained, as tubular headers stop a lot of reversion and they permit the gases to flow quickly from the hottest area so afterburn is significantly decreased.

To give you some idea of just how clean modified engines can be without trick tuning we will look at a couple of examples. The first is a Corvette 350 with TPI injection. It was being tuned for good power and good driveability, but economy and expense was of little concern to the owner. Basically, the modifications are as follows: Phase III cam and budget roller tip rockers, Brodix aluminium heads left unported, 9.5:1 compression ratio, 400 Chev crank to raise capacity to 383 cu in, enlarged throttle body and revised manifold runners, modified electronics for fuel injection and ignition, stock exhaust manifolds with modified CAT and big bore free flow exhausts and mufflers. Table 14.4 sets out the test results. Clearly the car passed easily, in fact if a "visual" had not been necessary the CAT could have been left off and it would still have got through.

TABLE 14.4 Tailpipe emissions for a modified Corvette

		Standard requirement	Modified
Idle test	HC	150ppm	51ppm
	CO	1.2%	0.02%
High test	HC	220ppm	34ppm
(2500rpm)	CO	1.2%	0.01%

At the other end of the spectrum is the 4.1 litre Buick developed for good power, but without any regard for the law or expense. In its tested form the engine ultimately produced almost 350hp, so it was far from mildly tuned. However, it produced the tailpipe readings shown in Table 14.5. The engine was extensively modified: Dyer

TABLE 14.5 Tailpipe emissions for a supercharged Buick

		Standard requirement	Modified
Idle test	HC	150ppm	63ppm
	CO	1.2%	0.1%
High test	HC	220ppm	29ppm
(2500rpm)	CO	1.2%	0.07%

Roots type supercharger with 7 psi boost, Phase III cam, ported heads, 8.5:1 compression ratio, tubular headers and twin 2½in exhaust without CAT converter, Holley 600 cfm four barrel carb. The PCV system and charcoal canister were the only emissions equipment retained. In spite of all of these modifications the engine easily passed the sniff test. Of course a "visual" would soon put an end to this enthusiast's disregard for the law.

These examples are cited not to encourage disdain for the law, but to illustrate that pollution control and performance can co-exist. We all have to breathe the air on this planet so we must concern ourselves with the pollution problem and take steps so as not to contribute to it. By taking a conservative approach with our modifications and by keeping our vehicles properly tuned, good performance and economy, along with reduced emissions, can be realised.

CHAPTER 15
Dyno Tuning

We can very easily expend a good deal of time and money in search of power and economy, and then miss out on attaining this objective simply because we have overlooked a comprehensive dyno tuning session. There is no way an engine can deliver power and economy tuned by ear, particularly with all of the engine management controls and emissions gear common to today's engines. For sure dyno tuning isn't the "be all and end all" of engine tuning, for a number of reasons. You can't really check how crisply an engine will accelerate or what its throttle response will be like, for example, due to the nature of the load applied to the engine. Also, the usefulness of dyno tuning is largely determined by the integrity and experience of the dyno operator. In all areas of life there are "sharp" and/or inexperienced operators looking for easy money; the dyno tune business is no exception. Many dyno operators know very little about power tuning and nothing about economy tuning. In my experience they are frequently just everyday motor mechanics doing tune-ups; they replace spark plugs and ignition points, set the timing and valve clearances and then produce a dyno readout to prove to the customer that the tune-up was successful. The naive customer pays his money and drives off happy in the knowledge that his car is running at peak efficiency; it must be, he now has a piece of paper which shows the car to be 6hp, or whatever, more powerful than when he drove it into the workshop. Used in this manner a dyno is just a propaganda tool, contrived to provide the unwary motorist with tangible proof, in the form of a dyno readout, that the tune-up was a success, so the mechanic is obviously a good fellow who knows his stuff.

Due to ignorance many motorists are "caught" in this manner. Obviously to avoid the same pitfall you have to be able to identify the real operator from the fellow faking it. The knowledge that you have gleaned from reading this and other books should assist you to be able to have an in depth discussion with dyno operators to see who knows what they are talking about. Have a look at the kind of cars they have in the workshop, see who their customers are etc. Only after doing some investigating can you be sure that a dyno session will be really worthwhile.

There are two basic types of dynamometers, the engine dynamometer and the rolling road or chassis dynamometer. The rolling road is usually employed for tuning and minor developmental work on road cars. It is very convenient as you just drive the car on to a set of rollers and run the engine to determine the power and torque output. The engine dyno is used for major or very sensitive engine development. You can keep track of many things apart from horsepower and torque outputs; inlet air flow, fuel flow and exhaust gas temperature of each cylinder, for example. The chassis dyno is not so sensitive, but even so it is a useful tuning tool when in the hands of an experienced operator. You can find, for example, that carburation changes give a little more power whereas comparison of the fuel flow figures could indicate that there has been disproportionate increase in fuel consumption which may not be acceptable. An increase in turbo boost may seem like a good idea but on the dyno there may not be very much power increase indicating restrictive manifolds or cylinder head. The power may suddenly fall off at higher rpm and at the same point fuel flow reads the same as it did 500rpm lower in the range. This could indicate the drop off was due to a lean-out. Perhaps the injectors, the fuel pump or the fuel filters have reached their flow limit. On the other hand there could be a "bug" in the electronics which is limiting fuel flow.

There are several types of dynos in use and while they will do a good job in helping a dependable dyno operator to set up an engine properly, do not take a lot of notice of the power figures. Even among so-called "calibrated" dynos variations of up to 10% from one dyno to another are not uncommon. The reason for this can be that various dyno manufacturers calibrate their units a little differently. Also, many tuning companies do not have the money to outlay on the latest, most sophisticated dynos. Instead, they use older units, or perhaps new less sophisticated types. This in itself is not such a bad thing providing the operator knows his business and the dyno will give consistent figures from day to day. The main thing is not to try to compare the power figures from one dyno to another; do your tuning on the same dyno. Otherwise you may try out some new modification and find that it gives you 10hp more, when in fact you had lost power. It was simply that this dyno was reading higher than the one on which the engine was first tested. Table 15.1 shows the result of tests on two dynos with a 350 Chev race engine.

TABLE 15.1 Dyno comparison of 350 Chev

	Dyno A		Dyno B	
rpm	hp	Torque	hp	Torque
5500	472	451	478	456
6000	505	442	533	466
6500	568	459	561	453
7000	601	451	582	437
7250	606	439	583	422
7500	612	428	585	410
7750	622	422	551	374

Note: this engine was not altered in any way between tests. The hp and torque figures have been corrected to compensate for changes in air density.

When an engine is run on the dyno, a record is made of its output each 250 or 500rpm over its operating range. These output figures are then converted to tell us what the hp and torque is, as only newer dynos are interfaced with a computer to give a direct reading. At the time these calculations are being made a "correction factor" is also introduced, to keep the output figures standard. If this was not done we would have no way of accurately comparing the engine's power level on another occasion when the atmospheric conditions are likely to be quite different. Throughout the test session a check is made of the barometer reading and at frequent intervals wet and dry bulb air temperature readings are taken, as these factors influence the air density. Obviously, the cooler the air and the higher the air pressure, the more oxygen and fuel you can cram into the engine, which in turn produces more power. Conversely, if the temperature is high and the barometric pressure low, the power will fall. To compensate for this factor during the dyno session, and to give a true comparison with earlier and also possibly subsequent tests, a correction factor is added to the conversion formula.

The conversion formula to calculate the torque on one particular type of dyno is this:-

$$\text{Torque} = \frac{W \times 26.26 \times C/F}{2}$$

where W = readout indicated by dyno needle

C/F = correction factor.

For example, if the dyno indicated the twisting force (W) to be 7.31, and the barometric pressure was 30.06ins, with a wet and dry bulb temperature of 48°F and 68°F respectively, the engine would be producing the following torque:-

W = 7.31

C/F = 1.016 (found from tables using the atmospheric figures above.)

$$\text{Torque} = \frac{7.31 \times 26.26 \times 1.016}{2}$$

= 97.52 ft/lbs.

Torque is a measure of the twisting force at the crankshaft expressed as pounds-foot force (commonly called just foot pounds). For example, if an engine is producing torque of 100lbf ft it means that it will lift a load of 100lb with a lever 1ft long connected to the crankshaft. If the engine moves this 100lb load through one revolution, work is being done; in this example 628ft/lbs (twisting force x revolutions x lever length x π). Power is the rate at which this work is being done, hence,

$$\text{Power} = \frac{\text{work}}{\text{time}} \text{ (torque x revolutions)}$$

215

In the Imperial system, power is measured in pounds/feet per minute. However, since these units are very small, the unit we know as horsepower is used today. One horsepower equals 33,000lb/ft per minute. James Watt worked this out as a result of his experiment using strong dray horses. Obviously, because power is the rate at which work is done, two motors both producing 100lb/ft torque could have vastly different power outputs. For example, if one engine lifted its 100lb load twice as quickly as the other it must have double the horsepower. Engine speed is measured in revolutions per minute, so this is the time factor we use in calculating horsepower.

$$HP = \frac{\text{torque x rpm}}{5252}$$

Another unit which I regularly use is called brake mean effective pressure (BMEP). This figure gives a true indication of how effectively an engine is operating, regardless of its capacity or its operating rpm. It is, in fact, a measure of the average cylinder pressures generated during all four engine strokes, and is calculated using the formula:

$$BMEP = \frac{HP \text{ x } 13000}{L \text{ x rpm}} \text{ or } \frac{\text{torque x } 13000}{L \text{ x } 5252}$$

where L = engine capacity in litres.

The average engine runs at a BMEP of about 130–145 psi, while a good street engine should run at 160–185 psi.

Another measure used to analyse combustion efficiency is called brake specific fuel (BSF). This is worked out by dividing the engine's fuel flow (lbs of fuel per hour) by its horsepower output. If the engine was consuming 100lb of fuel per hour at 4500rpm and the power output at that rpm was 250hp, the BSF would be 0.400 (100 ÷ 250 = 0.400). Obviously the less fuel the engine is using for each horsepower produced, the more efficient combustion must be, because more energy is being extracted from every lb of fuel. As the numerical value of the BSF decreases, the combustion efficiency improves, up to the point where subsequent reductions in the BSF causes reductions in horsepower.

During any test session, whether it be on the dyno or out on the road, you should make only one change at a time. This is the sole way that you are going to find out to what the engine is responding. With just one variable introduced for each test it is often difficult to know just what step to take next, so you will understand that the introduction of two or three changes will make it virtually impossible to know where you are heading with your tuning. At times, tuning can be extremely frustrating, because you seem to keep going up so many dead end streets. However, if you stick with it, and go about your tuning in a systematic manner, you are sure to have the engine responding better and using less fuel than before you started. The thing you must remember is to make just one change at a time, and keep accurate notes of any changes. Do not let over-enthusiasm cause you to rush; take your time and make absolutely certain to think everything through.

Chapter 16
Gearing

One area where I am frequently at variance with car makers is in regard to gearing. Not so many years back when we had three and four-speed manual and three-speed auto gearboxes, we had to put up with cars which were noisy and thirsty at freeway speeds in order to achieve sparkling acceleration through the twisty bits. Nowadays as the majority of transmissions are either four and five-speed manual, or four-speed auto, there is no reason to sacrifice quiet, effortless cruising and good fuel economy in the quest for brisk acceleration. However, a number of manufacturers have gone too far with overdrive top gears, so much so that many cars actually attain maximum speed in the next lower gear. Worse, such a high top gear brings an increase in fuel consumption due to a lot of throttle being necessary to maintain speed over hills. Additionally, with manual transmissions driver fatigue and also gearbox and clutch wear are increased, due to all the extra gearshifting required.

At one time I owned a factory high-performance vehicle which I personally considered was badly over-geared. Cruising at 75-80mph on twisty roads the fuel consumption was around 22mpg; driven hard this dropped still further to 18mpg! Not too good considering the car's light weight and small 1.6 litre engine. The gearbox ratios were quite suitable so the manufacturer's parts lists were consulted to find an alternative suitable crown wheel and pinion option. They did not list any but I found that other types of vehicle from the same manufacturer used similar differentials with lower (numerically higher) gearing. My axle had a 3.8:1 ratio but there was also a 3.95:1 and 4.15:1 ratio in other models and a commercial vehicle was listed as having a 4.4:1 axle.

Next I did my sums to determine which ratio would be most suitable, considering the type of roads on which I would spend most of my time. The engine really got going at 4000rpm and began to run out of puff at 6000. I wanted the engine well into the power band at my desired cruising speed of 75-80mph. The 4.15:1 crown wheel and pinion would have the engine spinning at about 4400-4500rpm at this speed so it was chosen. The car was transformed; hill climbing improved dramatically   217 and fuel economy went to 28mpg. Top speed was now 112mph compared with 107mph previously. Apart from the diff the only other changes made to achieve these results were a slight richening of the carburettor accelerator pump jets and main jets. The speedo drive gears were also changed to keep it reading correctly.

Usually a change of axle ratio would not bring such a big improvement but this example does illustrate just how much performance and economy can be gained by a simple crown wheel and pinion swap. Also it is a modification which the law and other peering eyes can not detect easily. Manufacturers claim that they gear their cars to achieve the quietest possible running and best economy at freeway cruising speeds. However, many cars are seldom, if ever, driven on freeways, hence the need to take a careful look at the gearing to determine if it could be robbing you of performance and economy. In truth, many cars are geared to help the manufacturer pass emission tests and achieve high fuel economy figures while running on a wheel dyno without the effects of wind resistance etc. These "economy" figures are then used for advertising purposes and to pass government-legislated corporate fuel consumption laws. For these reasons in some lands it is illegal to change the axle ratio as the vehicle technically would no longer pass these tests. Also for some models auto transmissions only are available as manually shifted vehicles tend to pollute more in certain operating modes, so you can appreciate what the makers are up against in attempting to satisfy the various, usually conflicting, requirements imposed upon them.

At times though, a simple crown wheel and pinion change alone will not give the desired results, especially if the engine has been treated to a fairly warm cam. In this example the owner had spent one third of his new car's purchase price modifying it before he had even taken delivery. It was a performance auto only model which he had had modified by fitting a heavy duty five-speeder, a head job and cam, plus extensive suspension parts. The end result was a car which was undriveable in top gear at anything less than freeway speeds and which guzzled fuel at the rate of 17.5mpg. The top speed was only 6mph better than the standard auto transmission model because top gear was far too high.

The first task was to track down a suitable crown wheel and pinion but the car makers didn't list any options. However, another manufacturer who used this same differential assembly had two other ratios available, 3.7:1 and 4.1:1. The 4.1:1 would have been desirable in view of the 0.76 overdrive top gear in the five speed box but first gear with a 3.58 ratio would then have become useless. Reluctantly, the 3.7:1 crown wheel and pinion was fitted in place of the standard 3.15:1 set. The car was much more pleasant to drive, which was encouraging, fuel economy improved to just over 20mpg and top gear speed rose by 6mph. Encouraged by the results, the gearbox manufacturer was consulted to find if a different overdrive ratio was available. A 0.84:1 ratio gear was selected and fitted. Again the car improved in every respect. Fuel economy was now almost 22mpg, top gear speed increased by another 5mph and top gear was completely useable.

By now you are probably thinking "how do I determine if my car is overgeared?" Well, there are no written rules; often is it as much a matter of driving conditions, driving style and personal preference. Also, remember that some cars have gearing which is just right, particularly if someone has been smart enough to order it with a performance ratio option, and some will be actually undergeared. Keep in mind too that low profile tyres change the gearing unless there has been a corresponding

The owner of this car was smart enough to order it with the 3.36:1 performance axle and LSD instead of the standard 3.08:1 gears. Note also the large diameter rear stabiliser bar fitted to reduce body roll and balance the handling.

increase in wheel diameter to compensate. For example, a change from a 175/75 profile to a 195/60 profile will lower the gearing by about 5%, so a 3.5 axle becomes equivalent to 3.68:1.

A car which spends the major part of its time on two lane twisting roads with a speed limit of 60–70mph will naturally require lower gearing to one running on freeways without any speed restrictions. A car which is very aerodynamic can be geared much higher than a car similar in size and weight but shaped like a barge. A car with a wide power range will tolerate high gearing much better than a car with a similar engine size but having a narrower power band.

Personally I prefer gearing which allows the car to get about 500rpm into the power band at my chosen cruise speed and which attains maximum speed at peak power rpm or maybe up to 300rpm lower. Such gearing will usually yield the best fuel efficiency and reduce gear changes. For outright performance the gearing would normally be lower than this to allow the engine to run up to or within a couple of hundred rpm of the manufacturer's maximum recommended engine speed.

Table 16.1 indicates the road speed per 1000rpm which would usually give the best performance/economy compromise for a variety of engine/gearbox combinations on good two lane unrestricted speed roads.

TABLE 16.1 – Gearing for performance and economy

Engine capacity (litres)	Road speed mph per 1000rpm			
	4 speed (m)	**5 speed** (m)	**3 speed** (a)	**4 speed** (a)
1.2-1.4	15-16.5	17-18		
1.6-1.8	17-18	18-19		
1.9-2.2	18-20	19-21.5		
2.5-2.8	20-22	21-23		21.5-24
3.0-3.4	22-23	23-25.5	22-24	24.5-27
3.8-4.2	23-25	24-27	23-26	25-28
5.0-5.8	24.5-26	25-28	24-26	26-28.5

The formula used to calculate road speed in mph is as follows:–

$$mph = \frac{rpm \times Td \times \pi}{GR \times 1050}$$

where Td = tyre diameter in inches

GR = overall gear ratio (gearbox ratio x axle ratio)

π = 3.1416

By transposing the formula we can find with the aid of Table 16.1 possible suitable rear axle ratios to attain a relaxed cruising speed along with peak economy and good performance.

$$GR = \frac{rpm \times Td \times \pi}{mph \times 1050}$$

where rpm = 1000

mph = speed from Table 16.1

To find the axle ratio required we must then divide GR by the gearbox gear ratio in top gear.

Fitting the correct axle ratio to increase the usefulness of top gear and improve economy also generally brings a marked improvement in acceleration. The gearbox and axle are really just torque multipliers. Hence an overall gear ratio (gearbox ratio x axle ratio) of 3:1 multiplies the engine torque by three, giving three times as much twisting force at the wheels as compared with what is available at the flywheel. Lowering the gearing to 4:1 would increase the twisting force by one third and enhance acceleration significantly. Table 16.2 reveals the effect correct gearing can have on acceleration and general performance. In this example if the original gearing had been retained, probably another 20hp would have been required to achieve the acceleration times of the car with revised gearing. A bigger cam would be necessary to

TABLE 16.2 – Effect of correct gearing on performance/economy

Engine capacity 3.0 litres

hp 175 @ 5300rpm

Torque 192 @ 3600rpm

		Performance with 3.15:1 axle and 0.76 overdrive top gear.	Performance with 3.7:1 axle and 0.84 overdrive top gear.
Maximum speed	1st	38mph @ 5800rpm	32mph @ 5800rpm
	2nd	65mph @ 5800rpm	56mph @ 5800rpm
	3rd	100mph @ 5800rpm	85mph @ 5800rpm
	4th	136mph @ 5800rpm	116mph @ 5800rpm
	5th	127mph @ 4100rpm	138mph @ 5800rpm
Acceleration 0–60		9.1 sec	8.4 sec
0–80		14.9 sec	14.0 sec
standing ¼ mile		16.6 sec	15.8 sec
Fuel economy		17.5mpg	21.9mpg

pick up 20hp and as a consequence the original fuel consumption and general driveability problem referred to earlier would have been further aggravated. Selecting suitable gearing is as important as selecting any performance part or modification. The wrong choice can spoil a fine car; the correct choice can transform a sluggish car into a real performer.

Chapter 17
Suspension and Brakes

You are probably questioning why a book about economy and performance has a few pages devoted to suspension and brakes? Well, a little money spent in these areas can contribute as much to performance in particular, and to a lesser extent to economy, as a large amount of money expended solely on the engine. To illustrate the point, consider the outcome of race circuit testing to determine the best power/handling/cost compromise for a popular family sedan. Three cars were used for the test; one was stock standard and two had a variety of engine and suspension modifications. The standard car had a good strong 150hp 3 litre engine and safe handling. The standard tyres were average "grocery getting" type 185/75 on 6in wide wheels. These tyres were probably the weakest link in the package but even so the standard car was quicker around the circuit than sporty sedans with good grippy tyres and 125hp engines, and a lot less weight. The second car had the factory performance suspension package and the engine had been modified to develop 196hp. The factory suspension pack included stiffer dampers, stiffer springs 1in lower than stock and 205/65 performance tyres. Additionally, this car had optional rear disc brakes fitted in line with its 135mph top speed (18mph faster than standard). The car should have been clearly superior to the stock version, and it was, to the tune of 2.5 seconds per lap.

The third car had been lightly modified to put out 171hp. Most of this power increase was the result of modifications to the exhaust system and 6hp came from mild head work. A good deal of time was spent getting the suspension right. Firstly, high quality Koni dampers were fitted all around and then the biggest diameter stabiliser bars that could be found were added. The front bar was 2mm thicker than stock and the rear bar 6mm bigger. Next, the front springs were changed for springs 40% stiffer than stock and a half inch shorter. The rear springs were left stock, as they were designed to carry a good load of people and luggage. I don't like stiff rear springs on a road car as they tend to cause the back of the car to skip around a good deal on second class roads. Besides, the large rear stabiliser bar had been chosen to stiffen up the rear and balance out the understeer which would have resulted from fitting the heavy springs and thicker bar at the front. A limited slip diff (LSD) was also fitted and while this work was in operation the standard 3.45:1 crown wheel and pinion was changed to a 3.8:1 to improve acceleration and make fifth gear more useful. Top speed was 129mph, 6mph slower than the 196hp car but with the changed gearing its acceleration was almost the same as the more powerful car. The next change was to fit 7in wheels and high performance tyres, grippy BF Goodrich T/A 11's, size 205/60. To improve braking semi-metallic disc pads were fitted. The rear drums were left unchanged. In this form the car was only fractionally more expensive than the second car but on the circuit it was a full 2.2 seconds per lap faster in spite of having substantially less power. On the road it was more economical and far easier to drive due to the more flexible engine and the changed gearing. Also, because the car looked and sounded little different to stock, it could be cruised at high speed without attracting undue attention.

The order of changes required to the suspension will to some extent depend on personal preference and the specifications of the stock suspension. In the main today's cars have ample wheel width so that is not the place to start. Also, wide super high performance tyres are not practical for day to day driving, and they are far too expensive. To my mind a more functional place to begin suspension changes is with the dampers, frequently incorrectly called shock absorbers. Very few cars, except some expensive European jobs, have anything like adequate and reliable dampers. Without good dampers the tyres cannot maintain proper contact with the road surface so adhesion is reduced, even if the tyres are sticky Pirelli P700s or BF Goodrich T/A 11s. My personal choice is for Koni dampers, not the gas type but the standard heavy duty "Special D". These are quite expensive when compared with the standard dampers which car manufacturers fit. However, they are adjustable and repairable, so in the long run they are good value. The main disadvantage with Koni dampers is their slightly rougher ride at low speeds compared with gas dampers like Bilstein and de Carbon. On the road they handle and ride every bit as well as these usually more expensive gas dampers.

For most cars the next place I would make a change is with the stabiliser bars. Stabiliser bars reduce roll without much increase in ride harshness, and they are usually quite inexpensive. The disadvantage of a thicker front stabiliser bar is that like stiffer front springs, it causes more understeer, so more steering lock will be required to get around corners at higher speeds. To offset this a thicker rear bar can be fitted but this move can create another problem; in front wheel drive cars a bigger rear bar can get you into an instant oversteer tail slide if you lift-off the throttle mid-corner at high speed; with rear wheel drive a bigger rear bar can cause the inside rear wheel to lift off the road so you lose drive out of tight corners at high speed unless a limited slip diff is fitted. This is not intended to scare you off heavy stabiliser bars as few people ever drive hard enough for either problem to surface. However, it is good to be aware of what can happen so as to avoid, or be prepared for, such problems.

Personally I like big stabiliser bars so that I can get good handling with smoother riding soft springs. Just how big you can go will depend on what is available from the suspension suppliers and how rugged the stabiliser bar mountings are. On small 1.6–1.8 litre front wheel drive cars I would be looking to fit 22mm bars front and rear, and possibly up to 24mm either at the front or the rear, to get the handling balance that I want. For rear wheel drive cars of the same size the bars would be 24mm front and about 16–18mm rear. Mid-size rear wheel drive with 2.8–3.5 litre six cylinder engines require 26–28mm front stabiliser bars and 18–21mm rear bars. With a heavy 5 litre V8 in the front the bar size increases to 33–36mm front and 21–24mm rear.

Before you pay a lot of money for a bar from a suspension manufacturer, check to determine if the car manufacturer has optional stabiliser bars available, or bars of the same shape off another model, because the original manufacturer's bars will, as a rule, be much cheaper. For example, one car which I frequently modify has a 24mm front bar and a 14mm rear. The suspension people make 27mm and 18mm replacement bars at what I consider to be outrageous prices. On checking the car manufacturer's parts listings I found that they fit 26mm front and 18mm rear bars on vehicles built for the Police. Further investigation revealed that on one particular station wagon model they fit a 20mm rear bar. The 26mm stabiliser is less than one third the cost of a 27mm bar from the various suspension parts manufacturers, and the 18mm Police and 20mm wagon rear bar is one fifth the price of their 18mm bar!

With good dampers and heavier stabiliser bars in place I turn my attention next to tyres and wheels. If the standard wheels are a suitable width and diameter to suit the tyres I wish to use, these are retained. I like the look of wide alloy wheels, but they are not good value for money. I'm not too keen on all the effort necessary to keep them clean and looking good either. I know a lot is written about how much light alloy wheels reduce upsprung weight and how this factor improves the handling, also the cooling slots are designed to improve brake cooling, but it is only on the race track where these advantages are really noticeable. A steel wheel is heavier, but it supports the tyre just the same as an alloy wheel, it is easier to keep clean, and it can be nudged into kerbs without cracking. Also, for little expense many wheel specialists will remove the standard width rim and weld a wider one-piece rim onto the standard steel centre. In this way you can gain the advantage of extra rim width for better tyre support.

With the money saved on fancy wheels you will be able to afford better quality tyres, but here again be sure to buy only as much tyre as you need and can regularly use. Wide, sticky tyres work fine on the race track but they can be an expensive nuisance, and quite dangerous, on the road. If you think that your car's suspension is as sophisticated as, say, a Porsche 944 Turbo or a BMW M535, go ahead and fit wide and expensive tyres. Remember, however, that once the tyres are half worn the fellow with skinny tyres will overtake you if the road is wet. If there is a hint of snow leave the car at home. Even in the dry on public roads a fairly even mannered car can be transformed into a twitchy beast with excessively wide tyres, no matter how good their quality. Few rear suspensions are well enough located to cope with rough tarmac and wide rubber. When the Opel Manta 400 with a 145hp 2.4 litre engine and Cosworth 16 valve head was released with 225/50 Pirelli P7 tyres, the journalists raved about how well it handled. They must have done their testing at the race track or on smooth freeways because on ordinary twisty roads at high speed the car was a pig, switching from understeer to vicious oversteer in an instant. Changing to 205/60 tyres changed it markedly. I think anyone who has followed a well-driven Mercedes 560 would marvel

at how quickly it can be pushed along for a big, heavy car with a suspension compromised to give a luxury class ride. Yet it rides on comparatively skinny 205 section tyres with a 65 profile height. Clearly there is more to handling than merely fitting big, wide, and expensive tyres.

Table 17.1 sets out what I consider to be the best tyre compromise for a number of applications. The tyres are probably much narrower and of a higher profile than you thought you needed. I don't consider that low profile tyres are necessary in the smaller

TABLE 17.1 Recommended tyre sizes

Engine size	Car weight	Minimum tyre	Handling/ride tyre	Handling tyre
1.2–1.4 litre	1700–1900lb	155/75	165/70	175/70, 175/65
1.6–1.8 litre	2000–2200lb	175/70	175/70, 185/70	185/65
2.0–2.3 litre	2100–2400lb	185/70	185/65, 195/65	195/60
2.0–2.3 litre	2500–2800lb	185/70	195/70, 195-65	195/60, 205/60
2.8–3.3 litre	2800–3200lb	195/70	205/65	205/60, 215/65
3.6–4.2 litre	3100–3300lb	205/65	215/65	215/60
5.0–6.0 litre	3200–3500lb	215/65	215/60	225/60

widths as small tyres are stable enough if the pressures are right, without reducing the wall height. Low profile tyres are more expensive and the ride rougher. To overcome the rough ride many people use less pressure, which in turn just reduces the tyres' responsiveness to that of a higher profile tyre running more pressure. Keep in mind that changing the tyre size, either section width or profile, can alter the gearing. A standard rule is that for each two sizes of increase in width the profile height must come down one number to retain approximately the same gearing eg. changing from a 185/70 tyre to a 205/65 tyre will keep the gearing the same as standard.

The construction of the tyre, the rubber compound, and the tread pattern is far more important than the actual size. Unfortunately there is no way of grading these things, so often it is a matter of listening to someone else's advice when it comes to making a tyre choice. The first thing that you can look for is a good open tread with at least two wide water channels running all the way around the tyre. Additionally, there should be good, full depth, drainage grooves running from these channels to both the inner and outer edge of the tyre. Some so-called performance tyres leave a lot to be desired in this respect. To give stability to the tread blocks some tyre makers do not mould these drains more than half tread depth. Then, when the tyre is half worn, there is no water drainage away from the large channels. Other tyre companies, in an effort to increase the area of rubber in contact with the road, leave the outer third of the tyre a semi-slick. This is fine while the road is dry, but as the tyre wears and the rain comes you will wish for better drainage.

Most cars are not capable of more than 130mph so "HR" speed rated tyres are suitable. "VR" rated tyres are much more expensive so unless you need a tyre which is VR rated you will generally be wasting your money. To obtain a VR rating the tyre construction and also the rubber compound is changed to enable the tyre to run at over 130mph without flying apart. Some companies offer their high performance tyres in both HR and VR ratings. The VR tyre doesn't grip any better, it's designed not to   225

Goodyear Eagles exhibit the sort of tread pattern to look for; good water channels running all the way around the tyre and drainage grooves to both the inner and outer edges from these channels.

fracture at higher speeds. Unfortunately though, some manufacturers only supply their best handling tyres with a VR rating, so if you want that additional grip there is no alternative but to pay the extra in this instance.

Of course not to be neglected when discussing tyres is tyre pressure. Generally, if you want sharp high speed handling you will have to use considerably more pressure than the manufacturer of the vehicle recommends. Personally I have found with front engine cars that I prefer pressures of about 33–36 psi front and 27–28 psi rear. The high front pressures give sharp steering, a secondary benefit is reduced steering effort so power steering isn't needed on most cars with 4 and 6 cylinder engines. This means that there is reduced power wastage and reduced fuel consumption. The lower rear pressures reduce the tendency of the rear end to jump about on rough surfaces and give a more comfortable ride. Also, the tyres wear more evenly, contributing to a longer life which saves you some money.

To help the tread maintain proper contact with the road, wheels of the correct width are required. If the wheels are narrow, the tread will squirm, reducing grip and increasing tread wear. If the wheels are too wide, the ride will become harsh and the aerodynamics of the car will be spoiled, increasing fuel consumption at higher speeds. Table 17.2 indicates the rim widths which should be aimed for. Remember that tyres of the same size can vary greatly in tread width. For example, a 205/60 tyre can have a tread width of 6.1 to 6.7in. Naturally this influences the rim width required. Unless the tyre has very low walls I normally like to see the rim width at least equal to the tread

TABLE 17.2 Recommended rim widths

Tyre size	Minimum width (in)	Preferred width (in)	Maximum width (in)
155/75	4.5	5.0	5.5
165/70	5.0	5.5	5.5
175/70	5.0	5.5	6.0
175/65	5.0	5.5	6.0
185/70	5.5	6.0	6.5
185/65	5.0	6.0	6.5
195/70	6.0	6.5	7.0
195/65	6.0	6.0	6.5
195/60	5.5	6.0	6.5
205/65	6.0	6.5	7.0
205/60	6.0	6.5	7.0
215/65	6.5	6.5	7.5
215/60	6.5	6.5	7.5
225/60	6.5	7.0	8.0

width to ensure good stability. Do take care if you decide to change the wheel width or the wheel offset of front wheel drive vehicles as the handling could finish up a disaster. In some lands it is now illegal to change the rim width or offset on all front wheel drive cars for this very reason.

The next modification would be to fit stiffer, but not necessarily lower, springs. Many cars have front springs which are far too soft. This permits plenty of body roll and allows the car to gently drift when cornering at normal speeds, so the tyres lose adhesion gradually rather than savagely. At the front I like the springs to be 20–50% stiffer than stock and give a ride height about a half to one inch lower than standard. With the nose dropped a little, the car becomes more aerodynamic. High speed stability is improved and fuel consumption shows a decrease. The stiffer springs reduce roll and increase steadiness under heavy braking. Because very few cars today have any camber adjustment, the front must not be dropped very much otherwise the front tyres will have too much negative camber, which will scrub the inside of the tyre tread in no time. For good tyre wear the front end should have 0–0.3° negative camber, and a maximum of 0.5° negative unladen. This reduces cornering grip a little but ensures a good balance between tyre life and adhesion. Also, straight ahead stability is better in cross winds with less negative camber.

At the rear I seldom change the ride height, otherwise very stiff, rough riding springs will be necessary to keep the car off the bump rubbers on anything but smooth roads. If the car is designed to carry a good load of luggage and people, the standard springs are probably heavy enough for fast driving with just a couple of people on board and a little light luggage. Fitting stiffer springs will give the rear dampers a lot more work and if the rear axle isn't too well located, most are not, then the dampers will have a lot of trouble keeping the back tyres in contact with the road. On rough corners the rear end will become very skittish and prone to sliding out (oversteer).

Some cars have what are called "progressive rate" springs, meaning that the springs are soft at their normal ride height and stiffen non-linearly as they compress. 227

The idea is good, in fact many rally cars use this type of spring at the front and rear. However, a number of car makers have gone overboard looking for a smooth ride so much so that the spring is initially far too soft, allowing excessive body roll. Such a spring may have a spring rate of say 170–310lb per in, very soft initially and finally quite stiff. A replacement spring for performance driving could have a rate of 230–290lb per in, stiffer initially but a little softer at full compression. If a single rate spring were used it would probably be about 255 or 265lb per in, which would give a harder ride and the same handling as the 230–290lb progressive spring.

Many suspension people are now advocating the replacement of rubber suspension bushes with bushes made of polyurethane or other hard plastic-like material. I'm not at all in favour of this because of increased noise and vibration within the car. Naturally there are some exceptions; the only general exception which applies to all cars is that the stabiliser bar "D" bushes and also the link bar bushes can be replaced without increasing harshness. Personally I feel that it is a waste of money replacing the rubber link bar bushes with polyurethane bushes. They are quite expensive. Equally effective is to fit thicker washers and wind the link bar rubbers down until they are fully compressed. This ensures that full suspension motion is transmitted to the stabiliser bar. If the bushes are left semi-compressed, as they are when the car leaves the factory, the suspension has to move at least half an inch before the stabiliser bar starts working. Another budget measure it to use rubber "D" bushes designed for a slightly smaller diameter stabiliser bar. Hence if the bar diameter is 28mm use bushes made for a 26mm bar. This pre-compresses the bush, ensuring that the stabiliser bar works more effectively.

One area where I do not believe in saving money is when it comes to deciding if a limited slip diff should be fitted. I firmly believe that any rear wheel drive car which is regularly driven in a spirited manner over wet or slippery roads should have an LSD. Without it the car will be dangerous to drive if it has more than about 110hp, particularly if the suspension is fairly stiff and tyre widths have been increased over stock. The LSD should not be a savage race-type unit, rather it should be a "soft" clutch or cone type with about 25% lock up torque. This means that 25% of axle torque will be transferred to the wheel which has traction. This ensures some drive out of the corners; without the LSD all of the torque would go to the spinning inside wheel. To help the LSD work properly and last a long time, use the correct type of LSD oil for your unit, and change the oil at least every 30,000 miles. It is not easy accurately to check if an LSD requires adjustment or is still working correctly. However, this is a quick check which I have found works well on many units. Raise one wheel off the ground and using a tension wrench determine how much pressure has to be applied before the wheel will turn. A new LSD will read about 80 lbf ft; less than 45 lbf ft usually indicates that repair is required.

Limited slip diffs are not really suitable for general road use in front wheel drive vehicles due to problems with torque steer. A lot of work is being carried out with viscous drives and as these become more reliable and freely available for a wide variety of front drive cars they should prove invaluable, particularly in powerful, torquey turbo cars.

Most new generation cars have excellent brakes which work quite well on the road at higher speeds. The usual arrangement is ventilated discs at the front and drums at the rear, although in recent years more vehicles are fitted with discs at the

Ventilated discs at the front provide the needed braking performance when backed up by fade-resistant semi-metallic pads.

rear. Personally I don't see the need to devote a lot of attention to brakes; very few roads require more than the occasional dab on the pedal to slow from 85mph to 50mph for a corner. This doesn't demand big, efficient and well-cooled brakes like a car on the race track, which may have to slow from 130mph to 50mph at the end of the main straight every lap with very little time for cooling between each brake application.

Some people feel that they must have rear discs and competition brake materials. This can be a mistake. A big, heavy car weighing around 3200lb plus driven briskly on tight, twisty roads will benefit from being fitted with rear disc brakes. However, few public roads are so demanding that light vehicles require rear discs. After all, the front brakes do about 65 to 70% of the work on front engined cars, so the rear brakes do not have to be really powerful.

Competition or full-metallic brake materials must not be used on road cars. This type of material must be at a very high temperature before it gives good braking performance. In fact a number of racers do not use competition materials in short sprint races because the brakes do not get enough heat into the pads to work properly. For the best braking performance in road cars semi-metallic pads should be fitted. When dead cold these require more pedal pressure than the standard organic asbestos materials, but this is about their only disadvantage of any consequence. Semi-metallics are also more expensive and sometimes generate higher noise levels. Semi-metallic materials offer three times greater heat dissipation than organic linings and up to about 800°F they retain 90% of their braking coefficient of friction. Most asbestos linings have a maximum coefficient of friction no better than about 0.38 at 100°F and by 200°F they begin to fade so that at 400° the CF is down to 0.21. Semi-metallics on the other hand will show a CF of about 0.32 dead cold, 0.37 at 100°, rising to 0.41 all the way between 300 and 500°F and then falling to 0.35 at 800°. Hence they show clearly superior hot braking performance. However, of even greater benefit from my viewpoint is their wet performance. All of us have had that feeling that we were never going to stop in time when it has been wet. Often the problem wasn't tyres losing grip but wet brakes not working. With a light water spray the CF of conventional pads 229 drops to approximately 0.28, saturated the CF will fall all the way down to 0.15; far worse than hot brake fade. Semi-metallics record a CF up around 0.36 with light spray and even when fully saturated the CF is still around 0.29.

Some people worry about the heavy, dead pedal feel when semi-metallics are used on some cars. This can be easily overcome by applying the brakes a couple of times after you leave your garage. Once the brakes are up to 100°F, just above human body temperature, they work fine and the dead pedal sensation goes away. There are also a couple of other solutions. The first is to fit semi-metallics on the front only and use conventional material on the rear brakes. The other alternative, and this is a solution which some car manufacturers also use, is to fit just one semi-metallic pad on each side at the front. Care is needed when doing this for if you accidently fit two semi-metallics on one front brake and two organic pads to the other side front brake, you will be steered right off the road when under brakes, because of unequal braking. I prefer to fit the semi-metallic pads on the inside, because without water shields the inner pads get more water spray, hence I would paint "IN" on them to identify that they are to be installed on the inside of the caliper. The standard pads are marked "OUT" to indicate their location.

With semi-metallic linings, brake cooling is not of major importance for road cars. Because the front brakes do the lion's share of the stopping effort, I like to see reasonable air circulation around them, so the first modification is to remove the water splash shields when these are fitted. If the car is very heavy and you are still getting fade or fluid boil, you will need an air deflector, or trunking, to direct air flow onto the front discs. At the rear, heavy cars with drum brakes can benefit by having 1.25in holes in both the backing plate and the brake drum to permit air flow through the brakes.

If you are experiencing hot braking problems, do not automatically blame it on brake fade. Ordinary brake fluid absorbs water and in time the boiling point of the fluid will drop from 500°F to only 350°F. When the fluid boils, the pedal will go spongy and you will have to pump it to get any response. The moral is to replace the fluid regularly if you work the brakes hard.

The brakes can have a dramatic effect on fuel consumption; a little drag can cost a lot of mileage. When adjusting drum brakes don't adjust them up so much that it is only just possible to turn the wheels by hand. Instead, when the linings are just contacting the drum, stop any further adjustment. Then push the brake pedal down hard a couple of times to locate the linings properly and again check for binding. If the brakes are now slack, readjust them, but if they are dragging excessively let them off a little. Naturally disc brakes cannot be adjusted; however, they can drag excessively and increase fuel useage. Some disc calipers never give any trouble; you can wear out half a dozen sets of pads and the pistons still retract properly so that there is no brake binding. However, some caliper designs are notorious for brake drag so when checking the pad wear test for binding as well. With some types the seals harden and lose their ability to retract the pistons, which means that the brakes are partially applied all the time. Other designs, usually single large diameter piston fully-floating calipers, age in a different way. In time, the large diameter piston wears minutely, which allows it to cock sideways a little in the caliper and jam. Again the pad bears heavily against the disc and drags; fuel consumption increases. Either problem requires a full caliper overhaul.

Chapter 18
Economy and
the Driver

One of the most important elements in determining the fuel consumption of a particular car is the driving technique and habits of the individual behind the wheel. It is quite possible to drive quickly and smoothly and achieve excellent economy. Alternatively, many drive slowly, with poor technique, and are rewarded with heavy fuel consumption.

Smooth driving requires that the driver be in tune with his car, the road, and the prevailing weather and traffic conditions. It may be great fun blasting out of a tight corner with the car in the lowest possible gear to produce maximum acceleration, and correspondingly exciting engine and exhaust noises. However, just 15 minutes of driving like this could consume as much fuel as 30 to 40 minutes of quick but gentle driving. By driving in a gear which has the engine working in the "pulling range", usually about 2500 to 3500rpm, and using just light throttle applications, driving from point A to B can still be fun and an exhilerating experience. With the money that is saved on engine wear, transmission wear, tyre wear and brake wear, it will be an experience which you will be able to afford more frequently.

On the other hand economy driving doesn't mean sticking the vehicle in the highest gear and leaving it there. A good deal of fuel is wasted by people who by habit shift the transmission into overdrive fifth whenever they are driving on the open road. Obviously if its a multi-lane freeway with steady gradients and the vehicle isn't being buffeted by a roaring headwind, the highest gear will probably result in the best possible economy. Not all roads are like this; there may be steep grades and tighter corners to contend with, not to mention a vehicle loaded down with the family and holiday luggage. Under such conditions a car running in top gear will require pedal to metal type throttle application to maintain speed up hills, or to accelerate up to speed out of turns. Driving in such a manner can increase fuel consumption by 20 to 30%, and there is more risk of detonation and engine bearing wear. Good economy demands that the gear selected suits the road speed, the gradient, the load and the wind direction.

In addition to selecting the correct gear, drivers must also learn to anticipate hills and accurately evaluate the grade. When this isn't done, the car quickly loses speed and only wide open throttle and perhaps a down change will allow you to crest 231 the hill at a respectable speed. This too increases fuel useage. The correct method is to apply throttle progressively as the car approaches the foot of the hill such that it is actually in an acceleration mode as the climb commences. Approached in this manner the vehicle will maintain speed over the hill with just a small progressive increase in throttle opening.

Cruise controls are very poor in this respect. Sure, they make driving long distances on relatively straight roads easier. However, they do not anticipate grades so the road speed actually has to commence falling off before the sensor signals for more throttle. By then it is far too late; only a lot of throttle and a corresponding increase in fuel flow will keep the cruise speed up.

Many people complain of increased fuel consumption when an air conditioner is in use, but this is not always the case as careful use of the air conditioner can actually reduce fuel waste. With more emphasis being placed on aerodynamics by vehicle designers, some cars actually burn up more fuel when the windows are wound down to give some cooling effect. Even with less aerodynamic styles there is very little difference in fuel consumption at 60 to 80mph between a car with the air on or the windows down. Where fuel consumption is increased with the air conditioned vehicle is around town or at very high speed.

There are a number of things which should be done to ensure good economy with the air conditioner on. Obviously the windows should be wound all the way up to improve the slipperiness of the vehicle through the air and to keep the cold inside and the hot out. If the car has a big clutch fan or flex blade fan driven by the engine, get rid of it and fit an electric fan. Switch the air conditioner on only when needed. This may sound crazy but I'm amazed at the number of people who only switch the thing off when everyone in the car begins to shiver. Learn to take advantage of the terrain by turning the air on when the car is coasting down hills and turn it off when pulling up hill or when accelerating. Actually there is a vacuum-operated micro-switch available which does this for you. It is connected to the inlet manifold, opening the switch when the vacuum is low and closing when it is high. Most switches are preset to open at 8 to 10ins Hg, but adjustable switches are available.

For those who are questioning the point, tests have proved that at 60 to 80mph fuel consumption increases by 13 to 20%, depending on vehicle aerodynamics, when all the windows are down. All that buffeting and noise going on inside the car indicates the wind drag you are creating. Almost as serious is the drag which is caused by body attachments and wide wheels. In combination, a front or rear spoiler together with auxiliary lights, tyres which go out about an inch more than stock and a ski rack with two sets of gear create just a few percent less drag than open windows.

Carrying unnecessary weight also increases fuel useage, particularly in hilly terrain or stop and go situations where a lot of acceleration is involved. The message is don't use the car as a storage bin; carry only those items which are really necessary. If you regularly have to carry a lot of weight, so much so that the tail drops, consider altering the suspension to enable the car to slice more cleanly through the air. A car with the nose in the air presents a poor aerodynamic shape. To rectify the problem either stiffer rear springs or shorter front springs will be needed to give a level or nose down attitude. Actually, all cars are aerodynamically cleaner with the nose down a little, so if you can afford to sacrifice some front ground clearance and suspension travel this is a way of effectively improving economy particularly if you engage in many miles of high speed driving or regularly experience strong headwind conditions.

Binding brakes or a driver who rests his foot on the brake pedal or who leaves the park brake partly on also wastes fuel. In simulated tests a 2lb weight on the brake pedal increased consumption by just over 20%; a heavy price to pay for a bad habit or a minor mechanical problem. With drum brakes the shoes should just touch the drums when cold. If the brake shoes are bearing heavily against the drums, adjust them off. Most disc brakes cause very little trouble with binding, but those calipers which are prone to sticking pistons are a real problem. The only solution when the pistons do not fully release the pads from off the disc is to recondition the calipers. With a few varieties of calipers the internal seals harden with age and prevent the pistons from returning fully. This is simply fixed with new seals. The more usual problem is worn or corroded pistons, or corroded caliper bores.

Few new generation cars have a manual choke, but for those so equipped the driver must develop the good habit of pushing the choke control full in as soon as possible. In addition, when giving the engine a tune-up look to see that the choke is fully open with the control pushed in as some cables do bind and restrict the choke plate from opening completely. For those carburated cars with an automatic choke it is a matter of regularly noting that the choke opens in the time specified by the manufacturer; usually 3 minutes for electric types. A number of carburettors of Japanese manufacture give trouble in that with age they are difficult to adjust to open fully when the engine is up to temperature and close when it is cold. When this becomes a problem it is often best to fit a manual choke conversion.

Poor or irregular engine maintenance will give rise to fuel wastage. Engines which are equipped with an ignition distributor utilising a vacuum advance mechanism will lose 10% economy from a disconnected or fractured vacuum hose. A similar decrease can occur if any one of the ported emission control vacuum switches fail and deny the advance mechanism full vacuum. Incorrect timing will also sacrifice about 10% in wasted fuel. Under full engine load conditions old misfiring spark plugs can cost anything from 20 to 40% in lost economy. An air filter clogged with dust may up fuel consumption by 7% and leaky injector nozzles or a leaky needle and seat can push consumption up by more than 50%.

Many people, fortunately few of them enthusiasts, get caught out purchasing so called fuel-saving devices. These simply do not work, or at least I've never come across one that did. Cynics claim that these devices are not fitted by the factory because the oil companies have a pact with car manufacturers to make it worth their while ensuring that their models use more fuel. Naturally the factories want to keep fuel consumption as low as possible; it helps sell cars. Now that some governments are insisting that manufacturers further reduce fuel useage in their engines, millions are being spent to achieve this goal, but you won't find any of these weird devices being used because they plain do not work.

There are a few things which do reduce consumption. Friction-modified engine oil is worth 2 to 3%. A wheel alignment cuts tyre scrub and improves economy. Radial tyres have less rolling resistance than crossply tyres, so cut consumption by a similar amount as friction modified oil; but surely there isn't anyone still using crossplys? However, the biggest contribution to economy comes from smooth driving technique and regular maintenance.

Appendix

Table of useful equivalents

1 inch = 25.4mm   1mm = 0.03937in

1 cubic inch = 16.387cc   1 litre = 61.024cu in or 1000cc

1 horsepower = 0.7457 kilowatts   1 kilowatt = 1.341hp

1 pound foot torque = 1.3558 Newton metres 1 Newton metre = 0.7376 pound foot

1 pound inch torque = 0.11298 Newton metres

1 psi = 6.89476 kilopascals

     or 68.95 millibars

     or 2.0345 inches of Mercury (Hg)

     or 27.67 inches of water

$$°F = (\frac{9}{5} \ x \ °C) + 32 \qquad\qquad °C = (°F - 32) \ x \frac{5}{9}$$

1 gallon (Imperial) = 160 fluid oz   1 fluid oz (Imperial) = 28.4cc
                  or 4.546 litres

1 gallon (US) = 128 fluid oz   1 fluid oz (US) = 29.57cc
                  or 3.785 litres

Index

A

Accelerator pump 88, 103
Acetone 38, 210
Advance:
    camshaft 12, 54-59
    centrifugal 131, 133-137
    ignition 9, 130-140, 154, 203, 209, 234
    initial 129, 131, 140
    vacuum 131, 132, 137-139, 204, 234
Air:
    bleed jet 87
    cleaner 92, 93, 209, 234
    conditioner 233
    density 91, 92, 215
    flow meter 116, 122, 123
    air-fuel ratio 82, 109, 118, 124
    temperature sensor 114, 117
AIR (air injection reactor) system 12, 21, 206
Alcohol 210
Anti-freeze 189, 190
APH (air pre-heat) system 200, 201
Avgas 34, 35, 37, 38
Auxiliary air valve 113
Auxiliary venturi 86

B

Balancing 175
Bearings: 177-179, 232
    clearance 178
    material 177, 178
Benzol 38
Black preparation 177
Boost pressure 153-159, 163
Boring 30, 171, 177
Brake mean effective pressure 216
Brake:
    adjustment 234
    cooling 231
    disc 228-231
    drum 230
    fluid 231
    material 230
Brake specific fuel 166, 216

C

Cam followers: 62, 63
    flat 62, 63
    hydraulic 62, 63, 69, 70
    Rhoads 62, 63
Camshaft:
    accuracy 56, 61
    drive arrangements 59, 60
    flat tappet 60, 62
    hydraulic tappet 60, 62, 69, 70
    lobe profile 47, 60, 61
    lobe wear 12, 60, 62
    lubrication 60
    mushroom tappet 62
    roller tappet 60, 62
    running-in 60
    surface treatment 60
    timing 13, 14, 45-59
Capacitor discharge ignition 145
Carbon monoxide 195, 199, 206, 207, 209-211
Carburettor:
    accelerator pump 88, 103
    basic operation 10, 83-90
    Carter 89, 100, 103, 106
    choke 83, 84, 234
    electronic controls 12, 118
    Holley 87, 89, 100, 103, 105
    emission controls 199, 200
    idle system 84
    main system 85, 103
    metering rods 87, 103, 106, 107, 118
    needle and seat 82, 209, 234
    pollution controls 104-106
    power system 87, 88, 103

Quadrajet 89, 100, 103, 105, 118
size 89, 90 99-101
SU 89, 90, 99
tuning 101-107
Weber 87, 89, 90, 93, 99, 103
Castor oil 184
Catalytic converter 37, 38, 207-209
Centrifugal advance 131, 133-137
Chevrolet:
    cylinder head 15-19, 22-24, 29
    exhaust manifolds 75, 76
    inlet manifolds 94, 95
Clearance:
    big end 178
    main bearing 178
    piston 169
    piston pin 176
    piston ring groove 171
    squish 42
    valve 68-70
    valve to piston 174
    valve to valve guide 28
Close loop 118
Coil 144-147
Combustion chamber:
    bath-tub 26
    grinding 26
    pentroof 27
    polishing 15
    semi-hemi 27
    squish clearance 42
    volume 39-42
Combustion rate: 27, 29, 42, 43, 56
    abnormal 29, 34, 91, 141, 163, 232
Compression ratio:
    calculation 39-42
    permissible 35-39
Compressor – turbo 153-158
Con-rod: 175-177
    bolts 176
    polishing 176, 177
    shot peening 177
Consumption – brake specific fuel 166, 216
Coolant temperature sensor 114, 117
Cooling:
    fan 193, 233
    oil 185
    water 189-194
Crankcase emissions 198
Crankshaft 174, 175
    balancing 175
    material 174
    stroking 175
    tuftriding 175
Cruise control 233
Cylinder:
    bore accuracy 171
    block preparation 177
    honing 171
    reboring 30, 171, 177
Cylinder head:
    gasket 29, 30, 193
    milling 29
    porting 15-21
    sealant 30
    tension 30

D
Damper – crankshaft 179, 180
Deck clearance 42
Detonation 29, 34, 91, 141, 163, 232
Distributor advance 9, 130-140, 154, 203, 209, 234
Dynamometer 214

E
EFE (early fuel evaporation) system 12, 91, 201-203, 210
EGR (exhaust gas recirculation) 97, 98, 130, 144, 205, 211
Electronic ignition 129, 131, 140, 146, 147
Emissions:
    carbon monoxide 195, 199, 206, 207, 209-211
    crankcase 198
    evaporative 198, 199
    exhaust 199-207
    hydrocarbons 195, 199, 200, 206, 207, 209-211
    nitrogen oxides 46, 56, 195, 199, 205, 207, 210, 211

Emission systems:
    AIR (air injection reactor) 12, 21, 206
    APH (air pre-heat) 200, 201
    carburettor 199, 200
    catalytic converter 37, 38, 207-209
    EFE (early fuel evaporation) 12, 91, 201-203, 210
    gearing 218
    PCV valve 198
    ported vacuum 204
    retarded ignition timing 203
Emission testing:
    car manufacturers 196
    sniff test 196, 209-211
    visual inspection 196, 197, 205, 206, 208
Emulsion tube 87
Ethanol 210
Evaporative emissions 198, 199
Exhaust:
    emissions 199-207
    flow 79-81
    header 71-79
    manifold 75-79
    muffler 80
    oxygen sensor 37, 117, 118, 124, 125
    port 15-21
    turbo 80, 81, 154
    valve 17-19, 24, 25, 167
    valve rotator 66
    valve seat 24, 27, 28, 167

F
Fan-cooling 193, 233
Filter:
    air 92, 93
    fuel 113
    oil 186
Float-carburettor 82
Flywheel 180
Foller cam 62, 63, 69, 70
Four stroke operation 14
Fuel:
    acetone 38, 210
    air ratio 82, 109, 118, 124

Avgas 34, 35, 37, 38
benzol 38
distribution 94, 96
ethanol 210
filter 113
lead 31
map 115
methanol 210
methyl benzine 38
Motor test 32-35
octane booster 37, 38
octane rating 31-35
Research test 32-35
sensitivity 32, 33
test engine 32
tuluol 38
Fuel injection: 14
    air flow meter 116, 122, 123
    air temperature sensor 116, 117
    auxiliary air valve 113
    closed loop 118
    coolant temperature sensor 114, 117
    electronic control unit 114, 115, 125
    engine speed sensor 117
    exhaust oxygen sensor 37, 117, 118, 124, 125
    filter 113
    idle mixture adjustment 126
    idle speed adjustment 126
    injectors 14, 120, 123, 234
    leak testing 119
    map 115
    open loop 118
    pressure regulator 113, 122
    PROM chip 118, 124
    pulse width 114, 115, 120-122
    pump 113, 120
    throttle body 113
    throttle position switch 115, 117, 124

G
Gasket:
    head 29, 30, 193
    sealant 30
Gearing 154, 218
Gudgeon pin 175, 176

H

Harmonic balancer 179, 180
Headers 71-79
Heptane 32
Holley carburettor 87, 89, 100, 103, 105
Hone – cylinder 171
Horsepower 215, 216
Hydrocarbon emissions 195, 199, 200, 206, 207, 209-211

I

Idle system 84, 126
Ignition:
    abnormal 29, 34, 91, 141, 163, 203, 209, 232
    advance 130-140, 154, 203, 209, 234
    coil 144-147
    conventional 127
    cross firing 148
    electronic 129, 131, 140, 146, 147
    knock sensor 38, 140, 163
    leads 147
    points 128, 129
Intercooling 159-163
Initial advance 129, 131, 140
Inhibitor – cooling system 189
Injectors – fuel 14, 120, 123, 234
Inlet:
    manifold 90, 93-99
    port 15-21
    valve 17-19, 22, 23
    valve seat 23, 27
Iso-octane 32

J

Jet:
    accelerator pump 102, 103
    air corrector 87
    idle 84
    main 85, 87, 103, 104
    power 87, 103

K

Knock sensor 38, 140, 163

L

Lifter:
    hydraulic 62, 63, 69, 70
    Rhoads 62, 63
    solid 62, 63
Limited slip diff 228
Lubrication:
    camshaft 60
    filter 186
    oil 181-184, 234
    sump baffles 187
    turbo 167, 181, 185

M

Main bearing:
    clearance 169, 178, 179
    installation 178, 179
    specification 177
Main jet 85, 87, 103, 104
Manifold:
    exhaust 71-79
    inlet 90, 93-98
    inlet modification 99
    inlet polishing 99
Methanol 210
Methyl benzine 38
Mineral oil 182
Muffler 80

N

Needle and seat 82, 209, 234
Nitrogen oxides 46, 56, 195, 199, 205, 207, 210, 211

O

Octane rating 31-35
Oil:
    additives 183
    castor 184
    change period 183
    diesel 183
    filter 186
    friction modified 234
    mineral 182

pipes 185
polymers 182
pressure 186
pump 186
service rating 181
splash shields 29
sump baffles 187
surge 187
synthetic 182, 183
temperature and cooling 185
viscosity 182
Open loop 118
Overboring – cylinder 171

P
PCV valve 198
Piston: 167, 169, 170
alignment 170, 176
clearance 169
crown shape 43
pin 175, 176
rings 167, 171-173
Points – ignition 127-129
Polishing:
combustion chamber 15
con-rods 176, 177
inlet manfiold 99
ports 15
Port:
exhaust 15-21
inlet 15-21
Power:
measurement 214
system 87, 88, 103
valve 87, 103
Pre-ignition 141, 163
Pressure:
cooling system 191
fuel 113, 120, 122
oil 186
PROM chip 118, 124
Pump:
accelerator 88, 103
fuel 113, 120
oil 186
Pushrod 63

R
Radiator:
inhibitor 189, 190
oil 185
sealant 190
water 191
Rear axle torque 220
Reboring – cylinder 171
Ring – piston: 167, 171-174
bedding-in 173
fitting 171, 172
gap 171
material 171
Rocker:
arm 64
arm ratio 64
shaft 65
stud 64, 65
Roller:
camshaft 60, 62
rocker arm 64
tappet 62, 63
RRM limit 13, 219
Running-in:
camshaft 60
engine 173
Rust inhibitor 189

S
Sealant:
cooling system 190
Hylomar 30
Permatex 30
Silastic 30
Seal – valve stem 29
Shot peening 177
Silencer 80
Sniff test 196, 209-211
Soluble oil 190
Spark advance 130-140, 154, 203, 209 234
Spark plug:
cleaning 145
electrode style 142-144
gap 144, 145
heat range 141-144
leads 147

misfiring 143-145, 210, 234
reading 104, 142, 143
Spring:
    valve 66-68
    valve retainer 66
Squish clearance 42
Stroking – crankshaft 175
SU carburettor 89, 90, 99
Sump baffles 187
Suspension:
    bushes 228
    camber 227
    dampers 223
    springs 227, 233
    stabiliser bar 223, 224
    tyres 223-226
    wheels 223, 224, 226

T
Tappet:
    flat 60, 62
    mushroom 62
    roller 62
Temperature:
    cylinder head 191
    Oil 185
    water 191, 192
Tension – cylinder head 30
Thermostat 191, 192
Throttle body 113
Throttle position switch 115, 117, 124
Timing:
    camshaft 13, 14, 45-59
    ignition 9, 130-140, 154, 203, 204, 209, 234
    marks 180
Toluol 38
Torque:
    engine 215
    rear axle 220
Turbo:
    AIR system 21
    boost pressure 153-159, 163
    compressor 153-158
    exhaust system 80, 81, 154
    ignition advance 154
    intercooling 159-163

lag 149, 151, 152
lubrication 167, 181, 185
map 157
reconditioning 167, 168
spark plugs 144
turbine 152, 164-166
wastage 158

V
Vacuum advance 131, 132, 137-139, 204, 234
Valve:
    burning 22, 28, 37, 66
    clearance 68-70
    exhaust 17-19, 24, 25, 167
    guide 18, 22, 25, 28, 49, 64
    inlet 17-19, 22, 23
    material 22, 25
    pocket 18, 21, 27
    seat 18, 19, 21, 22, 27, 28, 37, 167
    shape 22-25
    size 12, 18, 22, 25
    spring 66-68
    spring retainer 66
    stem seal 66
    throat 18, 21
    train 64-66
    to piston clearance 174
Venturi:
    auxiliary 86
    main 85-87, 90
    manifold 97
Visual inspection 196, 197, 205, 206, 208
Volumetric efficiency 158

W
Wastegate 158
Water:
    cooling 189-194
    injection 38
    radiator 191
    temperature 191, 192
    Thermostat 191, 192
Weber carburettor 87, 89, 90, 93, 99, 103
Wires – ignition 147